ATLANTIC SEASHORE FIELD GUIDE

Florida to Canada

J. DUANE SEPT

STACKPOLE
BOOKS

Published by
STACKPOLE BOOKS
5067 Ritter Road
Mechanicsburg, PA 17055
www.stackpolebooks.com

Printed in the United States of America

10 9 8 7 6 5 4 3 2 1

First edition

Cover design by Caroline Stover
Cover images by the author
Photos by the author except where noted
Additional photo credits on page 319

Library of Congress Cataloging-in-Publication Data

Names: Sept, J. Duane, 1950- , author.
Title: Atlantic seashore field guide : Florida to the Arctic / J. Duane Sept.
Description: First edition. | Mechanicsburg, PA : Stackpole Books, 2016. | Includes
    bibliographical references and index.
Identifiers: LCCN 2015036228 | ISBN 9780811714211
Subjects: LCSH: Seashore biology—Atlantic Coast (North America) | Seashore
    animals--Atlantic Coast (North America)—Identification. | Seashore plants—
    Atlantic Coast (North America)—Identification.
Classification: LCC QH102 .S47 2016 | DDC 577.70975—dc23 LC record available at
    http://lccn.loc.gov/2015036228

CONTENTS

INTRODUCTION

The Western Atlantic is well known for its diverse intertidal marine life. Thanks to a combination of wave exposure, shoreline type, and plentiful food, a rich abundance of animal and plant life can be found along the intertidal zone—the narrow strip of land that lies between the highest and lowest tide lines. Intertidal sites are best viewed when the tide reaches its lower levels.

TIDES

Tides are caused by the gravitational effects of the moon and sun acting upon the world's oceans. The moon's influence is stronger because of its proximity to earth. High tides occur when the moon is closest to the ocean, and the water level rises in response to the gravitational pull of the moon. When both the sun and moon are in the same orientation toward earth, the gravitational pull is greatest on the nearest oceans. When a low tide occurs at one side of earth, the opposite side experiences a high tide to compensate for the change in water level.

In the northern portion of the Western Atlantic, the tides are renowned for their high fluctuations. In Minas Basin, Nova Scotia, the height of the tide fluctuation can reach an incredible 53' (16 m). In Pensacola, Florida, however, the tides reach a maximum height of 2.0' (0.6 m) and a minimum height of -1.0' (-0.3 m)—a maximum fluctuation of 3' (1 m).

INTERTIDAL HABITATS

Several types of seashore may be found along our beaches. Each of these habitats is home to species whose physical features are specialized for that environment. Our shorelines have several intertidal zones, each inhabited by a particular combination of creatures and plant life. These zones are (from top to bottom) the spray zone, high intertidal zone, middle intertidal zone and low intertidal zone. Some species may be found in more than one type of habitat or intertidal zone.

ROCKY SHORES
Rocky beaches can contain a wide variety of creatures, including various anemones, limpets, chitons, and tunicates. While tidal zones are present in all tidal areas, they are most evident on rocky shorelines.

SANDY SHORES

Sandy shores are often found on exposed beaches; however, they may also be found in sheltered locations such as in bays. Creatures found on sandy shores will only be found in either exposed or sheltered sites but not both. Marine life forms that are found on sandy beaches include the Atlantic surfclam (p. 171), Carolinian ghost shrimp (p. 220), and iridescent sandworm (p. 36).

MUDDY SHORES

Muddy shores are typically found in sheltered sites such as in lagoons. Creatures found on muddy beaches include the softshell-clam (p. 190), eastern oyster (p. 155), and eastern mud snail (p. 117).

INTERTIDAL ETIQUETTE

The marine lifeforms that inhabit our shores are fragile, so please ensure your visit is a positive one for the creatures you have come to enjoy. Be careful where you step, and replace any rocks that you turn over. Creatures that require a moist or wet environment can dry out quickly when exposed to sunlight. When you leave, take care to pack out everything you brought with you. This will help preserve the seashore environment for other visitors as well as for the marine residents.

HARVESTING SHELLFISH

One of the many ways to enjoy the seashore is to harvest shellfish. If you plan to do so, ensure that you have the necessary license, and check for local restrictions and limits. Local areas are sometimes closed to harvesting because of pollution or algal blooms such as red tide.

RED TIDE

During the warmer months of the year, tiny algae reproduce rapidly (algal bloom). Each of these algae can contain tiny amounts of toxins, which are then concentrated in the body tissues of various filter-feeding organisms, including oysters, clams, mussels, scallops, and more. Once the algae die, the filter-feeders begin to rid themselves of the toxins naturally, which takes as little as four weeks, although it can take as long as two years for some species. Algal blooms can produce a poison (saxitoxin) that is 10,000 times more toxic than cyanide. So if you eat a tiny amount of shellfish that have ingested these toxins, you can become seriously or even fatally ill with paralytic shellfish poisoning (PSP). Cooking does not remove this toxin. To inform the public, government authorities regularly monitor shellfish for toxin levels, and affected areas are closed to shellfish harvesting. This information is available at various sites on the web or by making a phone call.

PSP (RED TIDE) HOTLINES
Worldwide
www.issha.org/Welcome-to-ISSHA/Harmful-Algae-Links/General-Information#list-state

Canada
www.dfo-mpo.gc.ca/shellfish-mollusques/index-eng.htm

USA
Connecticut: www.ct.gov/doag/cwp/view.asp?a=1369&q=259178
Delaware: www.dnrec.delaware.gov/wr/Services/OtherServices/Pages/
    RedTideInformation.aspx
Florida: myfwc.com/REDTIDESTATUS
Maine: www.maine.gov/dmr/rm/public_health/closures/shellfishhotline.htm
Massachusetts: www.mass.gov/dfwele/dmf/recreationalfishing/
    rec_index.htm#shellfish
New Hampshire: 1-800-43CLAMS; www.wildlife.state.nh.us/marine/redtide.html
New Jersey: www.state.nj.us/dep/fgw/saltwater.htm
New York: 631-444-0480; www.dec.ny.gov/outdoor/345.html
North Carolina: www.ncfisheries.net/recreational/recguide.html
Rhode Island: www.dem.ri.gov/topics/mftopics.htm
South Carolina: www.dnr.state.sc.us/marine/shellfish/regs.html
Virginia: www.vdh.state.va.us/shellfish/index.asp

HOW TO USE THIS GUIDE

This book identifies the common animals and plants, including color photographs of the organisms, that you'll see along the Atlantic Coast, and contains important information that will help you identify each species. This next section highlights the criteria used under each heading to help in the identification of each organism.

PHYLUM
This classification comprises a very large group of living organisms, which are often divided further into many classes. For example, both humans and fish belong to the phylum Chordata, because both species have vertebrae, and both snails and clams belong to the phylum Mollusca because they share one or more internal or external shells, a muscular "foot," and an unsegmented body with a mantle or fold in the body wall.

CLASS/FAMILY
The class or family is a grouping of one or more genera (see Species Names below) with similar overall characteristics. All oysters, for instance, belong to the oyster family (Ostreidae), which includes several genera.

SPECIES NAMES
A common name and scientific name are presented for each species. Every living organism has a unique scientific name consisting of two parts: the genus or genera (plural)

and the species. Scientific names change occasionally as new information is discovered. This book contains the most current names. Common names are those used in everyday conversation by people who live in an area where the species occur, so many organisms have several common names.

AUTHORITY
This is the individual who has provided the initial account published for this particular species.

OTHER NAMES
Any additional common or scientific names known for the species are included here.

DESCRIPTION
This section provides the distinguishing physical features and behavior required in identifying the species.

SIZE
This section includes dimension(s) of the largest individuals or colonies commonly found; younger individuals are normally smaller.

HABITAT/ECOLOGY
The type of area where the species lives is provided, which is often helpful in making an identification.

GEOGRAPHIC RANGE
This section describes generally the area of the Atlantic where the species is found, as well as other countries or continents where this species resides or was introduced.

NOTES
This section provides further information of interest, usually relating to the natural history of the species or perhaps ways in which it is used by humans for food or other purposes.

SIMILAR SPECIES
If there are look-alike species that often create difficulties in the identification of that species, these are treated in the relevant species account at the end (or cross-referenced).

INTRODUCED SPECIES
I Introduced species are noted with a symbol that indicates that this species is not native to this area. This alien species has been introduced by accident or for a specific purpose by man.

Sponges
(Phylum Porifera)

Sponges are the simplest of marine organisms and in fact do not have specialized body tissues. Sponges have an internal skeleton that is made up of microscopic spicules (rods) that are comprised of either calcium or silicon. This gives them their shape and each species has their own type of spicule which is used to identify individual species.

Water circulates through the body by entering the body via minute pores called ostia (singular, ostium) and leaves through large pores called oscula (singular, osculum). Flagella (microscopic whip-like structures) pump water through a system of canals, which circulate the water within the sponge by their continual beating. Both food and oxygen accompany the water so that the sponge is able to feed and breath with this system. Body wastes exit the oscula along with the water. Sponges attach to solid objects such as rocks and so do not move around. They often grow best where water currents are the greatest.

Eyed Finger Sponge

Haliclona oculata

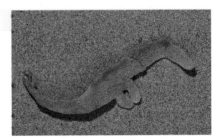

Authority: (Linnaeus, 1759)
Other Names: Also known as dead man's fingers, eyed sponge, finger sponge; formerly classified as *Chalina oculata*
Description: Color varies widely from tan to grayish brown, occasionally purple, rose, or reddish orange. The shape of this species varies with the number of its branches and their size. Its stalk is narrow, supporting several branches. Its pores (larger openings that allow water to exit the cavity) are large enough to be noticeable and scattered over its surface. Branches are generally flat but noticeably rounder south of Cape Cod.
Size: Height to 17.5" (450 mm); thickness to 0.5" (12 mm)
Habitat/Ecology: Attached to rocks; low intertidal zone to water 400' (124 m) deep
Geographic Range: Labrador to North Carolina
Notes: This species is often found washed ashore after a storm. Fresh specimens will often have much more color than older, sun-bleached individuals. This northern species is frequently found stranded on our shores. To identify many species of sponges, you need to look at the spicules with a microscope. This species, however, is easy to identify without a microscope.
Similar Species: Common Palmate Sponge (*Isodictya palmata*) is a smaller species, to 12" (30 cm) high, with conspicuous pores on the flat sides of the erect, flattened

branches. Its color ranges from yellowish to light brown or red-brown. This subtidal species ranges from Nova Scotia to North Carolina and is sometimes found washed up on the shore.

Northern Palmate Sponge (*Isodictya deichmannae*) is very similar to the common palmate sponge but requires a microscope to identify it with certainty. It ranges from Newfoundland to Rhode Island.

Purple Encrusting Sponge

Haliclona cinerea

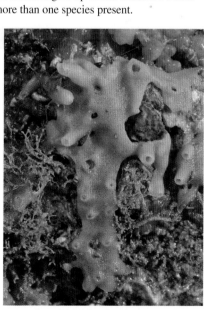

Authority: (Grant, 1826)
Other Names: Also known as purple sponge, volcano sponge; formerly classified as *Haliclona permollis*
Description: Its coloration ranges from pink to lavender or purple. Its surface is smooth and soft. Its volcano-like oscula may reach 0.25" (6.5 mm) on raised tubes.
Size: To 36" (91 cm) wide; 1.6" (4.1 cm) high
Habitat/Ecology: In protected waters, encrusted on rocks, in tidepools, and on floating docks; low intertidal zone to water 20' (6 m) deep
Geographic Range: New Brunswick to lower Chesapeake Bay; Washington to California
Notes: The wonderful color of this common sponge makes it easy to identify. It is also found in the Pacific Northwest where it lives higher up on the shoreline. Some authorities speculate that there may be more than one species present.

Bread Crumb Sponge

Halichondria panicea

Authority: (Pallas, 1766)
Other Names: Also known as crumb of bread sponge, crumb-of-bread sponge
Description: Two color forms are common—yellow and pale green. The texture of this species is firm, compressible, and easily torn. Oscules are regularly spaced at the tips of volcano-like mounds.
Size: Greater than 12" (30 cm) wide; 2" (5.1 cm) high
Habitat/Ecology: On exposed shores and in quiet bays, attached to rocks, wharves, pilings, and in tidepools; low intertidal zone to water greater than 1650' (500 m) deep

Geographic Range: Arctic to Cape Cod; Alaska to California

Notes: The crumb of bread sponge gets its common name from its scientific name, *panicea*, which means "made of bread," referring to its texture and the ease with which it breaks apart. This species has been called the most common intertidal sponge of our Atlantic Coast.

The green color is caused by symbionic microscopic algae called *Zoochlorellae* that live in sponge colonies. This sponge receives nutrients produced from the algae, and the algae receive shelter from the sponge. It's truly amazing that this intertidal sponge can also live at depths greater than 1650' (500 m) deep!

Bowerbank's Halichondria

Halichondria bowerbanki

Authority: (Burton, 1930)

Other Names: Also known as Bowerbank's crumb of bread sponge, bread sponge, crumb-of-bread sponge, yellow sun sponge

Description: Color ranges from yellowish to orange-brown or olive-green. This species is soft, with tissue that tears easily. It typically has a very irregular shape, and its surface is often raised in leaflike masses. This species forms somewhat thicker sponges than the new colonies of other sponges.

Size: To 6" (15 cm) across; 3" (7.5 cm) high

Habitat/Ecology: On sheltered shores, estuaries, lagoons, and in tidepools; usually in indirect light on pilings, rocks, shells, and seaweeds; low intertidal zone to shallow subtidal depths

Geographic Range: Bay of Fundy to Cape Hatteras

Notes: In May and early June, this common fouling sponge is most visible, but by late June and early July, it disappears for much of the summer. By late September, however, new colonies begin again, and soon afterward they may be found on rocks and shells.

If you look under the microscope at the spicules, they look like needles with one pointed end and one rounded end. This species can be difficult to separate from the sun sponge in the field.

Similar Species: Sun Sponge (*Hymeniacidon heliophila*) (see p. 5) is a southern species ranging from Cape Cod to Gulf of Mexico that is found in sites that receive direct sunlight. It is yellowish and grows to the same size as Bowerbank's halichondria. Looking under the microscope at this species, you will observe its spicules that resemble needles with two pointed ends.

Loosanoff's Haliclona (*Haliclona loosanoffi*) forms dark tan to gold crusts, with oscules on the chimneys that can grow to 1" (2.5 cm) high. Each sponge may reach 3" (7.5 cm) across, but several often fuse together to form large mats.

Sulfur Sponge

Aplysilla longispina

Authority: (George and Wilson, 1919)

Other Names: Also known as yellow sulfur sponge; formerly included with *Aplysilla sulfurea*

Description: Healthy sponges of this species have a distinctive yellow color; however, this color changes dramatically to purple on injured or dead individuals. This encrusting species has a soft consistency, with a glossy, lacquered look out of water. It also displays pointed projections arising from its upper surface, with no pores visible.

Size: To 8" (20 cm) in diameter; 0.8" (0.5 cm) in thickness

Habitat/Ecology: Encrusts rocks, wrecks, shells, and other sponges; low intertidal zone to water 82.5' (25 m) deep

Geographic Range: North Carolina to Florida, Caribbean, and West Indies

Notes: This sponge lacks the silica or calcium carbonate that is found in the "skeleton" of most sponges. Instead, thick, tough fibers of the protein spongin support this species and give it form. This characteristic is true for all members of the genus *Aplysilla.*

This species was formerly considered to be the same species as European sulfur sponge, *Aplysilla sulfurea.* New research has determined that the European sulfur sponge is from the Adriatic Sea and the western Mediterranean, and it is a separate species that is restricted to that area.

Sun Sponge

Hymeniacidon heliophila

Authority: de Parker, 1910

Other Names: Formerly classified as *Stylotella heliophila, Stylotella simplissima*

Description: Specimens living in sunlit areas are light yellow overall with a tint of olive green. In shady sites, however, they are often a bright orange to reddish orange. This species forms encrusting sheets with numerous erect, irregular, chimney projections. Large specimens are normally soft and easily torn, but small specimens are stiff and fleshy.

A sun sponge washed up on the beach

Size: Can exceed 16" (40 cm) across; to 1.5" (4 cm) high

Habitat/Ecology: On shells, sand flats, pilings, and rock jetties; low intertidal zone to subtidal depths

Geographic Range: North Carolina to the Caribbean

Notes: This species is one that can tolerate being exposed to direct sunlight and air. Its color pigmentation helps to protect it from becoming sunburnt. Specimens that have been found living in deeper waters appear not to produce chimney projections, likely due to currents in the ocean.

Redbeard Sponge

Clathria prolifera

Authority: (Ellis and Solander, 1786)
Other Name: Formerly classified as
  Microciona prolifera
Description: Red to orange in color. It
  grows with a distinctive, knobby,
  multibranched shape. Oscula are
  inconspicuous and scattered over the
  surface.
Size: To 8" (20 cm) or more high; 8" (20 cm) wide
Habitat/Ecology: In protected bays and estuaries; on rocks, pilings, shells, and other
  hard objects; low intertidal zone to shallow subtidal waters
Geographic Range: Prince Edward Island to Texas
Notes: This species is often found on the beach washed up after a storm. Individuals
  start out as small encrusting sponges that develop small lobes. As the sponge grows,
  the lobes mature into branches. The redbeard sponge is known for its ability to with-
  stand pollution and the low salinities within bays and estuaries.

Club-finger Sponge

Desmapsamma anchorata

Authority: (Carter, 1882)
Other Names: Also known as lumpy
  club finger sponge, overgrowing
  sponge; formerly classified as
  Fibularia anchorata
Description: Variably colored from
  purplish pink to salmon-pink. Produces
  upright branches that divide dichotomously with swollen processes. The oscules are
  abundant and visible on its branches, and this sponge's consistency is soft and
  compressible.
Size: To 14" (35 cm) high or more; to 6" (15 cm) in diameter
Habitat/Ecology: On stones, mangrove roots, and similar objects in sandy areas of
  shallow reefs and lagoons; subtidal depths to water 132' (40 m) deep
Geographic Range: North Carolina to Florida and the Caribbean; northwestern
  Europe and Africa
Notes: The club-finger sponge, like many other species, changes color because it oxi-
  dizes out of water. This species turns to black or dark brown. The skeleton of this
  species is greatly influenced by the quantity of foreign material, including sand,
  which is incorporated into the structure of the sponge. The club-finger sponge is
  often found washed up on our shorelines.

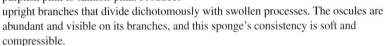

Sheepswool Sponge

Hippospongia lachne

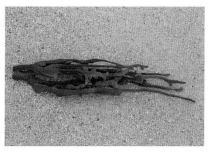

Authority: (de Laubenfels, 1936)
Other Name: Also known as sheep's wool sponge
Description: Color ranges considerably from olive to black. Its shape is round, with an irregular surface and large, raised pores.
Size: Width to 36" (91 cm); height to 24" (61 cm)
Habitat/Ecology: On rocky bottoms; subtidal waters to 150' (46 m) deep
Geographic Range: Florida to Mexico; Bahamas; West Indies
Notes: Like several other sponge species, this one is only found if it is washed ashore after a storm. This massive species has long been the focus of a major commercial sponge industry. At one time sponge diving was the way large numbers of sponges were harvested in Florida. Today natural sponges have been largely replaced with synthetic sponges. Tourists now purchase natural sponges as souvenirs. Fragments of this species are sometimes found washed up on the shore.

Brown Finger Sponge

Axinella pomponiae

Authority: van Soest and Rützler, 1998
Other Name: Formerly classified as *Homaxinella rudis*
Description: Color varies from dark purplish red to reddish brown. The branches are erect, flexible, and tapering with occasional lumps. The branches also commonly fuse together and are sometimes dichotomous at the tips.
Size: To 12" (30 cm) high; branches to 0.75" (2 cm) across
Habitat/Ecology: In sandy areas with hard bottoms near reefs; subtidal waters to 165' (50 m) deep
Geographic Range: North Carolina to Caribbean, Gulf of Mexico
Notes: Like many other sponges, this subtidal species is often found washed up on the shore. This species is very soft in consistency.

Yellow Boring Sponge

Cliona celata

Authority: Grant, 1826
Other Names: Also known as yellow
  sulfur sponge, sulfur sponge, boring
  sponge
Description: A yellowish body pro-
  trudes from holes in mollusk shells or
  coral.
Size: Diameter to 0.1" (3 mm); height to
  0.1" (2 mm)

Holes drilled in a shell by the yellow boring
sponge

Habitat/Ecology: On shells, coral, and
  occasionally concrete; low intertidal zone to water 132' (40 m) deep
Geographic Range: Gulf of St. Lawrence to Gulf of Mexico; Washington to
  California
Notes: The larvae of this remarkable sponge settle on calcareous shells and coral,
  where they secrete sulfuric acid, creating pits and galleries in the shells. This
  removes excess shells from the ocean that could otherwise overwhelm the ocean
  bottom.

  This sponge is recognized as a pest in oyster beds. Since it simply weakens the
  shells of the oyster, it is not a parasite, but in severe attacks it can exhaust and even
  kill its host. You may also encounter additional boring sponges, such as the red boring sponge (below).
Similar Species: Red Boring Sponge (*C. delitrix*) is orange-red in color. This species
  of sponge has been known to kill corals.

Cnidarians
(Phylum Cnidaria)

The phylum Cnidaria is made up of three classes of organisms that appear to be quite different from each other: sea anemones (Anthozoa), hydroids (Hydrozoa), and jellies (Scyphozoa).

All cnidarians produce their own nematocysts. These nematocytsts, however, vary greatly in their function. Some are sticky to capture prey, while others use small amounts of poison, and still others use them to "lasso" their prey. In fact, seventeen different types of nematocysts have been described. Most cnidarians are radially symmetrical, with their parts arranged around the center like the petals of a daisy. Only one opening is present: the mouth. It opens to their gastrovascular cavity. The mouth is surrounded by several tentacles to capture food. Wastes also exit through the same opening.

Members of this phylum are present in two forms. The polyp is the first form, which is represented by the sea anemone. Polyps are stationary, since they are attached to a substrate. The second form is the medusa, which is commonly found in the jellies. Medusae move by opening and closing, forcing water in and out, which moves the jelly in the opposite direction.

While some cnidarians are only present as a polyp or a medusa, many have alternating generations. This means that their life cycle includes both polyp and medusa generations.

CORALS AND SEA ANEMONES
(Class Anthozoa)

Sea anemones are soft-bodied organisms that possess unbranched tentacles around their mouth used to obtain food. Reproduction is normally sexual, but some species reproduce asexually. Although sea anemones appear to be sedentary, they actually can glide about surfaces slowly on their pedal disks. You'll find two types of coral: soft and hard. **Soft corals** (octocorals) may be shaped like fans, bushes, or rods. Their polyps are present in scattered cups. The outer covering to their flexible fingers consists of a mesh-like calcium structure that surrounds an inner core of flexible protein called gorgonin. **Hard corals** (stony corals) on the other hand are colony based so that when one feeds, all nearby polyps benefit. Each individual in these colonies secretes calcium carbonate in the shape of a cup to form a solid structure that is characteristic for the species. Polyps are best viewed at night when they stretch to their full length to feed. During the daytime, they remain retracted and are difficult to see.

SOFT CORALS

Brilliant Sea Fingers

Titanideum frauenfeldii

Authority: (Kölliker, 1865)
Other Names: Also known as orange
  bush coral; formerly classified as
  Solanderia frauenfeldii
Description: Color varies from yellow
  to deep red. The colonies consist of
  stiff, cylindrical, rod-like, tapering
  branches. They are unbranched when small or moderately branched when larger.
Size: Height to 15" (38 cm); branches to 0.33" (.8 cm)
Habitat/Ecology: On sand-covered limestone; subtidal depths 60–100' (18–30 m)
Geographic Range: North Carolina to Cuba; northern Gulf of Mexico
Notes: This bushy soft coral is a deep-water species that attaches itself to hard surfaces with a holdfast. It has no "wood-like" stem like the related sea fans and sea
  whips do. It is commonly found stranded on the beach after storms.

Sea Whip

Leptogorgia virgulata

Authority: (Lamarck, 1815)
Other Name: Also known as colorful
  sea whip
Description: Color varies widely, purple
  to yellow or orange, tan, white, and
  red. It has cylindrical stems—slender,
  whip-like, and sparsely branched close to the base, with small pores.
Size: Height to 36" (90 cm); stems to 0.5" (1.3 cm) wide
Habitat/Ecology: Attaches to rocks, shells, as well as on floating docks, rock jetties,
  and oyster reefs; shallow subtidal depths to 100' (30 m) deep
Geographic Range: New Jersey to Florida; more common south of Cape Hatteras
Notes: This coral, like all soft corals, is comprised of colonies of tiny polyps, each
  with eight tentacles (hence the name octocoral). A tough outer rind and horny core
  are the basis for the flexibility of this species.

  Several organisms are often found living on this coral. The Atlantic wing-oyster,
  Pteria colymbus (see p. 151), is one that frequently attaches to a branch. The sea
  whip barnacle, *Conopea galeata* (see p. 206), lives on this species exclusively, where
  it is very often overgrown by host tissue. Another species, the single-toothed simnia,
  Simnialena uniplicata (see p. 91), may also be found as it clings to a branch. Since it
  feeds on the host, it actually incorporates the pigment of its host into its shell.

  The sea whip has inhibitors that help to protect it from the sea whip barnacle and a
  variety of bryozoans that try colonizing on this species' branches. These inhibitors,
  however, are not always successful.

Similar Species: Straight Sea Whip (*Leptogorgia setacea*) is a similar species except that it is unbranched. It's common from the Chesapeake Bay to Brazil, and its colors are also similar to the sea whip. It grows to 6' (183 cm) high. Cups are found crowded and irregularly spaced in two rows. Often grows unattached.

Regal Sea Fan

Leptogorgia hebes

Authority: Verrill, 1869
Other Names: Also known as false sea fan; formerly classified as *Lophogorgia hebes*
Description: Color ranges from red to purple or orange and dark yellow. This species is highly branched, with dome-like mounds and slit-like pores on somewhat flattened stems.
Size: Height to 18" (45 cm); stems to 0.25" (.6 cm) in diameter
Habitat/Ecology: On hardbottom; subtidal to waters 89' (27 m) deep
Geographic Range: Virginia to northern Florida and Gulf of Mexico to Aruba and Brazil
Notes: This coral attaches to hard substrates by a holdfast. Research in the Gulf of Mexico showed that this species begins to spawn in late August or early September. Sea fans can be aged just like trees—by counting the annual rings. Females begin their reproduction at two years of age while males do not begin until six years old. Interestingly, the sex ratio in the Gulf of Mexico favored females 2:1.

Common Sea Pansy

Renilla reniformis

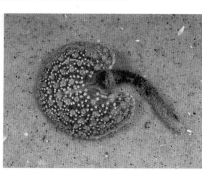

Authority: (Pallas, 1766)
Other Name: Also known as sea pansy
Description: The color of the heart-shaped frond is rose or pale purple, with white and yellow polyps on the dorsal surface. The stalk is purple and about the same length as the diameter of the frond.
Size: Frond to 1.5" (40 mm) wide; total length with stalk to 3" (75 mm)
Habitat/Ecology: It anchors itself in soft sand; low intertidal zone to water 360' (108 m) or more deep
Geographic Range: Cape Hatteras to Brazil, Caribbean
Notes: The common sea pansy uses its anchoring stem to keep it in place. It is capable of repositioning itself if it becomes covered with sand. It can also free itself from its location by extending and contracting its muscular stem. The yellow polyps on the frond are the feeding polyps that capture food. The white polyps are used as water pumps that can expand the body when it is deflated.

If the common sea pansy is disturbed, it emits a strong bioluminescent light that is only visible at night. One stimulus that evokes bioluminescence is the presence of a striped sea slug called the tiger armina (*Armina tigrina*), which is a predator of the common sea pansy.

HARD CORALS

Northern Star Coral

Astrangia poculata

Authority: (Ellis and Solander, 1786)
Other Names: Also known as star coral, northern stony coral; formerly classified as *A. astreiformis*, *A. danae*
Description: Normally white or pink, the northern star coral turns brownish when symbiotic algae are especially abundant inside its tissues. It forms encrusting masses with a distinctive star-like pattern.
Size: Colony diameter up to 12" (30 cm), but normally to 5" (12.7 cm)
Habitat/Ecology: On rocks and other hard surfaces; subtidal depths to 130' (28 m)
Geographic Range: Cape Cod to Florida
Notes: This encrusting stony coral does not form reefs but forms compact colonies instead. This subtidal species is often found washed up on the shore. Symbiotic algae (*Zooxanthellae*) are present within this stony coral, and as a result, they are able to survive in deeper waters with less light requirements than soft corals. Minute white bumps found on the surface are clusters of stinging capsules that are used to capture prey.

Compact Ivory Bush Coral

Oculina arbuscula

Authority: Agassiz, 1864
Other Names: Also known as compact ivory tree coral, ivory bush coral
Description: Color is normally white on the beach after being bleached by the sun. In life, the colonies range from tan to dark brown. This species has finger- or pencil-shaped branches with many cups.
Size: Colonies occasionally reach up to 3' (1 m) but are normally much smaller; branch diameter to 0.75" (20 mm)

Habitat/Ecology: On hard bottom; subtidal 20–328' (6–100 m)

Geographic Range: North Carolina to Georgia

Notes: Compact ivory bush coral is comprised of polyps (individuals) that shape their colonies with many branches that bear raised coral cups.

A living specimen

Each cup is produced by a single polyp. The polyps of this species, and others, obtain most of their nutrients by feeding on tiny animal plankton. The presence or absence of *Zooxanthellae* determines the actual color of live individuals.

Similar Species: Diffuse Ivory Bush Coral (*Oculina diffusa*) displays a few widely separated large and shallow cups. It is found from Florida to Bermuda, as well as in the Bahamas and the West Indies.

SEA ANEMONES

Sea anemones possess unbranched tentacles, which are used for feeding. These tentacles are normally retracted when the anemone is out of water at low tide. As a result, the anemone may resemble a soft blob rather than an anemone out of water.

Some species also have acontia (thread-like structures) found at the mouth or pores in the column, which are activated when the animal is disturbed. Acontia are densely armed with nematocysts and are used for defense. Sea anemones reproduce sexually, and a few also reproduce by asexual means.

Warty Sea Anemone

Bunodosoma cavernatum

Authority: (Bosc, 1802)

Other Names: Also known as American warty anemone, warty anemone; formerly classified as *Bunodosoma cavernata*

Description: The color of the column is variable, ranging from olive green to brown. The tentacles are colored with yellow-green and dark olive green. Approximately forty longitudinal rows of small warts are present on its muscular column, surrounded by a hundred sticky tentacles.

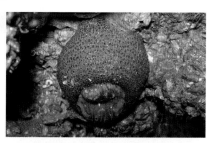

Individual with retracted tentacles

Size: Height to 4" (10 cm); oral disk to 2" (5 cm) in diameter

Habitat/Ecology: On rocks or other hard substrates with sandy or gravelly bottoms and jetties; low intertidal zone

Individual with fully extended tentacles

Geographic Range: North Carolina to Florida and Texas; West Indies
Notes: The warty sea anemone is normally contracted during daylight hours, appearing only as a dark lump. At night, however, its tentacles are fully expanded and ready to catch prey. It feeds upon any creatures that happen to come into contact with its tentacles. In one area, scorched mussels (*Brachidontes exustus*) (see p. 145) have been found inside this species, suggesting that it feeds upon them.

Painted Anemone

Urticina felina

Tentacles extended

Authority: (Linnaeus, 1761)
Other Names: Also known as northern red anemone, dahlia anemone, Christmas anemone; formerly classified as *Urticina crassicornis, Tealia felina* (occasionally misspelled *Telia felina*)
Description: Color is quite variable: red to yellow, chestnut or purplish, orange, green and white (solid or mottled). The column is smooth, graced with 100–160 thick, blunt tentacles within, in several rings surrounding the mouth; shell and gravel fragments are rarely attached to the column.
Size: Height to 5" (127 mm); width to 3" (76 mm)
Habitat/Ecology: On rocks or other hard surfaces in protected sites; mid intertidal zone to water 990' (300 m) deep

Tentacles retracted

Geographic Range: Arctic to Cape Cod; Alaska to central California; northern Europe
Notes: This circumarctic-boreal species is found in several locations in the Northern Hemisphere. The painted anemone broods its juveniles until they reach the twelve to twenty-four tentacle stage. This predator uses its tentacles to feed upon small fish, urchins, crabs, and other invertebrates. This species has been known to live to at least eighty years.

Silver-spotted Anemone

Aulactinia stella

Authority: (Verrill, 1864)
Other Names: Also known as gem anemone; formerly classified as *Bunodactis stella*
Description: The column is translucent olive to bluish green or occasionally

pinkish. The tentacles are also olive to bluish green, with a white ring around the base. The oral disk normally has white radial stripes originating from the mouth. The column is covered with several rows of sticky warts to which shell fragments and pebbles adhere. The smooth, tapered tentacles range in number from 48–120.

Size: Height to 1.5" (38 mm); width to 2" (51 mm)

Habitat/Ecology: On rocks near sandy shores and in tidepools; low intertidal zone

Geographic Range: Nova Scotia to the Gulf of Maine; Greenland

Notes: This is a small anemone that is easy to identify since it is wider than it is tall. The silver-spotted anemone's column is normally covered with sand, pebbles, and bits of shell. The shag-rug nudibranch (see p. 136) is one of this anemone's main predators. The nudibranch is able to attack the anemone by secreting mucus as a protection against the stinging tentacles, and thus, it does not become a meal of the anemone.

Ⓘ Orange-striped Anemone

Diadumene lineata

Authority: (Verrill, 1869)

Other Names: Also known as striped anemone, green-striped sea anemone, lined anemone, orange-striped green anemone; formerly classified as *Haliplanella luciae*

Description: The color of the column ranges from green to brown, with vertical pinstripes ranging in color from white to orange or red. A total of twenty-five to fifty long, delicate tentacles surround the oral disk.

Size: Height to 1.25" (3 cm); to 1.2" (3.5 cm) in diameter

Habitat/Ecology: On rocks mussel shells, oyster shells, and pilings; in protected areas and on mud in salt marshes; high intertidal zone to shallow subtidal depths

Geographic Range: Bay of Fundy to Texas

Notes: This species was introduced from the Western Pacific region (Japan, China, and Hong Kong) into Connecticut around 1892. Since that time, it has expanded its range along the Atlantic Coast tremendously. Research on the orange-striped anemone in Maine revealed that this species has become cold adapted to its new "home" by being active at and below 32° F (0° C).

This species has also been introduced to the Eastern Pacific, Europe, New Zealand, and Indonesia as well as the Atlantic Coast.

Short Plumose Anemone

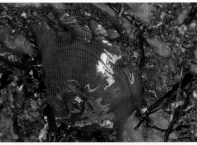

Metridium senile

Authority: (Linnaeus, 1761)

Other Names: Also known as frilled anemone, plumose anemone, common sea anemone, northern anemone, sun anemone, white plumed anemone, plumed anemone, powder puff anemone, orange anemone, fluffy anemone, white plume anemone; formerly classified as *Metridium dianthus*

Description: Overall white, yellow, orange or brown in color, with up to a hundred tentacles. The column is smooth, without any warts.

Size: Height to 4" (10 cm); width to 2" (5 cm) in diameter at base

Habitat/Ecology: On hard objects such as wharves, dock pilings, and rocks; in protected waters; low intertidal zone to subtidal waters 98' (30 m) deep

Geographic Range: Arctic to Delaware; Alaska to California

Notes: Although the short plumose anemone may be found attached to rocks, it is more often observed at the

dockside. Here, you can view this species with its tentacles fully extended, waiting for its next meal. If you are lucky enough to find it attached to a rock or other hard surface at low tide, you will notice that it looks much different and is much more difficult to identify.

This species reproduces sexually, as most anemones do. It also reproduces asexually by leaving a small bit of tissue behind when it is moving about. The tissue left behind is able to produce an identical genetic clone of the original anemone.

Hermit Crab Anemone

Calliactis tricolor

Authority: (Lesueur, 1817)

Other Name: Also known as tricolor anemone

Description: Column color normally ranges from brown with cream streaks to olive, cream, orange, red, or purple—often with dark spots at the base and occasionally with longitudinal stripes. Tentacles are pink, orange, tan, whitish, or gray-green. Up to 500 slender tentacles surround the oral mouth.

Size: Height to 2" (51 mm); width to 2" (51 mm)

Habitat/Ecology: Attached to the shells of various hermit crabs and occasionally onto the shells of living snails or large crabs; low intertidal zone to water 99' (30 m) deep

Geographic Range: North Carolina to Florida and Texas; Caribbean; Brazil

Tentacles retracted

Notes: This sea anemone favors attaching to the shells of several hermit crabs: the flat-clawed hermit crab (see p. 222), the giant red hermit crab (see p. 224), and occasionally the striped hermit crab (see p. 223). The hermit crab anemone forms a symbiotic relationship with its host. This relationship is beneficial to both partners. The anemone gains access to more food by its increased mobility, and the hermit crab gains increased protection from predators, with the anemone's nematocysts.

The hermit crab anemone often transfers from one shell to another on its own. It has also been observed that when a hermit crab moves to a larger snail shell, it frequently assists the anemone to transfer from the old shell to the new one.

Onion Anemone

Paranthus rapiformis

Authority: (Lesueur, 1817)

Other Name: Also known as sea onion

Description: Column with an opalescent glossy sheen that is cream to pinkish; may also be brown or greenish gray. Its shape resembles a freshly peeled onion when it is not anchored. Its column bears fine grooves, 144–180 tentacles, and a small pedal disk. It lacks acontia.

Size: Height to 3" (75 mm) when extended

Habitat/Ecology: In sand, in quiet water; low intertidal zone to shallow subtidal waters

Geographic Range: Massachusetts to Florida; Gulf Coast

Notes: The shape and texture of this anemone make it one of the easier species to identify. If it becomes disturbed, it simply detaches itself from its substrate and floats off, looking like a peeled onion! It can anchor itself in sand with its pedal disk shaped like an upside down mushroom or onto a buried shell or similar object. This burrowing anemone can extend its column down 14" (35 cm) or greater into an elongated worm-like shape. This species is also neutrally buoyant so that if it is dislodged from its anchor point, it simply shortens its body and retains water inside to form a round, onion-like shape. It can then float to a more suitable sandy location.

Pale Anemone

Aiptasia pallida

Authority: (Agassiz in Verrill, 1864)

Other Name: Also known as brown anemone

Description: The entire anemone is white or brown. Two sizes of elongated tentacles are present—many shorter outer ones, with a few much longer central ones. Tentacles total approximately one hundred.

Size: Height to 2" (51 mm); width 0.5" (13 mm) across at the narrowest point

Habitat/Ecology: On rocks, algae, sponges, mangrove roots, and floating docks; mid intertidal zone to shallow subtidal waters

Geographic Range: North Carolina to the Caribbean

Notes: The presence of a unicellular alga (*Symbiodinium microadriaticum*) that lives inside the tissues of the anemone's body causes its brown color when abundant. This species commonly creates clones of the same sex due to pedal laceration—when a portion of tissue is left behind when the individual moves.

Similar Species: Red-spotted Anemone (*Aiptasiogeton eruptaurantia*) has distinctive red spots on its column and lines on the oral disc. This intertidal species bears sixty-four or more tentacles and is only found from North to South Carolina.

Saltmarsh Anemone

Nematostella vectensis

Authority: Stephenson, 1935
Other Name: Also known as starlet sea anemone
Description: White or transparent with numerous white bands when extended; normally with sixteen tentacles, but they can range from twelve to twenty that are cylindrical—tapered but not knobbed. Eight lengthwise grooves are present on the column and a physa (a swollen, bulb-like structure at the column base).
Size: Height to 0.6" (15 mm); diameter to 0.1" (2.5 mm) at base
Habitat/Ecology: In salt marsh tidepools; high to mid intertidal zones
Geographic Range: Nova Scotia to Louisiana
Notes: The saltmarsh anemone is able to tolerate very low salinities of about 18 percent or less. This mud-dwelling burrowing anemone is usually buried in mud up to its tentacles. It is capable of locomotion with short peristaltic-like movements. This species has been introduced to the Eastern Pacific (Northern California to Oregon). It is now commonly used as species for a variety of laboratory studies.

The genus *Nematostella* is the only group of anemones with nematosomes—free-swimming bodies found in the cavity of these anemones. The purpose of these bodies is unknown.

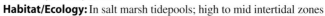

HYDROZOANS (Class Hydrozoa)

Hydrozoans are a large and diverse class with seven orders and numerous species. Within this class, there are hydroids, hydromedusae, and others. Each is comprised of a colony of organisms forming a larger external shape. Many species require microscopic examination for identification.

Zig-zag Wine-glass Hydroid

Obelia geniculata

Authority: (Linnaeus, 1758)
Other Name: Also known as knotted thread hydroid
Description: Color whitish overall; the stems are simple and unbranched, rising in an alternating zig-zag pattern. A sheath is found around the reproductive buds that is urn-shaped, with a collar.

Size: Height of polyp colony to 1" (2.5 cm); width greater than 12" (30 cm)
Habitat/Ecology: Attached to rocks, kelp, and other algae; in shallow waters
Geographic Range: Arctic to Florida and Texas; West Indies; British Columbia to California
Notes: Many individual polyps make up this colonial animal, which uses its small tentacles to capture food. The polyp is responsible for reproduction to produce small buds. These buds develop into free-swimming medusa which in turn produce fertilized eggs. Swimming planula (larvae) develop out of the eggs to complete their life cycle.

It has been observed that the medusae of the zig-zag wine-glass hydroid often swim with their bell turned inside out resembling wind-blown umbrellas.

Wine-glass Hydroids

Campanularia spp.

Authority: Lamarck, 1816
Other Name: Also known as campanularian hydroids
Description: Color is whitish; stems upright with wine-glass–shaped polyps that may be branched or unbranched and lack a zig-zag shape.
Size: Height of polyp colony to 10" (25 cm); width to 6" (15 cm)
Habitat/Ecology: On rocks, pilings, and seaweeds; low intertidal zone to water 1380' (420 m) deep
Geographic Range: Labrador to Florida; Bermuda; Bahamas; West Indies to Venezuela; Alaska to California
Notes: This hydroid can be found in its polyp stage from late spring to early fall. Detailed laboratory examination is necessary to identify individual species.

Graceful Hydroid

Lovenella gracilis

Authority: Clarke, 1882
Other Name: Also known as coquina hydroid
Description: The overall color of this species is light brown. The filaments are simple and divided as the main stem extends itself, and there are regularly located constrictions. This species is only found on the little coquina where it lives as small tufts. Colonies are normally found on many individuals of little coquinas.

Size: Colony to 0.75" (2 cm) high, 0.5" (1.2 cm) wide
Habitat/Ecology: On sandy shores; low intertidal zone
Geographic Range: Cape Cod to Gulf of Mexico
Notes: The graceful hydroid is a common species that lives in close association with the little coquina (see p. 182). This species is only found where the little coquina is present at the low intertidal zone during the summer months. Not much is known about this species. The presence of this hydroid likely affects the movement of the little coquina up and down the beach. It is unclear if the relationship between these species is parasitic, mutualistic, or commensal.

Portuguese Man-of-War

Physalia physalis

Authority: (Linnaeus, 1758)
Other Name: Also known as Portuguese man o' war
Description: The float is an iridescent blue, pink, and/or purple, with a blue flange with a pink edge above; blue tentacles trail behind underwater. The wing-like flange or crest can be inflated with gas so that it catches the wind to transport the entire organism in the ocean.
Size: Float to 12" (30 cm) long; height to 6" (15 cm). Tentacles to 165 ft (50 m) long. The tentacles of beached specimens are normally broken off and appear much shorter.
Habitat/Ecology: Pelagic; floats on the surface of the ocean in tropical and subtropical waters
Geographic Range: Worldwide in tropical waters; Florida to Texas and Mexico; Bahamas; West Indies; storms from the Gulf Stream push strandings as far north as Cape Cod
Notes: The Portuguese man-of-war is a **highly toxic** species whether alive in the water or dead on the beach. In the water, the long tentacles are difficult to see and certainly a hazard to swimmers. When stranded on the beach, this species still packs a punch—so **caution is advised**. Do not touch this organism with any part of your body! It can cause severe pain, sending a person into shock. Consult a physician at once if you are severely stung.

Deflating its wing-like flange changes the Portuguese man-of-war's capability to catch the prevailing wind. This species has commensal relationships with other species. The man-of-war fish (*Nomeus gronovii*) feeds on the Portuguese man-of-war's tentacles while avoiding its stinging cells. Research has determined that this fish can tolerate venom ten times the strength of other fish. At the same time, the fish relies on its speed and agility to avoid being stung. The Portuguese man-of-war can easily regenerate its tentacles, so it is not harmed; it actually benefits by using the fish to lure other fish into its tentacles.

The predators of this species include loggerhead sea turtles (*Caretta carette*) (see p. 278) and leatherback sea turtles (*Dermochelys coriacea*).

By-the-wind Sailor

Velella velella

Authority: (Linnaeus, 1758)
Other Names: Also known as by the wind sailor; formerly classified as *Velella mutica*
Description: The color is transparent overall with blue or violet tentacles. The float is oval with a transparent crest set diagonally on top of the cellophane-like float. Numerous tentacles hang from the edge of the float. Individuals that have been beached for a while lose their blue colors.
Size: Float to 4" (103 mm) long, but normally much smaller; height of crest to 2" (51 mm)
Habitat/Ecology: Pelagic; tropical and subtropical waters
Geographic Range: Florida to Argentina; occasionally as far north as Cape Hatteras; Pacific Coast, occasionally north to British Columbia; cosmopolitan
Notes: The by-the-wind sailor is a "natural" in the sailing world since it tacks at about 45 degrees away from the prevailing wind when viewed with its long axis at right angles to the wind direction. There are two types of sails for this species, as one is an exact mirror to the other. Those with a right-angled sail will sail in the opposite direction to those that have a left-angled sail in the same wind. As a result, you will only find left- or right-angled sails on any one beach after a storm. The other angled sail will be found on another beach at some other location in the world!

Blue Button

Porpita porpita

Authority: (Linnaeus, 1758)
Other Name: Formerly classified as *Porpita linneana*
Description: Overall color is blue with blue-green tentacles; occasionally you'll encounter yellow individuals; the float has a black margin with dark radiating lines. The float is round and flattened, with tentacles attached to the outer rim. No sail is present.
Size: Diameter to 1" (25 mm) across; height to 0.25" (6 mm)
Habitat/Ecology: Pelagic; tropical and subtropical waters
Geographic Range: Cape Hatteras to the Gulf of Mexico; the Caribbean
Notes: Like the Portuguese man-of-war and by-the-wind sailor, this species is not a true jellyfish, but a colonial animal made up of many individuals, called zooids, that make up the organism. A single mouth is found underneath the float where the tentacles bring the food to be ingested. This species is sometimes found washed up on beaches in the Atlantic. Farther south, in tropical waters, it may be viewed in the thousands, coloring the water with blue for miles.

Whitecross Hydromedusa

Staurostoma mertensii

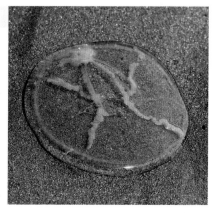

Authority: (Brandt, 1834)

Other Names: Also known as whitecross jellyfish; formerly classified as *Staurophora mertensi*, *S. mertensii*

Description: The entire medusa is transparent, with a milky white cross in the center. Larger individuals may show more colors in various parts of their medusae. The radial canals of the gastro-vascular cavity are shaped into a conspicuous cross when viewed from above. There can be 4,000 tentacles or more on large specimens; however, there are many less on smaller individuals.

Size: Bell diameter to 12" (30 cm), height to 2" (5 cm); normally much smaller

Habitat/Ecology: On the surface of the ocean; large bells are at the surface at night, at depths of 495' (150 m) in the daytime

Geographic Range: Arctic to Cape Cod, occasionally to Rhode Island; the Falklands and South Orkneys in the South Atlantic Ocean; Japan; southern Alaska

Notes: This species is considered bipolar, favoring the cool waters of both hemispheres. The medusae dine upon various small crustaceans as well as other medusae.

TRUE JELLIES (Class Scyphozoa)

True jellies alternate between two phases or stages: the polyp and the medusa. The medusa, or jelly-like, sexual stage is the dominant form. Individuals in this group lack a velum (veil-like ring), which is present in members of the class Hydrozoa. The animal moves by repeatedly contracting the muscles of the bell, which pushes water out and propels the jelly forward.

The main diet includes zooplankton, phytoplankton, larval fish, and other jellies. Various fishes, loggerhead turtles, and other sea creatures feed on jellies. So do humans, particularly in Japan and China, where jellies are eaten in salads and considered a delicacy.

Sea Wasp

Tamoya haplonema

Authority: O. F. Müller, 1859

Description: The whitish body is comprised of two parts. The umbrella is tough and rigid with a high dome shape. The tentacles are found at four points at the edge of the umbrella— each in groups of up to nine tentacles.

Size: Bell diameter to 2.1" (5.5 cm); height to 3.5" (9 cm)

Habitat/Ecology: Pelagic

Geographic Range: Long Island to Brazil

Notes: Although the sting of the sea wasp is not lethal, it can be quite painful. **Caution is advised** with this species. If you encounter a sea wasp while swimming, treat the area affected by washing it with seawater (not freshwater) to remove any cells that have not been discharged. The medusa has been observed in near shore waters during every month from May through December.

Lion's Mane Jelly

Cyanea capillata

Authority: (Linnaeus, 1758)

Other Names: Also known as lion's mane, red jelly

Description: The medusa is translucent: brown to red or deep purple with a flat-topped shape. It has its long tentacles arranged into eight clusters that hang from the outer edge of the cap.

Size: Bell diameter to 96" (244 cm); height to 24" (61 cm)

Habitat/Ecology: Pelagic

Geographic Range: Arctic to Mexico; Alaska to California

Notes: The lion's mane jelly is the largest jelly in the world. Specimens have been found that were 8' (2.4 m) in diameter with tentacles that could extend for 200' (60 m). It is possible that this large of a specimen may represent another closely related species. This species displays a variety of colors as it ages.

Atlantic Sea Nettle

Chrysaora quinquecirrha

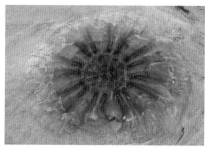

Authority: (Desor, 1848)
Other Names: Sea nettle, East Coast sea nettle
Description: Bell color varies from milky to pink with radiating reddish stripes; bell margin with scalloped clefts; four elongated oral arms below bell with ruffles.
Size: *Bay form:* bell diameter to 4" (10 cm); height to 2" (5 cm)
  Outer coast form: bell diameter to 10" (25 cm); height to 20" (50 cm)
Habitat/Ecology: Usually found floating near the surface of the water and occasionally stranded on the beach
Geographic Range: Cape Cod to the Gulf of Mexico

Notes: Depending on the habitat, you may encounter two forms of this species. In estuaries a small form exists that only reaches 2" (5 cm) in diameter. This is a milky form which can become especially abundant in Chesapeake Bay and other estuaries. On the outer coast a larger, brighter form exists that may be found at least 10 km offshore. **Be cautious** with this species, as its powerful nematocysts can easily penetrate human skin. As in many other species of jellies, Atlantic sea nettles can cause painful reactions. Swimming in areas with high densities is not recommended. Stranded specimens can also cause reactions.

North Atlantic Moon Jelly

Aurelia aurita

Authority: (Linnaeus, 1758)
Other Name: Formerly included with *Aurelia marginalis*
Description: The medusa is large, translucent, and comprised of an umbrella-shaped, flat bell with four circular gonads or "moons" visible from above. The gonads are found in yellow, pink, or brown. Four relatively long arms with ruffles hang below the bell. Numerous small tentacles are found on the margin of the bell. The mouth is in the shape of a cross.
Size: Bell diameter to 19.5" (50 cm); height to 3" (7.6 cm)
Habitat/Ecology: Pelagic
Geographic Range: Arctic to New Jersey

Notes: The North Atlantic moon jelly is a cold water jelly that was once believed to be found in waters as far south as Florida. This common species is often abundant in dense aggregations.

Similar Species: South Atlantic Moon Jelly (*Aurelia marginalis*) bears four shorter arms that hang from its bell. Its range extends from Delaware to the Gulf of Mexico.

Cannonball Jelly

Stomolophus meleagris

Authority: Agassiz, 1862

Other Names: Also known as jellyball, cabbagehead jellyfish

Description: The cap is milky blue to yellowish with a spotted brown ring around the outer margin; cap is deep, hemispherical, and very tough. The sixteen oral arms under the cap are fused.

Size: Bell diameter normally to 7" (18 cm); height to 5" (13 cm)

Habitat/Ecology: Usually found floating near the surface of the water and occasionally stranded on the beach

Geographic Range: Massachusetts to Florida and Texas; Bahamas; West Indies; uncommon north of Chesapeake Bay

Notes: The solid nature of this common species is uncommon in jellies and likely the reason for the name "cannonball." This tropical medusa has been observed during the warmer months of summer and fall in the Cape Hatteras region and year round in the Gulf of Mexico and south. It feeds upon a wide range of juvenile invertebrates found suspended in the water. It is a favored food for sea turtles.

Juvenile six-spined spider crabs (see p. 232) are frequently found living happily under the bell of this jelly. It is believed that they settle there as larvae and live as a symbiont while they grow. Watch for them inside the bell of stranded cannonball jellies. This species is not toxic, so it is safe to touch.

Mushroom Cap Jelly

Rhopilema Verrilli

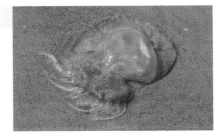

Authority: (Fewkes, 1887)

Other Names: Also known as mushroom cap, mushroom cap jellyfish

Description: The bell is creamy with brown or yellow markings present on the oral arms. The cap is deep, hemispherical, and firm. No tentacles are present on the margin, and numerous finger-like structures hang from the oral arms.

Size: Bell diameter to 14" (35 cm); height to 17" (44 cm)

Habitat/Ecology: Usually found floating near the surface of the water and occasionally stranded on the beach

Geographic Range: Long Island Sound to the Gulf of Mexico

Notes: Oral arms found below the cap on jellies are used for feeding. Long tentacles are often present on other species and used to obtain food, but these structures are not present on the mushroom cap jelly. Juvenile spider crabs (see p. 232) and blue crabs (see p. 236) may be found under the cap of the mushroom cap jelly. This species is not venomous to humans.

Ⓘ Australian Spotted Jelly

Phyllorhiza punctata

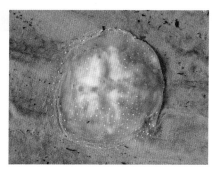

Authority: Lendenfeld, 1884

Other Name: Also known as Australian spotted jellyfish

Description: The bell color is milky (brownish in other populations), covered evenly with white spots. It is smooth with approximately one hundred lappets (small finger-like extensions that hang from the bell margin); eight oral arms (long projections) hang from beneath—each with elongated stinging cells attached.

Size: Bell diameter to 18" (45 cm) across; height to 24" (60 cm)

Habitat/Ecology: On or near the surface of the ocean near shore

Geographic Range: North Carolina to Florida; Gulf of Mexico

Notes: This jelly is an invasive species that is believed to have first appeared on the coast of Louisiana in 1993. This was possibly a result of a natural invasive population or more likely an accidental transplantation in the hulls of ships. Its first population explosion occurred in 2000, and it reappeared again in 2007 under favorable conditions. These cyclic appearances are likely a result of a combination of environmental factors favoring this species in certain years.

  The size of this Gulf Coast population is much larger than other populations around the world including: Western Australia, Eastern Australia, Western United States, and Puerto Rico. Each population found around the globe is unique enough in its appearance to identify it.

Comb Jellies
(Phylum Ctenophora)

Comb jellies look similar to jellies, except rather than opening and contracting a bell as jellies do, they use eight rows of ctenes (clusters of minute cilia) to move themselves in water. Comb jellies do not sting, but those that have tentacles use adhesive cells instead of stinging cells, while others may have two oral lobes (flaps next to the mouth), and still others have neither. There is no alternation of generations as there is in the bell-shaped jellies.

Comb jellies are voracious predators that capture small prey, especially plankton, although young fish and any other unlucky organisms may also become meals. They often occur in large swarms or blooms that arise overnight in sheltered waters.

Sea Grape Comb Jelly

Pleurobrachia pileus

Authority: (O. F. Müller, 1776)

Other Names: Also known as sea grape, sea walnut, sea gooseberry

Description: The body is transparent and iridescent. The shape of the body varies from round to oval, and two elongated tentacles are present, as well as eight rows of comb plates.

Size: Height to 1.1" (28 mm); width to 1" (25 mm)

Habitat/Ecology: On the surface of the ocean near shore

Geographic Range: Nova Scotia to Florida and Texas

Notes: Although the sea grape comb jelly is found along most of the Atlantic Coast, it is seldom found in estuaries—perhaps due to the reduced salinity found there. This species does not have bioluminescence. It is often found in large swarms. These swarms have been known to decimate large schools of young cod.

Similar Species: Arctic Sea Gooseberry (*Mertensia ovum*) is a pear-shaped, flattened, larger species, growing to 2" (51 mm) high and 1" (25 mm) wide. It can be found from the Arctic to the Gulf of Maine, and occasionally to Cape Cod during winter.

Beroe's Common Comb Jelly

Beroe cucumis

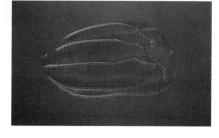

Authority: Fabricius, 1780
Other Names: Also known as pink
  slipper comb jelly, Beroid comb jelly
Description: In mature specimens, the
  elongated, transparent body is bluish
  overall with comb rows and a merid-
ional canal that has side-branches that fuse with opposing canals. The body can be a
variety of colors, including pink or rust, depending upon the age of the individual.
Size: Height to 2" (51 mm); length to 4.5" (114 mm)
Habitat/Ecology: On the surface of the ocean near shore
Geographic Range: New Brunswick to Cape Cod; Alaska to California
Notes: The diet of this species includes medusae and other comb jellies. Studies of
  this northern species have determined that it could not survive the temperatures
  found in the surface waters of the tropics. Beroe's common comb jelly is difficult to
  differentiate from the ovate comb jelly in the field, but their differing ranges are
  helpful.
Similar Species: **Ovate Comb Jelly** (*Beroe ovata*) (see below) is a similar species
  that can only be identified in adult specimens. Note range.

Ovate Comb Jelly

Beroe ovata

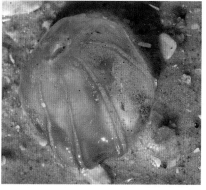

Authority: Bruguière, 1789
Other Name: Also known as Beroe's
  comb jelly
Description: In mature specimens, the
  elongated, transparent body is bluish
  overall with comb rows and a merid-
ional canal that has side-branches that
do not fuse with opposing canals.
Mature specimens are often pinkish,
but young individuals show brown or
yellowish spots on the circulatory canals and mouth. This species is bell-shaped and
strongly compressed from side to side.
Size: Length to 4.5" (112 mm)
Habitat/Ecology: On the surface of the ocean near shore
Geographic Range: Chesapeake Bay to Florida, Gulf of Mexico, and Caribbean
Notes: During daylight hours the ciliated rows are iridescent, as in many comb jellies,
  but at night this species is bioluminescent! The ovate comb jelly is commonly found
  in estuaries during the winter months. The genus *Beroe* originates from mythology,
  as Beroe was one of the sea nymphs, a daughter of Oceanus.
Similar Species: **Beroe's Common Comb Jelly** (*Beroe cucumis*) (see above) is a
  similar species that can only be identified in adult specimens. Also note the range.

Marine Worms

Marine worms have been grouped together simply because they are similar-looking phyla. They are unrelated, however. These worms belong to several different phyla including Flatworms (Phylum Platyhelminthes), Ribbon Worms (Phylum Nemertea), Segmented Worms (Phylum Annelida), Peanut Worms (Phylum Sipuncula), Spoonworms (Phylum Echiura), and Acorn Worms (Phylum Hemichordata).

FLATWORMS (Phylum Platyhelminthes)

Flatworms are noticeably flattened—hence their name. Members of this phylum are hermaphroditic and capable of both sexual and asexual reproduction. Their bodies have one opening, which serves as both a mouth and an anus. This primitive group does not possess eyes, but they may have numerous eyespots—light-detecting organs that help them find their way. Their length varies considerably, from the microscopic to 2' (60 cm).

Spotted Oyster Flatworm

Stylochus oculiferus

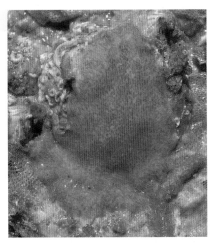

Authority: Girard, 1853
Other Names: Formerly classified as
S. floridanus, Imogine oculifera
Description: Overall brown to cream colored with small red to pink spots. Its large body has a distinctive ruffled edge. Eyespots are distributed along the edge of its entire body. Eyespots are also found on the tentacles, as well as on the body at the base of the tentacles and on the large area between the tentacles.
Size: Length to 2" (53 mm)
Habitat/Ecology: On oyster shells; low intertidal zone to shallow depths
Geographic Range: North Carolina to Florida
Notes: This large and beautiful species is uncommon and likely feeds upon oysters.

Speckled Flatworm

Pleioplana atomata

Authority: Girard, 1853

Description: The dorsal coloration ranges from brownish gray to chocolate brown overall, with fine streaks or blotches. Four clusters of ocelli, or eyespots, are present on the body, but ocelli are totally absent along its margin. No tentacles are present.

Size: To 1.5" (38 mm) long; to 0.75" (19 mm) wide

Habitat/Ecology: Under rocks, on algae, and in tidepools; low intertidal zone to subtidal waters

Geographic Range: New Brunswick to Cape Cod

Notes: The speckled flatworm is believed to be the most common northern flatworm on our rocky coast. This flatworm is a predator and has been reported to trap small invertebrates in the sticky slime trail it leaves behind. This species also occurs in Northern Europe.

Brown Ruffle-edged Flatworm

Phrikoceros mopsus

Authority: (Marcus, 1952)

Other Name: Formerly classified as *Pseudoceros mopsus*

Description: The background color is brown with small gray spots distributed over the entire body. A darker brown longitudinal band forms along the mid-dorsal area. A fine black line normally borders the outer edge of the oval body. Eyes are arranged in a triangular-shaped cluster of forty to fifty tiny eyes in the head area. Several additional clusters of eyes are also present elsewhere. Pseudotentacles are present and square-shaped.

Size: To 2" (5 cm) long

Habitat/Ecology: In rocky sites with tidepools and coralline algae; low intertidal zone

Geographic Range: Florida to Patagonia

Notes: The brown ruffle-edged flatworm is a common Caribbean species. The diet of this graceful predator includes clams and various other mollusks. It is the northernmost of the several species in the genus *Phrikoceros*.

RIBBON WORMS (Phylum Nemertea)

Ribbon worms lack segments and possess a body that is smooth, although their arrangement of gonads, which may be viewed through their translucent skin, may suggest the presence of segments. They are more advanced than flatworms, possessing a blood or circulatory system. They also possess eye spots (or ocelli) and sensory grooves located on the head. The eye spots are sensitive to light intensity.

Red Lineus

Lineus ruber

Authority: (O. F. Müller, 1774)
Description: The color varies greatly on the dorsal side, from dark red to green or brown, with a lighter ventral surface. The head displays a light edge. Its body is slender, slightly flattened, with a wider head than the remainder of body when it is not contracted. There are two to eight black eyespots and a slit on each side of the head.
Size: Length to 8" (200 mm); width to 0.1" (3 mm)
Habitat/Ecology: Under rocks and shells, on sandy mud habitats, in mussel beds, among barnacles, and in rock pools; high intertidal zone to shallow subtidal depths
Geographic Range: Arctic to Long Island Sound; Washington to central California
Notes: The red lineus is believed by some to be the most common ribbon worm found along our Atlantic Coastline. It feeds primarily on polychaete worms (annelids). As indicated above, it is present in a wide range of muddy habitats.
Similar Species: **Green Lineus** (*L. viridis*) is similar in coloration, from dark green to nearly black on its dorsal side, with a lighter ventral surface. Pale transverse lines are often visible along the length of its body.

Milky Ribbon Worm

Cerebratulus lacteus

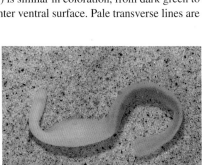

Authority: (Leidy, 1851)
Other Names: Also known as milky nemertean
Description: The body is pinkish to milky white or yellowish. The head is grooved on the ventral side (underside).
Size: Length to 48" (122 cm); width to 0.6" (16 cm)

This individual is much shorter than normal

Habitat/Ecology: Under rocks and similar objects in sand; low intertidal zone to subtidal depths
Geographic Range: Whole coast

Notes: This ribbon worm is capable of swimming using an undulating motion. During the breeding season, the males are bright red and females are brown. The skin of all ribbon worms contains both mucus-producing cells and ciliated cells. The mucus-producing cells produce a semi-permanent burrow that ribbon worms live inside.

SEGMENTED WORMS (Phylum Annelida)

The phylum Annelida includes three classes: Polychaeta, Oligochaeta, and Hirudinea. The majority of marine annelids discovered on intertidal shores are Polychaeta (segmented worms with bristles). One species of Oligochaeta (earth worms) is included here. No Hirudinea (leeches) have been included here. There are approximately 9,000 known species that belong to this phylum.

All members of this phylum are segmented, and each segment includes circulatory, nervous and excretory tracts. Segmented worms are considered to be a more advanced worm phylum because muscle contraction is localized allowing for a more complex organism.

POLYCHAETE WORMS (Class Polychaeta)

Polychaete worms are segmented worms with bristles, and they are a numerous and diverse group of annelids. This varied group ranges in size from a few centimeters to 10' (3 m) in length.

Tufted Twelve-paired Scaleworm

Lepidonotus squamatus

Authority: (Linnaeus, 1758)
Other Names: Also known as twelve-scaled worm; formerly *L. squamata*
Description: The body is tan, gray, or mottled and covered with twelve or thirteen pairs of scales. Roughened projections of several sizes are present on the scales. The tentacles and antennae are dark-banded with pointed tips.
Size: Length to 2" (51 mm); width to 0.6" (16 mm)
Habitat/Ecology: On and under rocks, shells, and on pilings; low intertidal zone to water 8,000' (2438 m) deep
Geographic Range: Labrador to Chesapeake Bay; Alaska to California
Notes: The tufted twelve-paired scaleworm is a species that often rolls up into a ball when it is threatened rather than shedding scales as other scaleworms often do. This species provides food for several fish species.
Similar Species: Commensal Twelve-paired Scaleworm (*Lepidonotus sublevis*) (see p. 34)

Commensal Twelve-paired Scaleworm

Lepidonotus sublevis

Authority: Verrill, 1873
Other Name: Also known as bristleworm
Description: Its grayish, greenish, or reddish brown body is covered with twelve pairs of scales. These scales bear low, uniform-size, conical projections.
Size: Length to 1.4" (35 mm); width to 0.4" (10 mm)
Habitat/Ecology: Living with hermit crabs, as well as in oyster beds and under rocks; low intertidal zone to subtidal depths
Geographic Range: Cape Cod to Florida and Texas
Notes: The commensal twelve-paired scaleworm gets its common name because it lives commensally in a shell with the flat-clawed hermit crab (see p. 222) and others.
Similar Species: Variable Twelve-scaled Worm (*Lepidonotus variabilis*) is a smaller species that reaches 1" (25 mm) long, with scales that are mottled gray or brown, each of which has its rear border edged in short hairs. It can be found among oyster shells and rubble from Florida to Texas and the West Indies.

Painted Fifteen-paired Scaleworm

Harmothoe imbricata

Authority: (Linnaeus, 1767)
Other Name: Also known as fifteen-scaled worm
Description: The overall color is variable and includes red, orange, brown, green, gray, and black— speckled or mottled. Some individuals also may have a black stripe down the back. It has a total of fifteen pairs of scales. Although two pairs of eyes are present on the frontal lobe, only one pair can be seen from above; the other pair can only be seen from below.
Size: Length to 2.5" (65 mm), width to 0.75" (19 mm)
Habitat/Ecology: Under rocks, in tidepools, on mussels, holdfasts, and similar locations, and estuaries; low intertidal zone to water 12,172' (3710 m) deep
Geographic Range: Arctic to New Jersey; Alaska to California; Europe; Indian Ocean; Arctic Ocean
Notes: The painted fifteen-paired scaleworm is a species that has been found in many areas around the globe. In some regions, females are known to brood their eggs beneath their scales. Females of various sizes are known to lay from less than 5,000 to 40,000 or more eggs. This species is able to live quite happily in brackish water. This opportunistic species also lives commensally with tubeworms, or inside the shells occupied by hermit crabs.

Similar Species: Four-eyed Fifteen-paired Scaleworm (*Harmothoe extenuata*) is larger—to 3" (76 mm) long and 0.75" (19 mm) wide—with similar colors. Both pairs of its eyes can be viewed from above. Its range is the same as the painted fifteen-paired scaleworm.

Two-gilled Bloodworm

Glycera dibranchiata

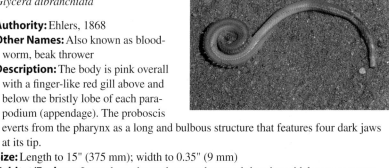

Authority: Ehlers, 1868
Other Names: Also known as bloodworm, beak thrower
Description: The body is pink overall with a finger-like red gill above and below the bristly lobe of each parapodium (appendage). The proboscis everts from the pharynx as a long and bulbous structure that features four dark jaws at its tip.
Size: Length to 15" (375 mm); width to 0.35" (9 mm)
Habitat/Ecology: In mud, sandy mud, or sandy gravel; low intertidal zone to water 1322' (405 m) deep
Geographic Range: Gulf of St. Lawrence to Florida and Texas; California to Mexico
Notes: Two-gilled bloodworms burrow in the mud with a technique that's unique to segmented worms. With great force, they propel their large and muscular pharynx into the substrate in front of them. They then contract their pharynx muscles, pulling their body forward, since their pharynx is anchored into the substrate ahead of them.

There are separate sexes for this species, and spawning occurs mid-June, just before high tide. Male worms are the first to spawn, followed by the females. Mature females have been known to produce up to ten million eggs; however, few are expected to reach maturity.

This species is commonly collected for fishing bait from Nova Scotia and Maine. Fishers and beachcombers alike should be cautious, since this species can deliver a nasty bite!

Leafy Shimmyworm

Nephtys caeca

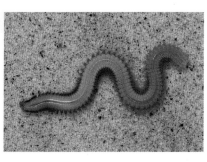

Authority: (Fabricius, 1780)
Other Names: Also known as red-lined worm, sand worm
Description: The body is green, white, or bronze, with extensions that resemble leaves found behind each pair of appendages.
Size: Length to 8" (20 cm), width to 0.6" (1.6 cm)
Habitat/Ecology: In sand and muddy sand; mid-intertidal zone to depths of 1,312' (400 m)

Geographic Range: Arctic to Rhode Island

Notes: The leafy shimmyworm does not have any eyes, and correspondingly *caeca* is the Latin term for blind. This shimmyworm has amazing regenerative abilities. If it loses one or more tentacles, it can regenerate them, or even its head!

The diet of this worm includes various intertidal invertebrates, including other polychaete worms. It can also digest any organic matter that it may ingest while it burrows. This species can live to six years.

Iridescent Sandworm

Alitta virens

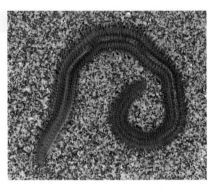

Authority: (M. Sars, 1835)

Other Names: Also known as clam-worm, ragworm; formerly classified as *Nereis virens*, *Neanthes virens*

Description: As its common name indicates, the color is an iridescent greenish or bluish from above, normally with small red, gold, or white spots. Its head has four pairs of tentacles that are all equal length. Its body tapers toward the rear, with a head section that is larger, and its proboscis bears a pair of strong, black jaws. Its head has four pairs of tentacles—all of equal length.

Size: Length to 8" (200 mm)

Habitat/Ecology: In sand, mud, clay, or peat in protected areas and estuaries; high intertidal zone to depths of 600' (175 m)

Geographic Range: New Brunswick to Virginia; entire Pacific Coast

Notes: Large specimens can be quite spectacular to view, with their rich opalescent green and other remarkable colors. This polychaete is known to make rather irregular burrows. It, like other members of its genus, feeds upon a variety of invertebrates, including other worms.

Similar Species: Common Sandworm (*Alitta succinea*) is colored greenish to brown toward its anterior portion and yellow to reddish toward its posterior. It also displays small parapodia near its head, and longer, flattened parapodia near its rear. This species' jaws are pale amber rather than black, and it builds a U-shaped burrow in sandy mud. Its length reaches 6" (150 mm), and it ranges from the Gulf of St. Lawrence to Cape Cod.

Plumed Worm

Diopatra cuprea

Authority: (Bosc, 1802)

Other Name: Also known as decorator worm

Description: Color of the worm is reddish to brown and speckled with gray. It has appendages that are yellowish brown or just yellowish. The most noteworthy characteristic of this species is its distinctive tube that is encrusted with various debris projecting from the upper portion of its tube. Its proboscis is armed with large jaws and segments four (or five) to thirty-five display bushy gills on their dorsal surfaces.

Size: Length to 12" (30 m); width to 0.4" (10 mm)

Surface view

Habitat/Ecology: On mud and sandy shores in protected areas; low intertidal zone to water 270' (81 m) deep

Geographic Range: Cape Cod to Brazil

Notes: The plumed worm builds and lives inside tubes that it secretes from its body. These black tubes have nothing attached to them beneath the surface; however, above ground this is not the case. There, the tube is camouflaged with plant fibers, shell fragments, seaweeds, sticks, and other debris that are bound to it. The conspicuous portion of this tube may reach several inches. This exposed section of the tube is normally downturned if it is long enough—a practice that is likely to prevent debris from falling inside the tube.

Northern Lugworm

Arenicola marina

Casting on beach

Authority: (Linnaeus, 1758)

Other Names: Also known as lugworm, northern lug worm; formerly classified as *Arenicola clavata*

Description: The gray or greenish body bears twelve to thirteen pairs of red gills.

Size: Length to 8" (20 cm); width to 0.75" (1.9 cm)

Habitat/Ecology: On sand or mudflats; low intertidal zone to shallow subtidal

Geographic Range: Arctic to Cape Cod

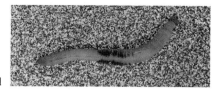

Notes: This is a common species in the North Atlantic. It is an easy species to detect, since it leaves its distinctive sand casting—a rope of sandy mud held together by mucus. Northern lugworms inhabit their burrows for a few weeks, until they have removed and digested the nutrients from the surrounding area immediately around them. Then they move on to a new site and build a new burrow. Occasionally lugworms can be found while they are outside of their burrows searching for a new homesite. During these times, they are vulnerable, and if disturbed they will cast off the hind section of their body, which can later be regenerated.

Similar Species: South Atlantic Lugworm (*Arenicola cristata*) is a large species—12" (30 cm) or more in length—that is reddish or greenish red in color with eleven prominent gills. The green pigment in the skin (arenicochrome) stains human skin when this worm is handled. In spring, this species produces an elongated amber or pink gelatinous egg mass that can reach 36" (90 cm) long from the burrow.

Collared Bamboo-worm

Clymenella torquata

Authority: (Leidy, 1855)
Other Name: Also known as
    bambooworm
Description: Two colors may be found: either cream with red joints or greenish. The head bears a flat top and an opercular plate to seal the sand tube.

Worm and tube

Large specimens display a collar on the fourth segment. The first segment bears six to eight setae.

Size: Length to 6" (150 mm)
Habitat/Ecology: In sand or sandy mud in protected sites; low intertidal zone to water 330' (100 m) deep
Geographic Range: Bay of Fundy to North Carolina
Notes: The tubes made by bamboo worms truly look like miniature bamboo poles. The collared bamboo-worm builds vertical tubes that may reach 10" (25 mm) in length in its sandy environment—the top of which may be observed at low tide. This species is found intertidally in the northern portion of its range but subtidally in the south. Other species are also present along the Atlantic Coast, but they are primarily subtidal. Bamboo worms are sometimes called "mud eaters" or deposit feeders.

There is also a crab, the bamboo worm pea crab (*Pinnixa longipes*) that sometimes shares the tube of this species. Together, they live in the same tube commensally.

Gould's Trumpetworm

Pectinaria gouldii

Tube.

Authority: (Verrill, 1874)

Other Names: Also known as ice-cream-cone worm, ice cream cone worm, trumpet worm, trumpetworm

Description: Pink overall with red and blue markings; head with two sets of golden bristles. The trumpet-shaped tube has a slight curve.

Size: Worm length to 2" (51 mm); width to 0.75" (19 mm)

Tube length to 2.5" (64 mm); width to 0.25" (6 mm) at large end

Habitat/Ecology: In sand and sandy mud in estuaries with low salinities; low intertidal zone to water 90' (27 m) deep

Geographic Range: Bay of Fundy to Florida

Notes: No finer stonemason work can be found than the intricate work performed by trumpetworms. A close look at their tubes will confirm that they have selected only the most perfectly sized and shaped sand grains for their home—meticulously gluing these together to build their tubes. As the worm grows, it adds slightly larger sand grains to its tube with amazing precision. Gould's trumpetworm lives upside down inside its cone-shaped tube, feeding on sand grains that are coated with microbes. Both ends of the tube remain open, with the small end facing up—exposed for breathing.

There are also two other trumpetworms that are found in the Atlantic's northern region, but these are found in subtidal waters.

Large Fringeworm

Cirratulus grandis

Authority: (Verrill, 1873)

Other Names: Also known as large fringed worm, orange fringed worm

Description: Color is yellowish, to red, orange, green, or brown; the contents of the gut are normally visible. Only segments number eight from the head and greater have clusters of long, slender filaments. There are no eyes present.

Size: Length to 6" (150 mm); width 0.25" (6 mm)

Habitat/Ecology: On mud flats; low intertidal zone to moderate subtidal depths

Geographic Range: Cape Cod to North Carolina

Notes: When viewing this large species, it can be difficult to differentiate between the gills and the feeding tentacles, as they appear similar. If the animal is disturbed, however, the tentacles are quickly withdrawn.

Similar Species: Eyed Fringeworm (*Cirratulus cirratus*) is a smaller species, 4.75" (121 mm) long, that bears two to nine pairs of eyes arranged in an arc on its bluntly pointed head. It can be found from Cape Cod to Maine.

Potter Spaghetti-worm

Amphitrite figulus

Authority: (Dalyell, 1853)

Other Names: Also known as Johnston ornate worm, Johnston ornate terebellid; formerly classified as *Neoamphitrite figulus*, *Amphitrite johnstoni*

Description: The body is orange, pink, red, or brown overall with many long, slender, yellowish orange tentacles extending from the head. The tapering body bears twenty-three to forty-five segments, with setae present on twenty-four to twenty-five segments.

Size: Length to 10" (25 cm); width to 0.5" (1.2 cm)

Habitat/Ecology: Under rocks; low intertidal zone to shallow subtidal depths

Geographic Range: Arctic to New Jersey

Notes: Seeking refuge from beneath a rock or similar object, the body of the Potter spaghetti-worm is normally hidden from view—and from predators. The feeding tentacles are normally all that is visible, as it uses them to sweep the surface for food. Living inside a tube composed of mucus, sand, or mud, it extends its grooved, mucus-covered tentacles to sweep the nearby area for food. Small organic particles return to the mouth conveyor belt style. Numerous similar spaghetti-worms are found in the area, and their identification can be difficult.

Similar Species: Ornate Spaghetti-worm (*Amphitrite ornate*) may also be encountered from Maine to North Carolina. This large species reaches 15" (38 cm), and it builds its tube underground to a depth of 12" (30 cm) or more.

Common Broom Worm

Pherusa affinis

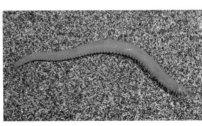

Authority: (Leidy, 1855)

Other Names: Also known as bristle-worm; formerly classified as *Trophonia affinis*

Description: The body is yellowish brown with large bristle-like palps at the anterior end.

Size: Length to 2.3" (58 mm); width to 0.2" (5 mm)

Habitat/Ecology: In silt, sand, and mud; low intertidal zone to shallow subtidal

Geographic Range: Bay of Fundy to Chesapeake Bay

Notes: The common broom worm secretes mucous that adheres to the surrounding sand, forming a tube to live inside. This species is quite tolerant of sludge and organic debris. Its predators include various crabs and fishes.

Dextral Spiral Tubeworm

Circeis spirillum

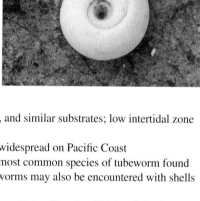

Authority: (Linnaeus, 1758)
Other Names: Also known as dextral spiral tube worm; formerly classified as *Spirorbis spirillum*
Description: The small shell is white and flattened, with a dextral or right-handed coil.
Size: Width to 0.25" (6.4 mm) across coil
Habitat/Ecology: On algae, stones, shells, and similar substrates; low intertidal zone to shallow subtidal waters
Geographic Range: Arctic to Cape Cod; widespread on Pacific Coast
Notes: The dextral spiral tubeworm is the most common species of tubeworm found on Atlantic shores. Other species of tubeworms may also be encountered with shells of varying shapes.
Similar Species: Sinistral Spiral Tubeworm (*Spirorbis spirorbis*) (see below)

Sinistral Spiral Tubeworm

Spirorbis spirorbis

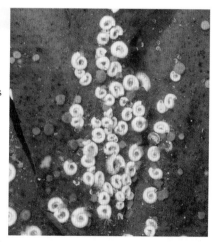

Authority: (Linnaeus, 1758)
Other Names: Also known as sinistral spiral tube worm; formerly classified as *Spirorbis borealis*
Description: The small shell is white and flattened, with a sinistral or left-handed coil.
Size: Width to 0.1" (3 mm) across coil
Habitat/Ecology: On algae, including rockweed and Irish moss, and rocks and similar hard objects; low intertidal zone
Geographic Range: Arctic to Cape Cod
Notes: Unlike most polychaete worms, The sinistral spiral tubeworm is hermaphroditic. In this species the forward segments of the abdomen are female and the rear ones male. In this way, if another worm is nearby, then its sex does not matter.
Similar Species: Dextral Spiral Tubeworm (*Circeis spirillum*) (see above)

Carnation Worm

Hydroides dianthus

Authority: (Verrill, 1873)
Other Names: Also known as Atlantic tube worm, limy tubeworm; formerly classified as *Hydroides uncinata*
Description: Whitish tubes are produced in irregular shapes. A red or mottled branchial plume is present.
Size: Length to 3" (76 mm); width to 0.1" (3 mm)
Habitat/Ecology: On stones, shells, and other hard surfaces; low intertidal zone to water 50' (15 m) deep
Geographic Range: Cape Cod to Florida and Texas; West Indies
Notes: The tubes of this species are distinctive as they straddle over any hard surface lacking patterns or coils. The tubes of this species are somewhat translucent, sometimes allowing the viewer to observe the greenish color of its green blood vessels.

Parchment Tubeworm

Chaetopterus variopedatus

At surface

Authority: (Renier, 1804)
Other Names: Also known as parchment worm, parchment tube worm
Description: Color of body is light yellowish overall. The body is divided into three sections: the head section is flattened, the mid-section has three enlarged parapodia used to pump water, and the last section has smaller segments.
Size: Length to 10" (25 cm); width to 1" (2.5 cm)
Habitat/Ecology: In mud, sandy mud, and eelgrass beds; low intertidal zone to shallow subtidal waters
Geographic Range: Cape Cod to North Carolina; occasional in Maine; West Indies (rare); cosmopolitan in warm seas
Notes: The parchment tubeworm is a blind polychaete worm that lives in a U-shaped burrow. Even though it lives in an opaque tube, it has an interesting defense mechanism: it will release a

Excavated

strikingly blue bioluminescent cloud if disturbed while it withdraws to the opposite end of its tube, leaving the intruder to experience the light show.

Two species of crabs are often "roommates" inside this species' tube in a commensal relationahip. Pairs of the eastern tube crab (*Polyonyx gibbesi*) (see p. 244) are often found inside the tube. Another species that

Worm removed from tube

may often be found is the parchment-worm crab (*Pinnixa chaetopterana*), which is smaller, whiter, and narrower, with a more rectangular carapace. Although these species live in similar ways inside the worm's tube, these crabs belong to two unrelated families of crabs.

Rarely, a third species of crab is found inside the tube, the squatter pea crab (*Tumidotheres maculatus*), which has a nearly circular shell.

Caterpillar Fireworm

Amphinome rostrata

Authority: (Kinberg, 1867)
Other Name: Formerly classified as *Amphinome lepadis*
Description: The color of the body ranges from brownish to black. It is graced with numerous white, bristle-like setae along its body. Tufts of orange filaments (gills) are also present along the sides of its body.
Size: Length to 5" (13 cm); width to 0.6" (1.5 cm)
Habitat/Ecology: Inside the valves of pelagic goose barnacles (see p. 205)
Geographic Range: Pelagic; North Carolina southward; Australia
Notes: This offshore, pelagic species is well named, as it looks much like a fuzzy caterpillar when it is viewed underwater. This species will only be found living in colonies of goose barnacles when they are washed ashore after a storm. Whole pelagic barnacles make up its diet. **Exercise caution** with this species, as touching its setae can cause a painful burning sensation if they break the skin.

Shingle Tube Worm

Owenia fusiformis

Authority: delle Chiaje, 1844
Other Name: Also known as roofing worm
Description: This bristleworm con-structs a burrow that is made out of sand, together with shell fragments, into a delicate, shingle-like arrange-ment. Its uniform shape extends along its entire body and bears tentacles that are only visible when extended.
Size: Length to 6" (15 cm)
Habitat/Ecology: In a sand-mud mix; low intertidal zone to water 990' (300 m) deep
Geographic Range: Maine to Brazil; Europe
Notes: This bristle worm lives in a dis-

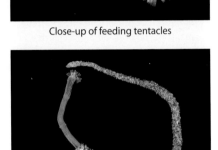

Close-up of feeding tentacles

tinctive shingle-like tube that tapers at both ends. While feeding, it extends itself approximately 0.5" (13 mm) above the substrate to filter and suspension feed on organic detritus.

AQUATIC EARTHWORMS (Class Oligochaeta)

Marine earthworms are related to the common earthworm. Their smooth bodies do not bear bristles as the class Polychaeta does.

Sludge Worms

Clitellio spp.

Authority: Savigny, 1820
Description: The body is pink to red-dish and may appear somewhat translucent. The segmented body is very slender and lacks all appendages.
Size: Length to 2.5" (63 mm)
Habitat/Ecology: In muddy sand in protected areas; high intertidal zone to subtidal depths
Geographic Range: Arctic to Florida
Notes: These species do not possess anterior appendages or parapodia (extensions) on the sides of their smooth bodies. They are generally reddish in color due to the pre-sence of hemoglobin. Individual species in this group are notoriously difficult to identify. Some species reach extremely high population levels providing an impor-tant food source for various birds on migration.

PEANUT WORMS (Phylum Sipuncula)

Peanut worms have only two body parts, one of which is much larger and more globular than the other. Only 320 species in this small group have been identified worldwide.

Rock Boring Peanut Worm

Themiste alutacea

Authority: (Grube, 1858)

Other Names: Also known as rock-boring sipunculan; formerly classified as *Dendrostoma alutaceum*

Description: The color is tan overall with yellowish tentacles. The body is pear-shaped, with dark hooks that are scattered along its trunk. The end of the introvert is circled with six short, branched tentacles.

Size: Length to 0.8" (20 mm)

Habitat/Ecology: Between rocks and rock crevices; low intertidal zone to water 99' (30 m) deep

Geographic Range: North Carolina to Argentina

Notes: This species lives among rocks. It is able to keep itself secured by swelling itself, which makes its removal quite difficult for a predator.

SPOONWORMS (Phylum Echiura; also known as Echiurida or Echiuroidea)

The echiuran worms, or spoonworms, are a small group of approximately 140 species worldwide. They are closely related to segmented worms, but spoonworms lack segments. A non-retractable proboscis (snout) is characteristic for this phylum, and the proboscis contains the brain. Echiura means "spiny tail" in Greek, a reference to the ring or rings of bristles that encircle the hind end of the worm.

Spoonworms

Thalassema spp. and others

Authority: Lamarck, 1801

Description: The sausage-shaped body is often pinkish in color. The proboscis is separated from the body with a constriction.

Size: Length to 10" (25 cm)

Habitat/Ecology: In mud and sand; low intertidal zone to subtidal depths

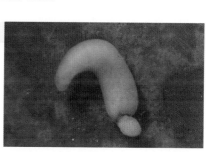

Geographic Range: The entire Atlantic Coast

Notes: Spoonworms move with alternating constrictions by continuous dilations of their body, This creates rhythmic pulsations that extend the full length of their body. They are particulate feeders that secrete mucous to their capture food. Most spoonworms build a burrow in which they live.

ACORN WORMS (Phylum Hemichordata)

The phylum Hemichordata is a small phylum with only a few species worldwide. It was once believed to be closely related to chordates, but that is not the case. Acorn worms have three parts to their bodies. They have a fleshy proboscis used for burrowing. They also have a loose, worm-like body or trunk and several paired gill slits on its dorsal surface. A collar is also attached to the body.

Kowalewsky's Acorn Worm

Saccoglossus kowalevskii

Authority: Agassiz, 1873

Other Names: Also known as helical acorn worm, northern acorn worm

Description: The color of the proboscis is white to pinkish along with an orange collar and a brown trunk. This species is very fragile.

Size: Length to 6" (15 cm); width to 0.25" (.6 cm)

Habitat/Ecology: In sand or mud flats; low intertidal zone to shallow subtidal levels

Geographic Range: Maine to North Carolina

Notes: Kowalewsky's acorn worm leaves distinctive mud castings on the shorelines it inhabits. They appear coiled and string-like, less that 0.8" (20 mm) in diameter, and frequently not piled up. These are small, fragile worms that are near impossible to collect whole, as they extend as far as 14" (350 mm) below the surface. The smell of medicinal iodine is often associated with acorn worms.

Golden Acorn Worm

Balanoglossus aurantiacus

Authority: (Girard, 1853)

Description: The color of the proboscis is whitish to yellowish with a collar that is orange. Its trunk has gold bands on a green or purple background. It bears projections that are flat and wing-like. The collar is the same length or longer that its proboscis.

Casting and tip of worm at surface

Size: Length to 3.3' (1 m); width to 0.4"
(10 mm)

Habitat/Ecology: On mudflats; low
intertidal zone to subtidal depths

Geographic Range: North Carolina to
Florida

Notes: This large species builds
U-shaped burrows that have a diameter
of approximately 0.2" (5 mm). One
opening to the burrow allows water to
enter while the other is used for the
removal of wastes.

Anterior portion of worm

Mollusks
(Phylum Mollusca)

Most mollusks (also spelled molluscs) have one or more internal or external shells, an unsegmented body, a mantle or fold in the body wall (which lines the shell or shells), and a muscular "foot." This diverse group of creatures includes snails, nudibranchs, clams, and octopuses. Scientists estimate there are as many as 130,000 species of mollusks in the world. Most of them are marine animals.

CHITONS (Class Polyplacophora)

Chitons are mollusks that are protected with eight shells, or plates, on their dorsal surface. Eyes are absent, but light-sensitive organs are present on the plates. Most species shun sunlight and are nocturnal, so they are usually found in the shade or under rocks. It is estimated that a total of 600 living species of chitons occur worldwide.

White Northern Chiton

Stenosemus albus

Authority: (Linnaeus, 1767)
Other Name: Also known as white chiton
Description: The overall color is yellowish to pale orange or light brown. The shape of the animal is elongated overall. The plates appear smooth to the naked eye. The girdle is covered with numerous elongated scales.
Size: Length to 0.5" (13 mm); width to 0.25" (6 mm)
Habitat/Ecology: On and beneath rocks; low intertidal zone to water 250' (76 m) deep
Geographic Range: Arctic to Massachusetts Bay; Alaska; Europe
Notes: The northern white chiton's scientific name *albus* refers to its white color. This is one of the easier species of chiton to identify in this area.

Northern Red Chiton

Tonicella rubra

Authority: (Linnaeus, 1767)

Other Names: Also known as red chiton, red northern chiton; formerly classified as *Ischnochiton ruber*

Description: The plates are normally a mottled reddish or brown with white, bluish, or brown zig-zag marks. The girdle is mottled reddish or brown and covered with minute scales. The animal's overall shape is oval. The valves' shape produces a ridge down the center of the dorsal side. The shells are pink inside.

Size: Length to 0.75" (19 mm) and occasionally up to 1" (25 mm); width to 0.4" (10 mm)

Habitat/Ecology: On and around rocks; low intertidal zone to water 450' (137 m) deep

Geographic Range: Arctic to Connecticut

Notes: Like many other chitons, this species feeds upon a variety of algae. The northern red chiton looks similar to the next species, the mottled red chiton. Their girdles differ greatly, with the mottled red chiton's girdle being noticeably smooth and leather-like. There is also no central ridge present in the mottled red chiton.

Similar Species: Mottled Red Chiton (*Tonicella marmorea*) (see below)

Mottled Red Chiton

Tonicella marmorea

Authority: (O. Fabricius, 1780)

Description: The plate color varies from tan to reddish brown, mottled with red, orange, purple, blue, or green. The girdle is smooth, dull, and leather-like. The animal's overall shape is oval. The head valve is flat to slightly convex and there is a slight ridge present along the center of the dorsal side. The shells are rosy pink inside.

Size: Length to 1.5" (38 mm); width to 0.75" (19 mm)

Habitat/Ecology: On rocks; low intertidal zone to water 300' (91 m) deep

Geographic Range: Greenland to Massachusetts Bay; Europe

Notes: The mottled red chiton feeds on a wide variety of sedentary organisms including algae, protozoans, sponges, hydroids, bryozoans, and others. A total of nineteen to twenty-six pairs of gills are present on the underside.

Similar Species: Northern Red Chiton (*Tonicella rubra*) (see above)

Eastern Beaded Chiton

Chaetopleura apiculata

Authority: (Say in Conrad, 1834)
Other Names: Also known as bee chiton, common eastern chiton
Description: Color varies from a dull yellow to green or brown. Specimens from the southern portion of its range often have a streak along the center. Numerous rows of tiny peg-like beads are present on the plates. The girdle is leather-like.
Size: Length to 0.75" (19 mm); width to 0.5" (13 mm)
Habitat/Ecology: On rocks, pen shells, slipper shells, and other hard objects; low intertidal zone to water 90' (27 m) deep
Geographic Range: Cape Cod, Massachusetts to west coast of Florida
Notes: This common species is sometimes called a bee chiton because the root word *apex* in its scientific name was mistakenly confused with *apis*, the Latin name for a bee. This chiton is regularly used for study in embryology. The eggs of this species are covered in numerous multi-branched spines, as well as numerous open pores that allow the sperm to enter.
Similar Species: **Mesh-pitted Chiton** (*Ischnochiton striolatus*) is a smaller tropical species that has an overall greenish or brownish coloration with white, green, brown, or black spots. Numerous irregular small bumps are found on its dorsal side. This tropical species can be found from the low intertidal zone to shallow subtidal sites, and it ranges from North Carolina to Brazil.

Florida Slender Chiton

Stenoplax floridana

Authority: (Pilsbry, 1892)
Other Name: Formerly classified as *Ischnochiton floridanus*
Description: Color varies from yellowish to grayish green, with white or brown spots. The body is slender, elongated, and covered with numerous rows of beaded riblets.
Size: Length to 1.5" (38 mm); width to 0.5" (13 mm)
Habitat/Ecology: Under rocks and shells; low to mid intertidal zone
Geographic Range: Southeast Florida to Panama
Notes: The Florida slender chiton is one of the easier species of chitons to identify simply by its slender shape, with a length approximately three times its width. Although its girdle appears smooth, it actually is covered with fine striated scales.

GASTROPODS (LIMPETS, SNAILS)
(Class Gastropoda)

Gastropods are mollusks that have a muscular "foot" that is present along the underside of the organism. They have a specialized tooth-bearing tongue, or radula, for feeding. Many mollusks also have a specialized organ called the otocyst. This organ is similar to our hearing apparatus, but it is located in the foot of many mollusks and used to help maintain balance.

KEYHOLE LIMPETS (Family Fissurellidae)

Diluvian Puncturella

Puncturella noachina

Authority: (Linnaeus, 1771)
Other Names: Also known as keyhole limpet, Linne's puncturella, little puncturella, Noah's punctured shell; formerly classified as *Puncturella princeps*
Description: The exterior shell color is dull white, and interior is glossy white. Slopes of the shell are steep, and a narrow slit is centered just in front of the tip. Sculpture is composed of sharp, radiating ribs.
Size: Length of shell to 0.5" (12 mm)
Habitat/Ecology: Under rocks; low intertidal zone to water greater than 5310' (1609 m) deep
Geographic Range: Circumpolar; Arctic to Cape Cod
Notes: Shells of this species are often found washed up on the beach. The genus *Puncturella* only includes those species with an opening near the apex but not at the apex of the shell.

Cayenne Keyhole Limpet

Diodora cayenensis

Authority: (Lamarck, 1822)
Other Names: Also known as little keyhole limpet; formerly classified as *D. altemata*
Description: Color is normally white but can also be buff and pinkish to dark gray. A small keyhole-shaped opening

is present at the apex of the shell. Surface sculpture consists of numerous radiating ribs—every fourth rib is larger.

Size: Length of shell to 2" (51 mm); width to 1.4" (35 mm)

Habitat/Ecology: On oyster reefs, floating docks, seawalls, and similar areas; mid intertidal zone to water moderately deep

Geographic Range: New Jersey to Brazil

Notes: The small opening, or anal aperture, that is present at the apex of volcano limpets is used as an outlet for water that has flowed over the gills, as well as for removing body wastes.

Lister's Keyhole Limpet

Diodora listeri

Authority: (d'Orbigny, 1847)

Description: Color is white to gray or buff, sometimes with darker rays. Every second radial rib is large. The concentric lines are more distinct, and when they cross the ribs, they form tiny squares. The radial ribs often have nodules on them. The opening at the apex has some black present and is wedge-shaped, with scalloped outer margins.

Size: Length of shell to 1.75" (45 mm)

Habitat/Ecology: On rocks and similar substrates; low intertidal zone to water 1650' (500 m) deep

Geographic Range: Florida to Brazil; Bermuda

Notes: Lister's keyhole limpet is most often encountered as a shell cast up on the beach.

Similar Species: Cayenne Keyhole Limpet (*Diodora cayenensis*) (see p. 51)

Dyson's Keyhole Limpet

Diodora dysoni

Authority: (Reeve, 1850)
Description: The dorsal side of the shell is white with black bands and with black present at the edge of the hole. The hole is shaped like a broad keyhole and is slightly off-center. A callus surrounds the orifice on the shell's interior. There are three or four small ribs between every strong rib and numerous concentric cords present on all ribs.
Size: Length of shell to 0.9" (22 mm)
Habitat/Ecology: Under rocks and on reefs; subtidal at approximately 6' (1.8 m) deep
Geographic Range: Florida, the Bahamas, and West Indies to Brazil; Bermuda
Notes: The shell of this subtidal species is sometimes found washed ashore, as with most keyhole limpets.

Jaume's Keyhole Limpet

Diodora jaumei

Authority: Aguayo and Rehder, 1936
Description: The dorsal side of shell is white to yellowish, with brown spots and no black present at the edge of the hole. The hole is round to oval-shaped and is at the apex. There is no black line around the hole on the shell's interior.

The ribs alternate between strong and weak ribs, and concentric cords are present as well. This limpet is rather low in profile.
Size: Length of shell to 0.75" (19 mm)
Habitat/Ecology: On rocks; low intertidal zone to water 1326' (402 m) deep
Geographic Range: Florida to the Lesser Antilles
Notes: Several keyhole limpets have a specific shape to the opening of their shell, and a careful look at that opening will help in the identification of many of Florida's keyhole limpets. Jaume's keyhole limpet has an oval-shaped opening.

Barbados Keyhole Limpet

Fissurella barbadensis

Authority: (Gmelin, 1791)
Other Name: Formerly classified as
Fissurella schrammii
Description: The dorsal side of the shell
is variable in color from pink to gray,
purple, or green, with brown blotches.
The shell's interior is off-white with
green rings. The hole is round or
slightly oval at the apex. The ribs are irregular, with both strong and weak ribs
sculptured with irregular knobs.
Size: Length of shell to 1.75" (44 mm)
Habitat/Ecology: On rocks of exposed shorelines; low intertidal zone
Geographic Range: Florida, Bermuda, and the West Indies to Brazil
Notes: This solid shell is often found on beaches, especially in the southern portion of
its range. In one study, the main time frames for the spawning of this species were
from September to November and from March to June.

Rosy Keyhole Limpet

Fissurella rosea

Authority: (Gmelin, 1791)
Other Names: Formerly classified as
Fissurella radiate var. *sculpta*,
Lucapina itapema
Description: The dorsal side of the shell
generally displays pink or purple rays
and a background of white and brown
or yellowish. The colors are variable,
however. The shell's interior is often greenish at the margins, white in the center, and
pink around the hole. The shell is relatively flat and narrower at the anterior end. The
hole is broadly oval and located at the apex. A callus surrounds the orifice on the
shell's interior.
Size: Length of shell to 1.5" (38 mm)
Habitat/Ecology: On and under rocks and similar objects; low intertidal zone
Geographic Range: Florida and the West Indies to Brazil
Notes: This is a relatively common keyhole limpet in the southern portion of its range.
Its coloration is extremely variable.
Similar Species: Barbados Keyhole Limpet (*Fissurella barbadensis*) (see above) has
a higher profile and a thicker shell.

LIMPETS (Families Lottiidae and Eoacmaeidae)

Tortoiseshell Limpet

Testudinalia testudinalis

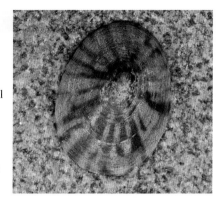

Authority: (O. F. Müller, 1776)

Other Names: Also known as Atlantic plate limpet, plant limpet, tortoise shell limpet, tortoise-shell limpet; formerly classified as *Acmaea testudinalis*, *Notoacmaea testudinalis*

Description: Color of shell's exterior is cream colored with irregular axial bars and streaks of brown. Some shells are greenish with the presence of algae. The interior is white or bluish white with a rather large, brown center spot and a checkered or solid border. The shell has a low profile with a smooth, oval shape.

Size: Length normally to 1" (25 mm) and occasionally to 2" (50 mm)

Habitat/Ecology: On rocks, pilings, shells, kelp stipes, and in tidepools; mid intertidal zones to water 165' (50 m) deep

Geographic Range: Arctic to Long Island Sound

Notes: The tortoiseshell limpet has displayed some homing behavior in the subtidal environment, but this has not yet been observed in the intertidal zone. Homing behavior is the practice of returning exactly to the same location on a rock to rest between feeding sessions. This species lives to three years. It lays its red eggs in the springtime in thin sheets.

Spotted Limpet

Eoacmaea pustulata

Authority: (Helbling, 1779)

Other Names: Formerly classified as *Acmaea pustulata*, *Patella puncturata*, *Patella pustulata*, *Patelloida pustulata*

Description: The exterior color of the shell is white, with numerous red, orange, or reddish brown spots or splotches—often with radial lines from the apex to the shell's edge. Fine, concentric threads are often present. The interior is white, often with an orange or yellow callus in the center. The shell is low, with a central apex and a base that is broadly oval or elliptical.

Size: Length to 1" (25 mm)

Habitat/Ecology: On and under rocks and on turtle grass; low intertidal zone to water 180' (54 m) deep

Geographic Range: Florida to the West Indies; Venezuela

Notes: This attractive limpet is easy to identify due to the irregular shape of its shell. The shell is sometimes found coated with a limy covering, which is easily removed by chipping it away with a fine-tipped tool.

Jamaica Limpet

Lottia jamaicensis

Authority: (Gmelin, 1791)
Other Names: Formerly classified as *Acmaea albicosta, Acmaea jamaicensis, Patella jamaicensis*; not a synonym of *Lottia leucopleura*
Description: The exterior of the shell features a brown to black background with five to ten white or yellowish raised ribs. The interior of the shell is white and features a brown or black callus (deposit). The apex is central on a shell with a high profile.
Size: Length to 0.74" (19 mm)
Habitat/Ecology: On smooth rocks; intertidal zone
Geographic Range: Florida to the West Indies; Panama
Notes: This striking species is more common in the Caribbean, and Florida is the northern limit for its range. Like most limpets, its shell is more often found washed up on the beach than the living organism.

LIMPET LOOK-ALIKE (Family Siphonariidae)

Striped Falselimpet

Siphonaria pectinata

Authority: (Linnaeus, 1758)
Other Name: Also known as striped false limpet
Description: The shell exterior is reddish brown with many radial ribs that are worn to white and branch near the shell's margin. The interior is glossy with the dark lines of the exterior showing through the shell.
Size: Length of shell to 1.25" (32 mm)
Habitat/Ecology: On algae-covered rocks, wood, and similar objects; above and below the high intertidal zone

Geographic Range: Florida to Texas; West Indies; Mexico; Portugal; African Mediterranean; West African coast to Angola

Notes: The striped false limpet is an air-breathing gastropod that is not closely related to true limpets or keyhole limpets but looks similar to those clans. Living high on the shoreline, it is often found on the same rocks as the northern interrupted periwinkle (see p. 68). Here, it grazes on microalgae, return-

ing to a "home site" or "scar" on its chosen rock during low tide. These home sites are depressions in the rock that closely fit the contours of the limpet's shell.

Some question whether this is a native species or an introduced species, which is widely distributed through Europe and Africa. Perhaps this question will be answered in the future. Only time will tell.

COILED SNAILS (Numerous Families)

Spiral Margarite

Margarites helicinus

Authority: (Phipps, 1774)

Other Names: Also known as helicina margarite, smooth top snail; formerly classified as *Margarita arctica*, *Margarites beringensis*

Description: The translucent shell is orange-brown with a green or purple iridescence. The shell is conical, low,

thin, and has a large body whorl that lacks ridges. The umbilicus, or navel, is open and deep.

Size: Height normally to 0.35" (9 mm); width to 0.4" (11 mm) and occasionally up to 0.5" (13 mm)

Habitat/Ecology: On rocks or algae; low intertidal zone to water 600' (183 m) deep

Geographic Range: Arctic to Massachusetts; Arctic to Alaska

Notes: The spiral margarite feeds on microalgae. It is found in the low intertidal zone in the northern portion of its range; however, it is found deeper in the southern portion of its range.

Northern Rosy Margarite

Margarites costalis

Authority: (Gould, 1841)
Other Names: Also known as boreal
rosy margarite, northern ridged
margarite, pearly top shell; formerly
classified as *M. cinereus*,
M. groenlandicus
Description: The color of the shell
exterior varies from rose to gray. The spiral-shaped shell displays a low spire with
spiral ridges crossed by fine axial threads.
Size: Height to 0.8" (20 mm); width to 0.8" (20 mm)
Habitat/Ecology: In sand; low intertidal zone to water 373' (113 m) deep
Geographic Range: Greenland to Cape Cod; Bering Straits to southern Alaska
Notes: Female northern rosy margarites are larger than males. Specimens from Alaska
are noticeably larger than Atlantic specimens. The shells of this species are occasionally found after they are washed ashore. This species is an important food for various
bottom-feeding fish and their shells have been found in these fishes' digestive tracts
by fishermen.

Beautiful Topsnail

Calliostoma pulchrum

Authority: (C. B. Adams, 1850)
Other Names: Also known as beautiful
top shell, beautiful top-shell, beautiful
top snail
Description: The color of the shell is
yellowish brown to reddish brown,
with a spiral row of small, dark red-
brown spots present. A beaded row
graces each whorl as it circles the shell.
No umbilicus or navel is present.
Size: Height to 0.5" (13 mm); width to
0.4" (10 mm)
Habitat/Ecology: On rocks; low
intertidal zone to water 1208' (366 m)
deep
Geographic Range: North Carolina to
the West Indies
Notes: The beautiful topsnail is a grazer that feeds on a variety of organisms,
including sponges. The shell is shaped like a child's top—just as its common name
suggests. The operculum, or "trap door," is thin, horny, and circular in shape.

Jujube Topsnail

Calliostoma jujubinum

Authority: (Gmelin, 1791)

Other Names: Also known as jujube top shell, jujube top-shell, mottled top shell, mottled topsnail

Description: The exterior of the shell is yellow to reddish brown of varying hues and white axial splotches. The shell is conical and high with flattened whorls and fine, beaded threads. The umbilicus, or navel, is white, narrow, and funnel-shaped.

Size: Height to 1.25" (32 mm); width to 1.25" (32 mm)

Habitat/Ecology: Under rocks and on offshore reefs; low intertidal zone to water at least 25' (7.5 m) deep

Geographic Range: North Carolina to Brazil

Notes: The shell of the jujube topsnail is relatively thick and strong. The scientific and common name of this species originate from its similarity to the fruits of the Chinese date (*Ziziphus jujube*). This tree produces small, 1" (25 mm) fruit with orange-brown skin. Ripe fruits are said to taste like a green apple; however, over-ripe fruits taste like a date.

Sculptured Topsnail

Calliostoma euglyptum

Authority: (A. Adams, 1855)

Other Names: Also known as sculptured top shell, sculptured top-shell, sculptured top snail

Description: The color of the shell's exterior varies from pale yellowish to pink or purplish pink. The sharply conical shell displays whorls that are somewhat flattened on the upper portion and slightly convex below. The body whorl is rounded at the edge. The sculpture includes several beaded spiral cords and six alternate, fine, weakly beaded threads. An umbilicus, or navel, is absent.

Size: Height to 1" (25 mm); width to 1" (25 mm)

Habitat/Ecology: Under rocks; low intertidal zone to water 195' (59 m) deep

Geographic Range: North Carolina to Texas and Mexico

Notes: The scientific name of the sculptured topsnail originates from a Greek adjective meaning "well sculptured," which refers to the strongly beaded cords on the shell.

Smooth Atlantic Tegula

Tegula fasciata

Authority: (Born, 1778)
Other Names: Also known as silky Atlantic tegula, silky tegula, smooth Atlantic tegula
Description: The color varies widely from cream to white background, mottled with light brown to dark brown or reddish irregular patches. In addition, there may be a red dotted line on the periphery of the shell. The shell's shape is distinctive: a rounded turban. A deep umbilicus is present, and there are two white teeth at the base of the columella.
Size: Width to 0.75" (19 mm)
Habitat/Ecology: On rocks, algae, sand, and in shallow seagrass beds; low intertidal zone to water 50' (15 m) deep
Geographic Range: Florida to Brazil
Notes: The shell of the smooth Atlantic tegula, like many other snails, is a favorite for hermit crabs to use.

Chestnut Turban

Turbo castanea

Authority: Gmelin, 1791
Other Name: Also known as cat eye snail
Description: The shell varies widely from gray, orange, or brown to yellowish orange, with irregular white or brown spots. The shell is high-spired and shaped with rounded, beaded whorls. The aperture is circular, with a white or pearly color. The operculum is thick and calcareous.
Size: Height to 1.75" (44 mm); width to 1.5" (38 mm)
Habitat/Ecology: On eelgrass and on and under rocks; low intertidal zone to water at least 4' (1.2 m) deep

Geographic Range: North Carolina to Florida, Texas, and the West Indies; Brazil
Notes: The chestnut turban grazes on algae. The empty shells and opercula of this turban are often found at the holes of octopuses.

Long-spined Star-shell

Lithopoma phoebium

Authority: (Röding, 1798)

Other Names: Also known as long-spined star snail; formerly classified as *Astraea longispina*, *Astraea phoebia*, *Astralium phoebium*

Description: The shell's exterior is white to yellowish, with an interior that is an iridescent silvery white. The shell has a flat profile that bears long, flat, saw-toothed spines at the edge of the whorls. Axial cords are also present on the whorls. The shell has a low profile that is nearly flat on the underside.

Size: Height to 1" (25 mm); width to 2" (50 mm) or more

Habitat/Ecology: In sand or mud on eelgrass flats; low intertidal zone to shallow subtidal waters

Geographic Range: Florida to the West Indies; Bermuda; Brazil

Notes: This species is often found in turtle grass and eelgrass beds. It is sometimes found exposed on the sand flats after low tides. The long-spined star-shell lives just beneath the surface of the sand or mud.

American Star Shell

Lithopoma americanum

Authority: (Gmelin, 1791)

Other Names: Also known as American star-shell, imbricated star shell; formerly classified as *Astraea tecta*, *Astraea tecta americana*

Description: The shell's exterior varies from white to cream or greenish. The cone-like spire is graced with several whorls that are slightly concave. Many strong ribs run obliquely across the

whorls to produce bulges at the whorl edges. A number of weak spiral cords are present at the base. The shell's base is flattened, with somewhat knobby spiral cords.

Size: Height to 1.5" (39 mm); width to 1.5" (38 mm)

Habitat/Ecology: Under rocks or in turtle grass; low intertidal zone to water at least 8' (2.4 m) deep

Geographic Range: Florida to the West Indies

Notes: Young specimens are occasionally quite colorful and are orange overall or pearly green.

Four-toothed Nerite

Nerita versicolor

Authority: Gmelin, 1791

Other Name: Also known as variegated nerite

Description: The shell color varies widely but often with red and black markings. The shell is low-spired and graced with several whorls. Many strong spiral cords are present on the whorls. The aperture has four (occasionally five) large teeth at the inner lip. The operculum is gray with fine beads.

Size: Height to 1.25" (32 mm)

Habitat/Ecology: On rocks; low intertidal zone

Geographic Range: Florida to the West Indies; Bermuda

Notes: The four-toothed nerite is normally found on exposed rocks with a greater wave action. Like other nerites, this species lays its eggs on rocks inside dome-shaped capsules.

Checkered Nerite

Nerita tessellata

Authority: Gmelin, 1791

Other Names: Also known as tessellate nerite, tessellated nerite

Description: Shell color is white with black checkers or black with white checkers. The columellar area is whitish. The shell is low-spired and graced with several whorls. Many spiral cords are present on the whorls. The aperture has two small teeth at the inner lip. The operculum is black with a slightly convex exterior.

Size: Height to 0.9" (22 mm)

Habitat/Ecology: On and under rocks; low intertidal zone

Geographic Range: Florida to Brazil; Bermuda

Notes: The checkered nerite is a common species that is found in areas that are protected from strong waves.

Antillean Nerite

Nerita fulgurans

Authority: Gmelin, 1791

Other Name: Also known as lightning nerite

Description: Shell color is black, with white or yellowish markings and blurred mottling. The columellar area is whitish. The shell is low-spired, roundish, and graced with several whorls. Numerous unequal spiral cords are present on the whorls. The aperture has two medium-size teeth at the inner lip.

Size: Height to 1.25" (32 mm)

Habitat/Ecology: On rocks, often in mangrove areas; low intertidal zone

Geographic Range: Florida to Brazil

Notes: The Antillean Nerite is a species that prefers living in protected areas with brackish water.

Similar Species: Checkered Nerite (*Nerita tessellata*) (see above) is darker, rounder, and smaller, with reduced teeth.

Virgin Nerite

Neritina virginea

Authority: (Linnaeus, 1758)

Description: Shell color is variable and may include green, black, white, red, or purple, and it is marked with various dots, streaks, or lines. The columellar area is white to yellowish. The shell is low-spired and graced with several whorls. The whorls are smooth, with a polished finish. The aperture has several irregular, small teeth at the inner lip. The operculum is normally black and smooth.

Size: Height to 0.75" (19 mm)

Habitat/Ecology: On rocks; low intertidal zone

Geographic Range: Florida to Brazil

Notes: The virgin nerite lives in brackish waters, mangrove areas, and at stream mouths. It remains out of the water for only short periods of time.

Olive Nerite

Neritina reclivata

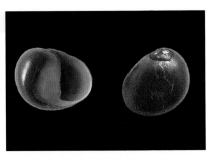

Authority: (Say, 1822)

Other Name: Also known as green nerite

Description: Shell color is olive with numerous dark, fine axial lines. The columellar area is whitish to yellowish. The round shell is low-spired and graced with several whorls. The whorls are smooth, without spiral cords. The aperture has small, irregular teeth at the inner lip. The operculum is black to brownish.

Size: Height to 0.5" (13 mm)

Habitat/Ecology: On mud or various plants and in tidepools; low intertidal zone

Geographic Range: Florida to Brazil

Notes: This species is herbivorous and has a record of a specimen found as far north as Beaufort, North Carolina. It is common in brackish water and sometimes found on coastal freshwater springs.

Northern Lacuna

Lacuna vincta

Authority: (Montagu, 1803)

Other Names: Also known as banded lacuna, chink snail, common northern chink shell, common northern lacuna

Description: The shell's exterior is yellowish or light brown, often with light or dark bands and darker spire in live specimens. The shell is thin and translucent, with four or five convex whorls, deep sutures, and a long, narrow, deep umbilical chink or crack. The head and foot are dark gray, but the tentacles are white.

Size: Height to 0.4" (10 mm); width to 0.25" (6 mm)

Habitat/Ecology: On eelgrass and algae; low intertidal zone to water 152' (46 m) deep

Geographic Range: Arctic to Rhode Island; Alaska to California; northern Europe

Notes: Unlike many snails, this species is more often found as a living organism crawling on kelp or other algae, rather than as a shell washed up on the beach. This species lives in salinities as low as 20 percent. It breeds from January through early spring, with a lifespan of less than one year. The northern lacuna lays its distinctive doughnut-shaped egg masses on seaweed.

Common Periwinkle

Littorina littorea

Authority: (Linnaeus, 1758)

Other Names: Also known as wrinkle-winkle, edible periwinkle, European periwinkle

Description: Shell exterior varies from gray to olive or brown, with dark brown bands. The shell is conical with a pointed apex; the aperture is round or oval, with one edge white and the opposite edge black. The animal is dark gray, with a cream-colored sole of the foot, and the tentacles have eyes at their base.

Size: Height to 1" (25 mm) and occasionally up to 2" (52 mm); width to 0.75" (19 mm)

Habitat/Ecology: On rocks and similar objects; high intertidal zone to water 198' (60 m) deep

Geographic Range: Labrador to Chesapeake Bay; California; Russia to northern Spain

Notes: The common periwinkle is a northern species that was believed to be introduced from Europe, but this belief was incorrect. This large periwinkle is a native species that was hit in the last Ice Age in the southern portion of its range but survived in a warm water refuge in Nova Scotia. Since that time, its range has increased and it has repopulated the areas where it previously lived.

Periwinkles are edible, and at one time they were called "Champlain's escargot"; their shells are occasionally found at old campsites from Mi'kmaq First Nation's people.

Their numbers can become exceedingly abundant, and at places such as Long Island Sound, numbers can exceed 1000 per square meter. The common periwinkle matures between two and three years of age and normally has a lifespan between five and ten years. Females may shed between 10,000 and 100,000 eggs directly into the sea. This species is our largest periwinkle.

Smooth Periwinkle

Littorina obtusata

Authority: (Linnaeus, 1758)
Other Names: Also known as northern yellow periwinkle, yellow periwinkle
Description: The color of the shell varies widely on the exterior from yellow to orange or brown, green or black; it's often banded. The spire is low and rounded, and the whorls are smooth. The operculum is yellow or dark orange.
Size: Height to 0.5" (13 mm); width to 0.5" (13 mm)
Habitat/Ecology: On macroalgae—especially northern rockweed (see p. 293) and knotted wrack (see p. 295); low intertidal zone to shallow subtidal waters
Geographic Range: Labrador to New Jersey; Europe
Notes: Research on the smooth periwinkle has shown that this species has a significant preference for feeding on northern rockweed over other species of algae. They actually feed on decaying algae.

The European green crab (see p. 234), is a common predator of the smooth periwinkle at some locations of the Northeast Atlantic. Research conducted on this periwinkle suggests that this new predator has triggered the smooth periwinkle to produce a thicker shell and become lower-spired for protection.
Similar Species: Rough Periwinkle (*Littorina saxatilis*, see below) displays a distinctive pointed tip on its spire.

Rough Periwinkle

Littorina saxatilis

Authority: (Olivi, 1792)
Other Names: Also known as northern rough periwinkle; formerly classified as *Littorina saxatila*
Description: The exterior color of the shell is gray or yellowish to dark brown—occasionally with spiral

stripes. The shell is globose with convex whorls that feature smooth spiral cords and a distinctive pointed tip on its spire.

Size: Height to 0.6" (16 mm); width to 0.5" (13 mm)

Habitat/Ecology: On rocks; splash zone to shallow subtidal waters

Geographic Range: Arctic to Chesapeake Bay; San Francisco Bay; Britain; Spain

Notes: The rough periwinkle lives primarily in the high intertidal and spray zone—areas that are subject to much less moisture than lower intertidal zones. To cope with this harsh environment, this snail minimizes moisture loss by moving to sites that provide shelter from the sun, including crevices and under various objects. It also is able to close its operculum for extended timeframes. The rough periwinkle is able to survive for an amazing forty-two days out of water. Its globose shape also helps to minimize water loss.

   This species can live for up to six years. Unlike the other northern periwinkles, females produce live, shelled young.

Similar Species: Smooth Periwinkle (*Littorina obtusata*) (see p. 66)

Lined Periwinkle

Echinolittorina jamaicensis

Authority: (C. B. Adams, 1850)

Other Names: Formerly classified as *Echinolittorina riisei*, *Nodilittorina mordax*

Description: The background color of the shell is white to cream with brown and approximately twelve wavy lines and bluish gray bands running over each whorl. These lines and bands cover much of the shell. The shell is broadly elongated, with convex whorls that have six to eight primary spiral grooves between sutures. The ratio of shell height to width is about 1.46:1. None of these characteristics alone should be used to identify this species, since they overlap with similar species; use several to identify a specimen.

Size: Height is 0.2" (5.8 mm) or greater; width to 0.15" (4 mm) or greater

Habitat/Ecology: On rocks and similar hard substrates; high intertidal zone

Geographic Range: Florida to Texas; Mexico; Jamaica; Barbados; Venezuela

Notes: The lined periwinkle is found throughout South Florida and throughout much of the Caribbean. Like many similar periwinkles, it is a herbivore that scrapes the rock surfaces in order to graze on microalgae and barnacle spat. Between December and May, it may experience high mortality of adult snails—up to 80 percent of the population. The average lifespan of this species is two years. This is one of five species recently described in the *Echinolittorina ziczac* species complex. All five species look similar but only three are found in Florida.

Similar Species: Zebra Periwinkle (*Echinolittorina ziczac*) is the largest species in the complex, to 0.8" (20 mm), and is primarily grayish white with brown lines. The bottom cord of the body whorl is indistinct.

Northern Interrupted Periwinkle

Echinolittorina placida

Authority: Reid, 2009

Other Names: Formerly included with *E. interrupta*, *Nodilittorina interrupta*

Description: The color of the shell's exterior is a white to light gray background and features blue-gray to black diagonal lines or zigzags and a wide black spiral band running around each whorl. The aperture is dark brown, with a light spiral band within the anterior portion. The shell is elongated and narrow and is sculptured with fine spiral lines. The aperture is oval and lacks a "spout" at the blunt end. The head and sides of the foot are black, and both pairs of head tentacles display two longitudinal black lines.

Size: Height to 0.8" (20 mm); height/width ratio 1.85:1

Habitat/Ecology: On rocks, jetties, and similar hard objects at sheltered sites; high intertidal zone

Geographic Range: North Carolina to Florida and Texas; Mexico

Notes: This is the third species of the *Echinolittorina ziczac* complex, a group of closely related species found in Florida; however, this is the only species found as far north as the Carolinas. This periwinkle originally ranged only as far north as a point on the mainland at the southern Gulf of Mexico and Yucatán Peninsula. This location is the northern limit of natural rock outcrops along the coast, however, this species has taken advantage of sea walls, jetties, and similar structures to increase its range as far as North Carolina.

The northern interrupted periwinkle is often misidentified as *Littorina ziczac* because of the similarity of its shell markings. The identification of these two closely related species includes shell morphology, differences in the anatomy of the penis, DNA data, and geographic separation.

Mangrove Periwinkle

Littoraria angulifera

Authority: (Lamarck, 1822)

Other Names: Also known as angulate periwinkle; formerly classified as *Littorina scabra angulifera*

Description: The color of the shell's exterior ranges from whitish or yellowish to orange or red-brown, with various irregular, reddish brown stripes. The columella is pale purplish with whitish edges. The shell has a sharp apex, six convex whorls, and the body whorl with numerous spiral cords.

Size: Height to 1.25" (32 mm); width to 0.6" (16 mm)

Habitat/Ecology: On trees and pilings in mangrove areas and in brackish water; above the high intertidal zone

Geographic Range: Florida to Brazil; Panama (Pacific)

Notes: The mangrove periwinkle is common on mangrove roots, bark, and leaves. This is one of the largest periwinkles found along our shorelines. Females lay numerous eggs that soon hatch to become free-swimming larvae.

Marsh Periwinkle

Littoraria irrorata

Authority: (Say, 1822)

Other Name: Also known as gulf periwinkle

Description: The shell's exterior is grayish white with small, short streaks of reddish brown between the spiral grooves. It is globular with a sharp apex and four to five nearly flat whorls. Many fine spiral grooves cover the whorls.

Size: Height to 1" (25 mm); width to 0.6" (16 mm)

Habitat/Ecology: On mud, marsh vegetation, and occasionally rocks and jetties; above high intertidal zone

Geographic Range: New York to Florida: Gulf Coast to Texas (except southern Florida, where it is replaced by the mangrove periwinkle (see above); formerly north to Massachusetts

Notes: The marsh periwinkle is occasionally covered with a fine algal growth that gives the shell an overall greenish tinge. Females deposit floating egg capsules.

Beaded Periwinkle

Cenchritis muricatus

Authority: (Linnaeus, 1758)
Other Name: Formerly classified as
Tectarius muricatus
Description: The shell's exterior is light
brown, gray, or white. The shell is
globular with whorls that are slightly
convex and a sharp apex. Several spiral
rows of whitish knobs cover the entire
shell.

Size: Height to 1.1" (28 mm)
Habitat/Ecology: On rocks; above the high intertidal zone
Geographic Range: Southern Florida and the West Indies to northern South America
Notes: The beaded periwinkle lives on the rocks near where the water splashes at the
shoreline. This species is able to remain out of water for an amazing length of time.
In one instance a specimen was revived after being out of water for a year!

Flat Skenea

Skeneopsis planorbis

Authority: (O. Fabricius, 1780)
Other Names: Also known as flat-coiled
skeneopsis, orb shell, orbsnail, planorb
skenea, trumpet shell; formerly classified as *Skenea planorbis*
Description: Color of shell's exterior is
brown to red-brown. This minute shell

is flat, coiled, and without much of a spire. The surface is smooth, and the umbilicus
is fairly wide and deep.
Size: Height to 0.24" (6 mm)
Habitat/Ecology: On algae, shells, stones; low intertidal zone to water 96' (29 m) deep
Geographic Range: Greenland to Florida; Russia to Azores; Mediterranean
Notes: Flat skenea carries its shell with a tilt—often rocking it side to side while it
crawls along the algae or other substrate. The shells of older individuals are often
completely encased in a mucous covering. This tiny species is often observed crawling on the surface film of water.

Common Wormsnail

Vermicularia spirata

Authority: (Philippi, 1836)

Other Names: Also known as common worm shell, West Indian worm shell

Description: The exterior color of the shell varies from yellowish brown to reddish brown. The shell is irregular with a worm-like shape. The first few whorls are tightly coiled, but that regularity soon disappears. The remainder of the shell becomes irregular and unpredictable in shape. Prominent longitudinal ridges are present along the outer face of the shell.

Size: Height to 6" (150 mm); width to 0.25" (6 mm)

Habitat/Ecology: On sand or mud shores; often grows among sponges or other colonial organisms; subtidal in shallow water

Geographic Range: Massachusetts to Florida; West Indies; Bermuda

Notes: The empty shells of this interesting gastropod are often washed up onto the shore. At first, this shell appears to be the residence of a worm; however, it is the shell of a mollusk. It has a head with tentacles and eyes and a radula, or toothed tongue, just like the rest of its clan, the snails. Several individuals are sometimes found growing together, forming one very tangled group.

Similar Species: Florida Wormsnail (*Vermicularia knorrii*) (see below)

Florida Wormsnail

Vermicularia knorrii

Authority: (Deshayes, 1843)

Other Names: Also known as Florida worm-shell, Knorr's worm shell

Description: The exterior color of the shell is buff-brown with a white tip. The shell is irregular with a worm-like shape. The first few whorls are tightly coiled, but the remainder of the shell becomes irregular and unpredictable in shape.

Size: Height to 3" (76 mm); width to 0.25" (6 mm)

Habitat/Ecology: In sponges; subtidal waters to at least 8' (2.4 m) deep

Geographic Range: North Carolina to Florida and the Gulf of Mexico; Bermuda

Notes: Like the common wormsnail, this species is only found washed ashore after a storm, as it lives in subtidal waters.

The Florida wormsnail feeds on suspended plankton and detritus. It grows in irregular shapes because it lives inside sponges, which dictate its uncoiled growth.

Similar Species: Common Wormsnail (*Vermicularia spirata*) (see above)

Common Sundial

Architectonica nobilis

Authority: Röding, 1798

Other Names: Also known as common American sundial; formerly classified as *A. granulata, Solarium granulatum*

Description: The exterior color is cream with reddish brown spots that are positioned along the spiral cords. Shell is heavy, resembling a top, and flat with six or seven whorls, each with four or five beaded spiral cords. The base is flattened.

Size: Height to 0.75" (19 mm); width to 2" (51 mm)

Habitat/Ecology: On sandy shores; subtidal—below low intertidal zone to water 122' (37 m) deep

Geographic Range: North Carolina to Brazil; Baja California to Peru

Notes: The common sundial buries itself in the sand, spire-down, during daylight hours to emerge at night and feed upon sea pansies (see p. 11). Their empty shells are sometimes found washed ashore.

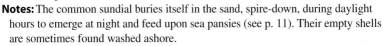

Beaded Sundial

Heliacus bisulcatus

Authority: (d'Orbigny, 1842)

Other Name: Also known as Orbigny's sundial

Description: The exterior of the shell is yellowish brown overall. The shell is flat with a low spire, four or five whorls—each with five rows of tiny, square-shaped beads.

Size: Width to 0.5" (13 mm)

Habitat/Ecology: On and in sand; low intertidal zone to water 1207' (366 m) deep

Geographic Range: North Carolina to Brazil; Bermuda; West Africa

Notes: This small sundial is uncommon and associated with soft corals in subtidal waters.

Atlantic Modulus

Modulus modulus

Authority: (Linnaeus, 1758)
Other Names: Also known as button
snail, buttonsnail
Description: The shell's exterior is
grayish white overall, often with purplish tinges and reddish brown spots or
lines. The shell is broadly conical with
three to four whorls, a low spire, and
sloping shoulders. A single small,
tooth-like spine is located on the lower
end of the columella or central axis.
Size: Width to 0.75" (19 mm)
Habitat/Ecology: On marine grasses in
sandy or rubble sites; shallow subtidal
waters

Geographic Range: North Carolina to
Texas and to Brazil; Bermuda
Notes: The Atlantic modulus feeds on minute plant life and detritus. It lays its eggs on
the grass blades in long, gelatinous tubes; the young emerge directly as miniature
snails without a planktonic larva stage. Their densities have peaked sporadically in
the seagrass beds of Florida Bay.

Ladder Hornsnail

Cerithideopsis scalariformis

Authority: (Say, 1825)
Other Names: Also known as ladder
horn shell, ladder horn snail
Description: The shell varies from gray
or red-brown to violet. It is sharply
conical with ten to thirteen well-
rounded whorls and numerous coarse,
axial ribs. A flared aperture lip also
graces the shell.
Size: Height to 1.25" (32 mm); width to
0.4" (10 mm)
Habitat/Ecology: On mud shores; near low intertidal zone to shallow subtidal waters
Geographic Range: South Carolina to West Indies; Bermuda
Notes: The ladder hornsnail feeds on algae and detritus. Their eggs are deposited in
gelatinous strings from which the young hatch as free-swimming larvae.

False Cerith

Lampanella minima

Authority: (Gmelin, 1791)
Other Names: Also known as black
  horn snail, Caribbean false cerith;
  formerly classified as *Batilaria minima*
Description: Shell exterior is highly
  variable and includes gray, black, or
  brown. It is often banded. Shell interior
  is dark brown.
  The shell is sharply conical, elongate
  with six to eight whorls, a sharp apex,
  and low, knobby ribs.
Size: Height to 0.75" (19 mm); width to
  0.25" (6 mm)
Habitat/Ecology: On mudflats and in brackish lagoons; low intertidal zone to shallow
  subtidal waters
Geographic Range: Florida to Brazil; Bermuda
Notes: The false cerith is often found in dense populations on mudflats. In the southern portion of this species' range, it provides a main food source for the flamingos
  that reside there.

Fly-specked Cerith

Cerithium muscarum

Authority: Say, 1832
Other Names: Also known as flyspeck
  cerith; formerly classified as *Thericium
  chara*
Description: The color of the shell's
  exterior varies from grayish white to
  yellowish or brownish gray, with rows
  of small chestnut spots on the spiral
  cords and threads. The shell is elongate-
  conical with a sharp apex. A distinctive
  spinal cord is present at the base of the
  body whorl.
Size: Height to 1" (25 mm)
Habitat/Ecology: In sandy or muddy shores; low intertidal zone to water 8.6' (2.6 m)
  deep
Geographic Range: Florida to the West Indies
Notes: The fly-specked cerith has numerous enemies that prey upon it. The predatory
  gastropods include the crown conch, lightning whelk, true tulip, and Florida horse
  conch. This species is normally found in bays or estuaries, especially near marine
  grasses.

Stocky Cerith

Cerithium litteratum

Authority: (Born, 1778)
Other Names: Also known as lettered horn shell; *C. literatum* is a misspelling
Description: The exterior shell color varies from white to gray, with spiral rows of black to reddish brown spots. The shell is conical and stout with seven straight-sided whorls and a pointed spire. The sutures are indistinct, and numerous coarse spiral threads are present. A prominent spiral cord, bearing numerous pointed knobs, is located just below the sutures.
Size: Height to 1.4" (35 mm); width is less than half the height
Habitat/Ecology: In sand or on rocks and rubble covered in algae; in subtidal waters
Geographic Range: Florida to Brazil
Notes: All ceriths feed on both algae and detritus. There are several species of ceriths that live as far north as Florida. They are similar is general appearance with several small differences. The most common species are included in this guide.
Similar Species: Dwarf Cerith (*Cerithium lutosum*) is a smaller, stout species that grows to 0.5" (13 mm) and occasionally to 0.75" (19 mm) high. The shell is normally dark brown and the apex is light colored. The spire whorls have three or four spiral rolls of numerous beaded cords.

Common Purple Sea-snail

Janthina janthina

Freshly stranded common purple sea-snail with its bubble raft

Authority: (Linnaeus, 1758)
Other Names: Also known as common janthina, common purple snail, violet snail
Description: The shell is two-toned with deep purple below and pale violet above. The shell is globular but flattened in height. It also has a D-shaped aperture.
Size: Height to 0.75" (19 mm); width to 1.5" (38 mm)
Habitat/Ecology: Pelagic
Geographic Range: Cape Cod to Florida and Texas; worldwide in all tropical and subtropical waters
Notes: The common purple sea-snail is a pelagic snail, like its close relatives the elongate janthina and pallid janthina. These snails are all pelagic species that roam the tropical and subtropical seas.

Like most snails, they are heavier than water, but unlike most species, they are able to produce a bubble raft that is entrapped in mucus to keep them afloat. These floating snails are predators to other pelagic organisms, including the by-the-wind sailor (see p. 22), Portuguese man-of-war (see p. 21), and blue button (see p. 22).

The common purple sea-snail is the most prevalent species of snail that is found washed ashore on our beaches.

Elongate Janthina

Janthina globosa

Authority: Swainson, 1822

Other Names: Also known as dwarf purple sea snail, elongate purple sea-snail, globe purple sea snail, globe violet snail

Description: The shell's color is entirely glossy violet to purple. The fragile shell is globose but higher than it is wide, with a rounded point on the aperture's lower lip.

Size: Height to 1.1" (28 mm); width to 0.9" (24 mm)

Habitat/Ecology: Pelagic

Geographic Range: Florida to Brazil; world wide tropical and subtropical waters

Notes: The elongate janthina, like all members of the genus *Janthina*, releases a violet pigment when disturbed. The Greeks used the violet fluid produced by these snails as a dye for their clothing. Although its species name is *globosa*, it is not the most globose shape of all the janthinas. The pallid janthina (below) is the most globose.

Similar Species: **Pallid Janthina** (*Janthina pallida*) has a whitish violet shell that is not glossy. The shape of its shell is globose, or very rounded. It grows to 1" (25 mm) across, with a large, round aperture and a smooth, rounded lip.

Western Atlantic Wentletrap

Epitonium occidentale

Authority: (Nyst, 1871)

Other Name: Also known as fine-ribbed wentletrap

Description: The shell's color is white—exterior and interior with a smooth and glossy finish. The elongated conical shell has a total of seven to eight rounded whorls with deep sutures and twelve to fifteen blade-like ribs that are sharply angled at the shoulder. The top of the shoulder is flattened, making the body whorl appear to be inset.

Size: Height to 1" (25 mm)

Habitat/Ecology: In sandy areas; subtidal to 373' (113 m) deep

Geographic Range: South Carolina to Brazil; Bermuda; Barbados

Notes: The western Atlantic wentletrap is one of the more common species of wentletraps found washed up on our Atlantic shores.

Humphreys Wentletrap

Epitonium humphreysii

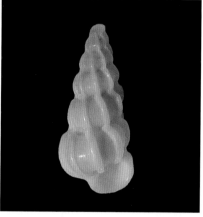

Authority: (Kiener, 1838)

Other Names: Also incorrectly named Humphrey's wentletrap; formerly classified as *Scalaria sayana*

Description: The shell's color is white, exterior and interior. The elongated conical shell has a total of eight to nine rounded whorls with deep sutures and eight to nine rounded, blade-like ribs. The aperture is broadly oval, with a thickened lip.

Size: Height to 0.9" (22 mm)

Habitat/Ecology: In sand or rubble; low intertidal zone to water 600' (183 m) deep

Geographic Range: Cape Cod to Texas

Notes: Many wentletraps may be found along our Atlantic shores. Approximately twenty-four species are present in North Carolina waters, and likely more in Florida. Humphreys wentletrap was named in honor of D. Humphreys Storer (1804–1891), a physician and naturalist from Boston. This species lays its eggs in small capsules that are covered with sand—similar to beads on a string.

Angulate Wentletrap

Epitonium angulatum

Authority: (Say, 1831)
Other Name: Formerly classified as
Epitonium arnaldoi
Description: The shell's color is shiny
white—exterior and interior. The
elongated conical shell has a total of
six to eight rounded whorls with deep
sutures and nine to ten thin blade-like
ribs that align with the above whorl's
ribs and are fused where they touch.
Size: Height to 1" (25 mm); width to
0.4" (10 mm)

Habitat/Ecology: In sandy areas; low intertidal zone to water 152' (46 m) deep
Geographic Range: New York to Uruguay
Notes: The angulate wentletrap, like all wentletraps, discharges a purple dye from its
dye gland. This is one of the wentletraps that is able to use this purple dye to
anesthetize its prey: living anemones.

Brown-band Wentletrap

Epitonium rupicola

Authority: (Kurtz, 1860)
Other Names: Also known as brown-
banded wentletrap, lined wentletrap;
formerly classified as *E. lineatum*
Description: The shell's exterior color is
white or yellowish with two brown
spiral bands on each side of the suture.
The elongated conical shell has a total
of eleven rounded whorls, with deep
sutures and twelve to eighteen blade-
like ribs that are weak or strong. The
aperture is nearly circular with a lip
that is slightly thickened.
Size: Height to 1" (25 mm)

Habitat/Ecology: In sandy areas; low intertidal zone to water 120' (37 m) deep
Geographic Range: Massachusetts to Florida and Texas; Suriname
Notes: The brown-band wentletrap is a species that is more common in the northern
part of its range. Wentletrap shells are a favorite of shell collectors. At least one collector has noted that when empty wentletrap shells are found, they often appear
along with empty three-lined basketsnail (see p. 117) shells. No explanation has been
found for this occurrence.

Many-ribbed Wentletrap

Epitonium multistriatum

Authority: (Say, 1826)
Other Name: Also known as multiribbed wentletrap
Description: The shell's color is white, exterior and interior. The elongated conical shell has a total of seven to ten rounded whorls with deep sutures and sixteen to nineteen thin blade-like ribs that are not angled at shoulder. The aperture is oval-shaped, with a thin lip.
Size: Height to 0.6" (15 mm)
Habitat/Ecology: In sandy areas; subtidal to 723' (219 m) deep
Geographic Range: Massachusetts to Texas; Bermuda
Notes: The shells of the many-ribbed wentletrap are uncommon along our coast, making them a real treasure to find on the beach.

White Hoofsnail

Hipponix antiquatus

Authority: (Linnaeus, 1767)
Other Names: Also known as hoof shell, white hoof shell, white hoof-shell
Description: The color of the shell is white or yellowish white, outside and inside. The shell is conical, solid, and heavy, with a concave base. The apex is pointed, with a blunt end and curved backward.
Size: Height to 0.9" (22 mm)
Habitat/Ecology: Clinging beneath rocks and shells; low intertidal zone to water 10' (3 m) deep
Geographic Range: Florida to Brazil
Notes: The white hoofsnail is somewhat variable in its shape as it attaches itself to a rock or dead shell, and the closer its shape matches its base, the better its attachment. This species is more often found on old shells that have been in relatively quiet waters.

Striate Cup-and-saucer

Crucibulum striatum

Authority: Say, 1824
Other Names: Also known as cup-and-saucer, cup and saucer limpet, cup-and-saucer limpet
Description: The shell's exterior is white, pinkish, yellow, or brown, and its interior is glossy yellowish white to pale orange. The shell is cap-shaped, with a curved apex that is off-center and a base that is almost round. Inside the shell, a cup-like process is attached to the anterior wall.
Size: Width to 1.4" (35 mm)
Habitat/Ecology: On rocks and shells; low intertidal zone to water 1208' (366 m) deep
Geographic Range: Nova Scotia to Brazil
Notes: The striate cup-and-saucer is common intertidally in the northern portion of its range, but south of Cape Cod it is rare and subtidal.

This species is a filter-feeder that dines upon minute animals, microalgae, and diatoms after they enter the mantle cavity.

Convex Slippersnail

Crepidula convexa

Authority: Say, 1822
Other Names: Also known as convex slipper shell, faded slipper shell
Description: The shell exterior is yellow to dark brown and often mottled with reddish brown. The interior is reddish brown with a white internal septum or deck that is set deep in the shell. The deck covers a third of the opening and has a concave edge. The shell is oval and cap-shaped, and the apex is strongly arched—enough for some to call it an "elf's cap."
Size: Height to 0.5" (12 mm); width to 0.3" (8 mm)
Habitat/Ecology: On shells, rocks, and similar hard objects; in quiet bays and lagoons; low intertidal zone to shallow subtidal waters
Geographic Range: Massachusetts to Florida; Texas; Yucatán; California

Notes: The convex slippersnail is a protandrous hermaphrodite, an individual that changes from male to female after it increases in size to reach a minimum size. Hormones dictate which sex it will become when mating with another individual. This species deposits its eggs with a capsule-shape onto a rock, and then it broods them until they hatch.

Common Atlantic Slippersnail

Crepidula fornicata

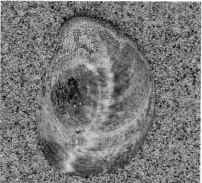

Authority: (Linnaeus, 1758)

Other Names: Also known as Atlantic slipper shell, boat shell, common slipper snail, quarterdeck

Description: The exterior color is white to tan with blotches or radiating lines of brown. The interior is shiny, and white, occasionally with brown marks.

   The shell is oval with an apex that has a strong arch. The underside features a shelf-like deck with a wavy edge that covers one-third to one-half the interior.

Size: Height to 2" (51 mm); width to 1" (25 mm)

Habitat/Ecology: On rocks, shells, and Atlantic horseshoe crabs (see p. 225); low intertidal zone to water 50' (15 m) deep

Geographic Range: Gulf of St. Lawrence to Florida and Texas; Europe; Washington to California

Notes: The common Atlantic slippersnail is most often found washed up on the beach, but it can also be found attached to a rock or shell. These slippersnails are famous for their habit of stacking themselves on top of each other, which have been found with up to nineteen individuals. Those on the bottom are females and those on top are males—in between are the hermaphrodites.

Spotted Slippersnail

Crepidula maculosa

Authority: Conrad, 1846
Other Name: Formerly included with
Crepidula fornicata
Description: The exterior shell color is
white and irregularly spotted with
purple-brown blotches or streaks. The
interior is shiny, white, and occasionally marked with brown. The shell
is oval with an apex that can be low to
strongly arched. A plate-like shelf is
present inside that covers one-third to
one-half of the interior. The platform
edge varies from wavy to straight or
may have a small central indentation.
Size: Height to 1.2" (31 mm); width to
1" (25 mm)
Habitat/Ecology: On rocks, shells, and
horseshoe crabs; low intertidal zone to
water 50' (15 m) deep
Geographic Range: North Carolina to
the Gulf of Mexico; Bahamas
Notes: The spotted slippersnail closely
attaches itself to its substrate. If its

substrate is irregular in shape—like that of a bivalve—its aperture will also be
irregular. This species, like the common Atlantic slippersnail (see p. 81), may be
found stacked on top of other individuals.

Spiny Slippersnail

Bostrycapulus aculeatus

Authority: (Gmelin, 1791)
Other Names: Also known as spiny
slipper shell, thorny slipper shell
Description: The exterior shell color is
brown to orange with white rays or
spots. The shell interior is light brown,
and the deck or shelf is white. The
shell is oval, with curved, radiating
spiny ridges covering the dorsal sur-

face. The shelf-like deck has a wavy edge and several folds.

Size: Height to 1.25" (32 mm)

Habitat/Ecology: On rocks, mangrove roots, shells, and other hard objects; shallow subtidal waters

Geographic Range: North Carolina to Brazil; California to Chile

Notes: The spiny slippersnail is one of the easier slipper shells to identify, with its prominent spines. It also

displays strongly spiraled early whorls. This subtidal species is often found washed up on the beach attached to empty shells.

Eastern White Slippersnail

Crepidula plana

Authority: Say, 1822

Other Names: Also known as eastern white slipper shell, flat slipper, flat slipper shell

Description: The shell is pure white, inside and out. Shell is oval and flat, or curved to fit inside large moonsnails or other large shells. A shelf or deck is present on the underside that takes up about half of the shell's length. The underside is polished.

Size: Height to 1.5" (38 mm)

Habitat/Ecology: On large shells, rocks, and similar hard objects; low intertidal zone to shallow subtidal waters

Geographic Range: Nova Scotia to Brazil; Bermuda

Notes: The eastern white slippersnail does not pile up as other slipper snails do. This species is also found attached to the Atlantic horseshoe crab (see p. 225). Males are small in size, while the females are much larger. They brood their eggs under their shell.

American Pelicanfoot

Arrhoges occidentalis

Authority: Beck, 1836

Other Name: Also known as American pelican's foot

Description: The exterior shell color varies from grayish to yellowish white, and the interior of the shell is shiny white. The shell's shape is conical and stout. A total of eight to ten well-rounded whorls are graced with several strong, curved axial ribs. The aperture has an outer lip that is expanded into a wing-like extension.

Size: Height to 2.5" (64 mm)

Habitat/Ecology: On sand or mud bottoms; subtidal from 30–1800' (9–549 m) deep

Geographic Range: Labrador to North Carolina

Notes: The American pelicanfoot is a subtidal species, and shells sometimes wash to the shoreline after a storm. Researchers in New Hampshire have discovered that this species burrows into the substrate during the winter months, when it does not feed. In February, it returns to the surface to feed once again upon macroalgae and diatoms.

West Indian Fighting Conch

Strombus pugilis

Authority: Linnaeus, 1758
Description: The exterior shell color is
deep yellowish brown, often with a
pale section in the middle of the body
whorl. Aperture color is a rich orange.
The interior and lip are glazed. The
shell is heavy and solid, with short
conical spire. A total of seven whorls
are present and rounded spines are
often present along with a flaring lip.
Immature specimens lack a flaring lip.
If shoulder spines are present, they are
found on the last two whorls.
Size: Height to 5" (127 mm)
Habitat/Ecology: On muddy shores;
low intertidal zone to shallow subtidal
waters
Geographic Range: Florida to Brazil
Notes: This species and the Florida
fighting conch are found with shoulder
spines and without. Individuals without
spines are more difficult to identify.
**Similar Species: Florida Fighting
Conch** (*Strombus alatus*) (see below)
has a lighter weight shell with rich red-
brown color, and the large spines are
only found on the last whorl.

Florida Fighting Conch

Strombus alatus

Authority: Gmelin, 1791
Other Name: Also known as fighting
conch
Description: The exterior shell color
varies from yellowish brown to dark
reddish brown. Aperture color is often
dark reddish brown. The interior and
lip are glazed. The shell is heavy and
solid, with a short conical spire. A total
of eight whorls are present, and
rounded spines also are often present
along with a flaring lip, which

immature specimens lack. If shoulder spines are present, they are only found on the last whorl.

Size: Height to 4" (102 mm); width to 2.5" (64 mm)

Habitat/Ecology: In sand; low intertidal zone to water 120' (37 m) deep

Geographic Range: North Carolina to Texas

Notes: The Florida fighting conch is more common in Florida than the West Indian fighting conch. The Florida fighting conch is an herbivore that feeds on red algae. It is occasionally brought up by offshore fishing trawlers.

Similar Species: West Indian Fighting Conch (*Strombus pugilis*) (see p. 85) has a heavier shell with brighter orange color, and the large spines are found on the last two whorls

Pink Conch

Lobatus gigas

Authority: (Linnaeus, 1758)

Other Name: Also known as queen conch

Description: The exterior shell color is yellowish white with various brown markings, and fresh shells have a fragile, brown periostracum that flakes off. The interior of the shell is a distinctive bright rosy pink. Interior and lip are glazed. The shell is heavy and solid, with eight to ten whorls and large, blunt spines on the last three whorls. The outer lip is thickened and flares extremely wide when the individual is mature.

Size: Height to 12" (30 mm); width to 8" (20 mm)

Habitat/Ecology: In sand normally near eelgrass; subtidal from 5–15' (1.5–5 m) deep

Geographic Range: Florida to Venezuela

Notes: Although the pink conch is a subtidal species, its shells occasionally wash up on the shore after a storm. This impressive species was once quite common in Florida; however, this is not the case today. It has been overfished for years for its meat and shell, and now they are rarely found. It is still common south of Florida, and this is the source for the shells that make their way to Florida for sale to tourists.

Milk Conch

Lobatus costatus

Authority: (Gmelin, 1791)

Other Names: Also known as harbour conch, ribbed stromb; formerly classified as *Strombus jeffersonia*

Description: The exterior shell color is yellowish white with a light brown periostracum that flakes off when dry. The shell aperture and lip are white and glazed. The shell is conical and stout, with approximately ten whorls and a pointed spire. Small rounded knobs are often present along with a flaring lip.

Size: Height to 7" (178 mm)

Habitat/Ecology: In sandy shores; in quiet waters and lagoons; subtidal to water 80' (24 m) deep

Geographic Range: North Carolina to Brazil; Bermuda

Notes: The milk conch is fairly common south of Florida, but its shells are not often found in Florida.

Similar Species: West Indian Fighting Conch (*Strombus pugilis*), **Florida Fighting Conch** (*Strombus alatus*) (see p. 85)

Hawk-wing Conch

Lobatus raninus

Authority: (Gmelin, 1791)

Other Name: Formerly classified as *Strombus bituberculatus*

Description: The exterior shell is light gray with irregular brown mottling. The aperture is salmon pink inside, bordered with white. The interior and lip are glazed. The shell is conical and stout, with eight convex whorls and a pointed spire. A series of knobs are present at the shoulder. A prominent "hawk-wing" or wing-like extension that projects forward is featured at the lip.

Size: Height to 5" (127 mm)

Habitat/Ecology: In quiet sandy waters; subtidal to 20' (6 m) deep

Geographic Range: Florida to Brazil; Bermuda

Notes: The scientific name *raninus* was derived from the Latin *rana* ("frog") and translates to "little frog"; it was chosen since the shell resembles a frog's warty back. Dwarf or miniature specimens, less than 2" (5.1 cm) high, were once named *Lobatus raninus nanus*. This designation has since been removed, and these specimens are simply included in the general variation within the species.

Coffee Bean Trivia

Niveria pediculus

Authority: (Linnaeus, 1758)

Other Name: Also known as coffeebean trivia

Description: The exterior shell is light brown to pinkish brown with three pairs of dark brown spots found on the dorsal side. The ventral side is lighter colored. The body whorl completely covers the spire, and sixteen to eighteen cords run from a slight central groove in the center of the dorsal side to the edge of the elongated central aperture. The red to yellow mantle of the living organism is often folded over the shell, which hides most of it.

Size: Height to 0.75" (19 mm); width to 0.5" (13 mm)

Habitat/Ecology: Under rocks; low intertidal zone to water 150' (46 m) deep

Geographic Range: North Carolina to Brazil

Notes: The coffee bean trivia is a carnivore that dines on tunicates. Egg capsules are deposited within the

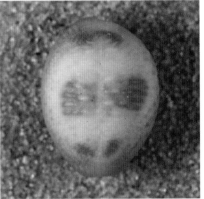

tunicate flesh, from which the free-swimming young emerge and begin their lives. This small shell is often featured in women's jewelry.

Similar Species: Four-spotted Trivia (*Niveria quadripunctata*) is a smaller shell, to 0.25" (6.5 mm) in height, with two to four tiny, dark red-brown dots along the center line of the dorsal side.

White Globe Trivia

Niveria nix

Authority: (Schilder, 1922)

Other Names: Also known as snowy trivia; formerly classified as *Trivia nix*

Description: The exterior color and the aperture are pure white. The body whorl completely covers the spire, and twenty-two to twenty-six cords run from a slight central groove in center of dorsal side to the edge of the elongated medial aperture.

Size: Height to 0.5" (12 mm)

Habitat/Ecology: Around rocks; subtidal waters 16.5–383' (5–116 m) deep

Geographic Range: North Carolina to Brazil

Notes: Little is known about the natural history of the white globe trivia. Its shells are sometimes found washed ashore after a storm.

Atlantic Yellow Cowrie

Erosaria acicularis

Authority: (Gmelin, 1791)

Other Names: Also known as yellow cowry; formerly classified as *Cypraea spurca acicularis*

Description: The exterior shell is glossy, orange-yellow, with yellow and brown spots on the dorsal surface; the ventral surface is white.

The shell is inflated and oval with no spire and a narrow aperture the length of the shell with strong teeth on both sides.

Size: Length to 1.25" (32 mm)

Habitat/Ecology: Under stones and coral; on reefs; low intertidal zone to water 2574' (780 m) deep

Geographic Range: North Carolina to Brazil; Bermuda

Notes: The Atlantic yellow cowrie is a species that was originally believed to be closely related to a similar-looking Mediterranean species. This cowrie is a night feeder. Females lay their eggs in crevices, where they protect them with their large, muscular foot. Native Americans used cowries as money for trading.

Measled Cowrie

Macrocypraea zebra

Authority: (Linnaeus, 1758)
Other Names: Formerly classified as *Cypraea exanthema, C. zebra*
Description: The exterior shell is glossy, light to dark brown, with white round spots on the dorsal surface; the sides have dark centers. The ventral surface lacks the white spots near the aperture, and the teeth are dark reddish brown. The shell is inflated and oval, with no spire and a narrow aperture the length of the shell with strong teeth on both sides. The live animal features a thick, light to dark brown mantle with numerous branched papillae that covers the shell completely.
Size: Length to 4.5" (114 mm)
Habitat/Ecology: On or near coral; low intertidal zone to water 462' (140 m) deep
Geographic Range: Florida to Brazil
Notes: The measled cowrie, like other cowries, has been over-collected and is not as common as it once was. Females guard their egg mass and use their proboscis to keep the eggs free of debris.
Similar Species: Atlantic Deer Cowrie (*Macrocypraea cervus*) (see below) features white spots on its sides and a shell that is rounder and wider.

Atlantic Deer Cowrie

Macrocypraea cervus

Authority: (Linnaeus, 1771)
Other Name: Formerly classified as *Cypraea cervus*
Description: The exterior shell is glossy, light to dark brown, with round, white spots on both the dorsal surface and the sides. The ventral surface lacks the white spots near the aperture, and the interior is purplish. The shell is inflated and oval, with no spire and a narrow aperture the length of the shell with strong teeth on both sides; the teeth are dark reddish brown. The live animal features a pinkish brown and white mantle covered with numerous short papillae that completely covers the entire shell.

Size: Length to 6.75" (171 mm)

Habitat/Ecology: Normally offshore on rocks; low intertidal zone (rare) to water 116' (35 m) deep

Geographic Range: Florida to Yucatán; Brazil

Notes: Like many cowries, the Atlantic deer cowrie is nocturnal, feeding on algae and various colonial invertebrates. Females lay a gelatinous mass of 500 to 1,500 egg capsules, which she broods. The Atlantic deer cowrie is the largest cowrie in the world. This shell occasionally washes onto ocean beaches.

Similar Species: Measled Cowrie (*Macrocypraea zebra*) (see p. 90) features white spots with dark centers on its sides.

Single-toothed Simnia

Simnialena uniplicata

Authority: (G. B. Sowerby II, 1849)

Other Names: Also known as one-tooth simnia; formerly classified as *Neosimnia uniplicata*

Description: The exterior shell is smooth and glossy; the color varies from yellow to deep rose, white or light purple. The shell is thin, nearly cylindrical, and lacks a spire. The aperture is long and narrow, with open canals at both ends.

Size: Height to 0.75" (19 mm)

Habitat/Ecology: On sea whips; shallow subtidal depths to 100' (30 m) deep

Geographic Range: Virginia to Brazil

Notes: The single-toothed simnia is a predator that lives on and feeds upon the sea whip (see p. 10). This subtidal species is occasionally found alive—clinging to a sea whip after it has washed up on the beach. Females lay their eggs on the branches of sea whips while males defend their territories there as well. The shell and mantle of this species usually take on the color of the sea whip on which it lives.

Milk Moonsnail

Polinices lacteus

Authority: (Guilding, 1834)

Other Name: Also known as milk moon shell

Description: The shell's exterior is milky white—smooth and polished. The shell's interior is white. A thin, brown or yellowish periostracum may be present on fresh shells. The shell is globe-shaped with three or four whorls and a well-rounded spire. The aperture is oval with a flattened inner lip. The umbilicus is deep, and half or more is filled by a thick, white button-like callus. The operculum, or trap door, is reddish brown.

Size: Height to 1.5" (38 mm)

Habitat/Ecology: On sandy shores; low intertidal zone to shallow subtidal waters

Geographic Range: North Carolina to Brazil

Notes: This small white treasure is often found washed up on the beach. It deposits its eggs in a distinctive spiral sand collar. Its scientific name *lacteus*, means "milk white," in reference to the color of its shell.

Similar Species: Immaculate Moonsnail (*Polinices immaculatus*) is a smaller species that lives in northern waters from the Gulf of St. Lawrence to North Carolina. Its white shell is smooth and shiny; it features three or four whorls and a short, pointed apex. It is a subtidal species with shells that may be washed to the seashore after a storm.

Shark Eye

Neverita duplicata

Authority: (Say, 1822)

Other Names: Also known as Atlantic moonsnail, lobed moon shell, shark's eye, sharkeye; formerly classified as *Polinices duplicatus*

Description: The shell's exterior is slate gray to tan with a dark bluish line that winds around the spire. The shell's interior is brown. Its mantle is dull gray, and it covers the shell when extended. A thin, brown or yellowish periostracum may be present on fresh shells. The shell is globe-shaped with four or five whorls and a low, well-rounded spire.

The aperture is elliptical. The umbilicus is partially or completely covered with a white to chestnut-brown lobe-like callus that is thick and wide. The operculum is horny, thin, and brown.

Size: Height to 2.5" (64 mm); width to 3.75" (95 mm)

Habitat/Ecology: On sand and sand-mud mixture shores; low intertidal zone to shallow subtidal waters

Geographic Range: Cape Cod to Texas

Notes: The shark eye is a common moonsnail with a distinctive bluish line that winds around the spire, creating the appearance of an eye on its shell. This line is darkest at its earliest whorls. This species is a carnivore that preys upon a variety of other mollusks. It uses its radula or raspy tongue, along with acids that it secretes, to drill neat, beveled, circular holes in their shells. Once the hole has been drilled, it inserts its proboscis to digest the soft tissues of its prey. Its prey includes the blue mussel (see p. 145), northern horsemussel (see p. 146), Atlantic surfclam (see p. 171), Arctic wedgeclam (see p. 174), Atlantic jackknife-clam (see p. 175), northern quahog (see p. 184), and softshell-clam (see p. 190). This species replaces the northern moonsnail south of New Jersey.

Similar Species: Northern Moonsnail (*Euspira heros*) (see below)

Semisulcate Moonsnail

Sigatica semisulcata

Authority: Gray, 1839
Other Names: Also known as scratched moon snail; formerly classified as *Natica fordiana*
Description: The shell's exterior is white, smooth, and polished. The shell is thin and globe-shaped with five whorls and a well-rounded spire finely grooved by several spiral lines. The aperture is oval. The umbilicus is deep, round, and lacks a callus. The operculum is corneous—with a few whorls.
Size: Height to 0.4" (10 mm)
Habitat/Ecology: In sand; in subtidal waters from 10–60' (3–18 m) deep
Geographic Range: South Carolina to Brazil
Notes: The semisulcate moonsnail spends its daylight hours buried beneath soft sand and emerges at night in search of food. This is an uncommon species.

Northern Moonsnail

Euspira heros

Authority: (Say, 1822)
Other Names: Also known as northern moon shell, northern moon snail
Description: The shell's exterior is gray to tan and smooth. The shell's interior is white, and its mantle is gray. A thin, yellowish periostracum may be present on fresh shells. The shell is globe-shaped, with five whorls and a well-rounded spire.
  The aperture is oval-shaped. The umbilicus is open. The operculum, or trap door, is light brown.

Size: Height to 4.5" (114 mm); width to 3.5" (89 mm)
Habitat/Ecology: On sand and mud flats; low intertidal zone to water 1200' (366 m) deep
Geographic Range: Labrador to North Carolina

Notes: The northern moonsnail is a voracious carnivore that wanders sand and mud flats, searching for its next meal. It moves along the surface with its enormous foot that can be retracted completely inside its shell. It deposits its eggs, like most moonsnails, in round, sand collar–like formations that are produced in the early summer months. They are often discovered at low tide while walking along the beach.

Similar Species: Shark Eye (*Neverita duplicata*) (see p. 92)

Northern Spotted Moonsnail

Euspira triseriata

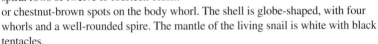

Authority: (Say, 1826)

Other Names: Also known as spotted northern moon shell, spotted northern moon-shell, spotted moon shell, spotted moonsnail; formerly classified as *Lunatia triseriata*

Description: The shell's exterior is cream and normally with two or three spiral rows of twelve to fourteen bluish or chestnut-brown spots on the body whorl. The shell is globe-shaped, with four whorls and a well-rounded spire. The mantle of the living snail is white with black tentacles.

Size: Height to 1.25" (32 mm)

Habitat/Ecology: On sandy shores; mid intertidal zone to water 350' (107 m) deep

Geographic Range: Gulf of St. Lawrence to North Carolina

Notes: The northern spotted moonsnail closely resembles the northern moonsnail (see p. 93); however, it normally features numerous spots on its body whorl and is significantly smaller in size.

Miniature Moonsnail

Tectonatica pusilla

Authority: (Say, 1822)

Other Names: Also known as miniature natica, southern miniature natica; formerly classified as *Natica pusilla*

Description: The shell's exterior is smooth and porcelain-like, white to tan, often with faint brown spots or bands. The shell is globe-shaped, with three whorls (body whorl expanded) with a depressed spire. The aperture is semilunar with a flattened inner lip.

The umbilicus is a tiny opening next to the rolled callus. The operculum is calcareous.

Size: Height to 0.3" (8 mm)

Habitat/Ecology: In sand or sandy mud; low intertidal zone to shallow subtidal waters

Geographic Range: Maine to Florida and Brazil

Notes: Shells of the miniature moonsnail are occasionally found washed ashore on the beach after a storm. This small moonsnail is similar to the shark eye, except that the miniature moonsnail

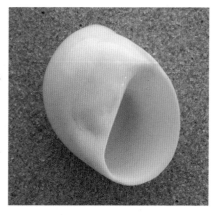

carries a corneous operculum or an operculum made from a horn-like material.

Similar Species: Shark Eye (*Neverita duplicata*) (see p. 92)

Colorful Moonsnail

Naticarius canrena

Authority: (Linnaeus, 1758)

Other Name: Also known as colorful Atlantic natica

Description: The shell's exterior is smooth and polished and is cream-colored to yellowish tan, with spiral chestnut or dark brown bars, stripes, or zigzag marks. The shell's interior is brownish. The shell is globe-shaped, with about four whorls, a depressed spire, and a small apex.

The aperture is semilunar, with a thin, flattened inner lip. The umbilicus is nearly completely covered by a thick, white, button-like callus. The operculum is calcareous, white, and thick with deep grooves.

Size: Height to 2" (51 mm)

Habitat/Ecology: On sandy shores; subtidal waters 3–50' (0.9–15 m) deep

Geographic Range: North Carolina to Uruguay

Notes: This beautiful shell is occasionally found washed ashore on the beach at low tide. Its colorful markings help to make it easier to identify.

White Baby Ear

Sinum perspectivum

Authority: (Say, 1831)

Other Names: Also known as common Atlantic baby's ear, common baby's ear, ear shell, white baby-ear

Description: The shell's exterior is milky white. The shell is elongate-ovate and flat. There are three to four whorls, with the body whorl making up nearly three-quarters of the whole shell, and a low rounded spire. The surface sculpture has numerous spiral growth lines. The body covers the entire shell, and a huge foot is present.

Size: Height to 2" (51 mm); width to 1.25" (32 mm)

The living animal

Habitat/Ecology: On sandy shores; low intertidal zone to water over 100' (30 m) deep

Geographic Range: New Jersey to Brazil. Not common north of Virginia

Notes: The white baby ear ploughs through the sand, using its large foot that often leaves a furrow. Its mantle is large, cream-colored with a hint of yellow, and it completely covers its thin shell. This species is a relative of the moonsnails, and it too is searching for bivalve prey.

Similar Species: Brown Baby Ear (*Sinum maculatum*) (see below)

Brown Baby Ear

Sinum maculatum

Authority: (Say, 1831)

Other Names: Also known as brown baby-ear, maculated baby's ear, spotted babyear

Description: The shell's exterior is totally brown or blotched with brown. The shell is elongate-ovate and flat. There are three to four whorls, with the body whorl making up nearly three-quarters of the whole shell, and a high, slightly pointed spire. The surface sculpture has numerous spiral growth lines. The body covers the entire shell, and a huge foot is present.

Size: Height to 1.2" (31 mm)

Habitat/Ecology: On sandy shores; subtidal waters from 1–86' (0.3–26 m) deep

Geographic Range: North Carolina to Brazil

Notes: The brown baby ear is a subtidal species that lives further out than the closely related white baby ear. Its shells are often found washed up on the shore.

Similar Species: White Baby Ear (*Sinum perspectivum*) (see p. 96)

Scotch Bonnet

Semicassis granulata

Authority: (Born, 1778)

Other Name: Formerly classified as *Phalium granulatum*

Description: The exterior shell color is cream, with spiral rows of yellow to reddish orange rectangular spots. The shell's interior is fawn-colored. The aperture is large, with canals at both ends. The outer lip is heavy and toothed inside. A thin periostracum may be present on fresh shells. The shell is globe-like with five whorls with a short spire and twenty spiral grooves crossed by numerous growth lines, creating a reticulated pattern.

The operculum is horny, crescent-shaped, and brownish. The mantle is cream-colored with dark spots.

Size: Height to 4" (102 mm); width to 3" (76 mm)

Habitat/Ecology: On sandy shores; shallow subtidal waters

Geographic Range: North Carolina to Uruguay

Notes: The Scotch bonnet is a much sought-after beach shell that is occasionally found after storms. This carnivore dines on such specialty items as sea urchins and sand dollars. In order to feed on them, it dissolves the urchin's shell with sulfuric acid to get to the meat inside. Females deposit their eggs in round "towers," and then they "sit" on them. The young eventually emerge to begin their free-swimming lives. The Scotch bonnet is an offshore species that is taken in scallop trawlers.

Emperor Helmet

Cassis madagascariensis

Authority: Lamarck, 1822

Other Names: Also known as cameo helmet, Clench's helmet, queen helmet; includes *Cassis madagascariensis spinella*

Description: The shell's exterior is brown and has a pale parietal shield that is smooth and porcelain-like, with a light peach-colored section and short bands of dark brown. The shell's aperture teeth are white with dark brown between.

The shell is heavy, massive, triangular, and helmet-like, with a large body whorl and a nearly flat spire. The body whorl includes three or more spiral rows of blunt knobs. The aperture is narrow and extends nearly the full length of the shell, with teeth on both sides.

Size: Height to 14" (36 mm); width to 12.5" (32 mm)

Habitat/Ecology: On sandy shores; subtidal waters from 18–59' (5.5–18 m) deep

Geographic Range: North Carolina to West Indies

Notes: Today, the shell of the emperor helmet is rarely found on our beaches. At one time it was caught in large numbers by scallop trawlers. It is now rare in Florida. This massive mollusk is a subtidal species that dines on sea urchins and sand dollars.

It is among the largest species of helmets that are living in the world today. Despite its scientific name, it is not found in Madagascar.

Reticulated Cowrie-helmet

Cypraecassis testiculus

Authority: (Linne, 1758)

Other Name: Also known as reticulated cowry helmet

Description: The shell's exterior varies from white to tan-orange with orange-brown to dark brown spots. The shell is solid and ovate with five to eight whorls—the body whorl makes up most of the shell—and a short spire. The shell's sculpture is made up of many axial ridges that extend over the entire shell. The aperture is long and narrow, with an outer lip that is rolled back and toothed within.

Size: Height to 3" (76 mm)

Habitat/Ecology: On sandy and rocky shores; subtidal waters from 3.3–83' (1–25 m) deep

Geographic Range: North Carolina to Brazil

Notes: Shells of the reticulated cowry helmet occasionally wash ashore. This subtidal species is a carnivore that eats sea urchins and sand dollars. Females deposit numerous elongated purple egg capsules—each of which contain many eggs. The young hatch to become free-swimming larvae in the nearby waters.

Giant Hairy Triton

Monoplex parthenopeus

Authority: (Salis Marschlins, 1793)

Other Names: Also known as giant triton, neapolitan triton, Von Salis' triton; formerly classified as *Cymatium costatum, C. parthenopeum*

Description: The exterior shell color is brownish yellow, often with spiral bands of darker brown becoming darkest at the thickened axial ridges. The shell's interior is white with the inner margin a bright orange to reddish brown.

The shell is spindle-shaped, with five to eight whorls, a pointed spire, and several prominent spiral cords.

A thick, hairy periostracum is prominent on fresh shells.

Size: Height to 6" (152 mm)

Habitat/Ecology: On rocks; below the low intertidal zone to water 208' (63 m) deep

Geographic Range: North Carolina to Uruguay; Japan

Notes: The giant hairy triton was often included with catches of the Atlantic calico scallop (see p. 159). The distinctive thick and hairy periostracum of fresh specimens makes its identification easy.

Atlantic Distorsio

Distorsio clathrata

Authority: (Lamarck, 1816)

Other Name: Formerly classified as *Distorsio robinsoni*

Description: The shell's exterior is yellowish white and the interior is white. The shell is spindle-shaped and distorted, with six or seven whorls, a pointed spire, and many axial and spiral ribs, giving the surface a checkered appearance. The aperture is small and irregular-shaped, with a flattened inner lip and teeth on both sides. A hairy periostracum is present on fresh shells.

Size: Height to 3" (75 mm)

Habitat/Ecology: On unknown bottoms; from just below low intertidal zone to water 200' (61 m) deep

Geographic Range: North Carolina to Brazil

Notes: The name of the genus *Distorsio* refers to the distorted appearance of its shell. This species has been found in areas where scallop shells have been dumped near shellfish factories. The shell of this species is occasionally found on the beach.

Giant Tun

Tonna galea

Authority: (Linnaeus, 1758)

Other Name: Also known as giant tun shell

Description: The shell's exterior is creamy white to light coffee brown. A varnish-like periostracum is present. The shell is globe-shaped, with three to seven convex whorls and a body whorl that dominates the shell. There are nineteen to twenty-one broad, evenly spaced spiral ridges and the spire is rounded. The aperture is large and lunar with a flared outer lip.

The animal has a yellowish body that is mottled with black, a rather large foot, and a rather long proboscis.

Size: Height normally to 6" (15.2 cm) but occasionally as high as 10" (25.4 cm)

Habitat/Ecology: On sandy shores; just below low intertidal zone to water 109' (33 m) deep

Geographic Range: North Carolina to Brazil; Indo-Pacific; Mediterranean

Notes: The giant tun is a carnivore that has the "enviable" distinction that it can swallow its prey whole. It then

secretes acid in order to digest its prey. Females deposit their eggs in fairly wide rows. On occasion, free-swimming, pelagic young can be found in beach drift in the springtime.

Atlantic Figsnail

Ficus papyratia

Authority: (Say, 1822)
Other Name: Formerly classified as *Ficus communis*
Description: The shell's exterior is cream to grayish with yellow-brown spots. The shell's interior is a polished orange-brown.

The shell is elongated, pear-shaped, and thin-shelled, with four whorls and a rounded spire. The aperture is elongate, with a thin outer lip and straight canal.
Size: Height to 5" (12.7 mm)
Habitat/Ecology: On sandy shores; low intertidal zone to water 604' (183 m) deep
Geographic Range: North Carolina to Florida and Mexico
Notes: The shells of the Atlantic figsnail are sometimes found washed onto the beaches in large numbers on the west coast of Florida.

Cabrit's Murex

Vokesimurex cabritii

Authority: (Bernardi, 1859)
Other Names: Formerly classified as *Haustellum cabritii, Murex maculatus*
Description: The shell's exterior is a uniform white to rose pink or yellowish. The shell is conical with about five whorls, including an inflated body whorl and a short spire. The body whorl is ornamented with three rows of three to seven elongated spines.

The aperture is small and oval, with the outer lip margin toothed and the inner lip smooth within. The canal is narrow and elongated, with several slender spines present.
Size: Height to 3" (7.6 mm)
Habitat/Ecology: In sand or rubble; subtidal waters from 109–422' (33–128 m) deep
Geographic Range: South Carolina to the West Indies
Notes: This beautiful and delicate shell is not often found on the beach without some damage to its spines. Cabrit's murex shells vary considerably with the length and number of elongated spines present on various individuals. In fact, some lack spines altogether.

Apple Murex

Phyllonotus pomum

Authority: (Gmelin, 1791)
Description: The exterior shell color is
yellowish tan with various brown
mottlings.

   The sturdy shell is spindle-shaped,
rough with five to nine whorls and a
pointed spire.

   The aperture is large and round, with
the outer lip thickened.

   Each whorl has three varices, or ridges, and there are two or three axial ribs be-
tween varices. Many spiral cords and fine threads instersect the ribs and varices.
Size: Height to 4.5" (114 mm); width to 2.25" (57 mm)
Habitat/Ecology: On rocks or sand; low intertidal zone to water 42' (12.6 m) deep
Geographic Range: North Carolina to Brazil
Notes: The apple murex is a predator that feeds upon several snails and bivalves, including the eastern oyster (see p. 155). The apple murex deposits its eggs in leathery
tower-like capsules onto rocks. These eggs hatch after approximately three weeks as
miniature crawling predators. These tiny carnivores begin this stage of their life
searching for immature mollusks to drill holes into their shells and remove the
contents.

Lace Murex

Chicoreus dilectus

Authority: (A. Adams, 1855)
Other Names: Also known as Florida
lace murex; formerly classified as
Chicoreus florifer dilectus
Description: The exterior shell color is
light brown to dark brown with a rough
finish. Young individuals are almost
totally pink.

   The shell is ornate and elongately
ovate with seven whorls and a pointed
spire. Each whorl has three varices that support scaly spines, with a low knob between
varices. The aperture is round with eight to ten leaf-like spines along the outer edge.
Size: Height to 3" (76 mm); width to 1.5" (38 mm)
Habitat/Ecology: In sand, in mud, or rocky areas; among mangroves; low intertidal
zone to shallow subtidal waters
Geographic Range: North Carolina to Panama
Notes: Like all murexes, this species is a predator that feeds on various bivalves by
drilling a hole into the shell and sucking out the soft tissues inside. The lace murex is
the most common murex present in southern Florida.

Florida Rocksnail

Stramonita haemastoma

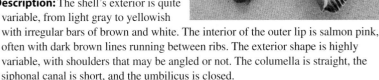

Authority: (Linnaeus, 1767)
Other Names: Also known as Florida rock snail, southern oyster drill, southern drill; formerly classified as *Thais haemastoma*
Description: The shell's exterior is quite variable, from light gray to yellowish with irregular bars of brown and white. The interior of the outer lip is salmon pink, often with dark brown lines running between ribs. The exterior shape is highly variable, with shoulders that may be angled or not. The columella is straight, the siphonal canal is short, and the umbilicus is closed.
Size: Height to 5" (127 mm); width to 2.5" (64 mm)
Habitat/Ecology: Attached to rocks or shells in rock jetties and oyster beds near inlets; high to low intertidal zones
Geographic Range: Virginia to Brazil
Notes: This common species feeds by boring holes in various mussels, oysters, barnacles, and clams. It lays its eggs on rocks and similar objects, including the shells of horseshoe crabs. Two subspecies are commonly encountered in our area. *Stramonita haemastoma floridana* (pictured) is found from Virginia to Florida. It is smaller in size, with less sculpture. The second subspecies, *Stramonita haemastoma canaliculata*, is found from Florida to Mexico. It has deeper sutures and is larger in overall size.
Similar Species: Tinted Cantharus (*Pollia tincta*) (see p. 110)

Atlantic Dogwinkle

Nucella lapillus

Authority: (Linnaeus, 1758)
Other Names: Also known as dogwinkle; formerly classified as *Thais lapillus*
Description: The exterior shell color is extremely variable and includes: white, pink, yellow, orange, brown, or black, occasionally with spiral stripes. The solid shell is ovate with five or six convex whorls and a short spire with a somewhat pointed apex. Each whorl has several low, rounded spiral cords that are often slightly knobby. The aperture is oval with a thick outer lip. The aperture is large and round, with the outer lip thickened. The operculum is brown and horny.
Size: Height to 2" (51 mm); width to 1.1" (28 mm)
Habitat/Ecology: On rocks, mussels, or seaweed; high to low intertidal zone
Geographic Range: Labrador to Long Island Sound; Europe

Notes: The Atlantic dogwinkle is a very variable species. Its many colors are largely influenced by diet. For the dogwinkles that frequently dine upon blue mussels (see p. 145) the shell color is normally dark. Lighter-shelled individuals may dine upon barnacles or some other light-colored prey.

Pitted Murex

Favartia cellulosa

Authority: (Conrad, 1846)
Other Name: Formerly classified as *Murex cellulosus*
Description: The exterior shell color ranges from yellowish to grayish white. The aperture is purplish or brownish within. The shell is spindle-shaped, with approximately six whorls and conical spire. The aperture is small and nearly round with a flattened outer lip. Each whorl has five to seven rough, fluted varices crossed by several small, scalloped axial ridges. The siphonal canal is short and open.
Size: Height to 1" (25 mm)
Habitat/Ecology: On sand or in rubble; often near oyster beds; low intertidal zone to shallow subtidal depths
Geographic Range: North Carolina to Brazil; Bermuda
Notes: The pitted murex is well named, since the shell appears to be very pitted. This species is frequently found in close association with oyster beds, where it is believed this species feeds upon young oysters.

Thick-lip Drill

Eupleura caudata

Authority: (Say, 1822)
Other Names: Also known as thick-lipped drill, thick-lipped oyster drill
Description: The exterior shell color varies from bluish white to reddish brown. The aperture is yellowish to pale reddish brown within. The shell is spindle-shaped, with a conical spire. There are about five whorls with approximately eleven strong axial ribs—two of which are enlarged (one bordering the aperture and another directly opposite) giving the shell a flattened look. The aperture is oval, with the outer lip thickened and with teeth.
Size: Height to 1.6" (41 mm)
Habitat/Ecology: On shelly substrates; near oyster beds; in shallow waters

Geographic Range: Cape Cod to Florida

Notes: The thick-lip drill is a predator of various mollusks including the eastern oyster (see p. 155). It is a major predator in the northern portion of its range. Females deposit their eggs in late winter and spring, and their young will crawl upon hatching.

Mauve-mouth Drill

Calotrophon ostrearum

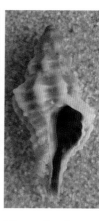

Authority: (Conrad, 1846)

Other Names: Also known as mauve-mouthed drill; incorrectly *Muricopsis ostrearum*, *Cantharus ostrearum*

Description: The exterior shell color is grayish white. The aperture is purplish to grayish pink within. The shell is spindle-shaped, with six whorls and a pointed spire. The whorls are decorated with seven to ten strong axial ribs crossed by irregular spiral cords. On each spire whorl there are two spiral cords on the lower section. The aperture is angled above, and below is pointed. The siphonal canal is long and open.

Size: Height to 1.25" (32 mm)

Habitat/Ecology: On rocks, shells, and similar hard objects; low intertidal zone to water 211' (64 m) deep

Geographic Range: Florida

Notes: At some locations albino specimens reach 25 percent of the population. This species is a carnivore that preys upon other mollusks.

Common Dovesnail

Columbella mercatoria

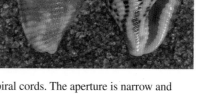

Authority: (Linnaeus, 1758)

Other Name: Also known as mottled dove snail

Description: The shell's exterior is white, with varying patterns or spots of yellow or brown. The shell is globe-shaped, with five to six whorls and a short, pointed spire. The whorls are sculptured with numerous low, rounded, spiral cords. The aperture is narrow and curved, with the outer lip thickened.

Size: Height to 0.75" (19 mm); width to 0.5" (13 mm)

Habitat/Ecology: On sand or stones; low intertidal zone to water 20' (6 m) deep

Geographic Range: Florida to Brazil

Notes: The common dovesnail is frequently encountered when washed up on the beach. Females deposit their eggs in single dome-shaped capsules, which take about a month to hatch into crawling miniatures of the adults.

Well-ribbed Dovesnail

Cotonopsis lafresnayi

Authority: (P. Fischer and Bernardi, 1856)
Other Names: Also known as well-ribbed dove shell; formerly classified as *Anachis lafresnayi, A. translirata*
Description: The exterior shell color is yellowish to light brown. The aperture is white within. The sturdy shell is elongate, with six to seven flat-sided whorls with a conical spire. The whorls are sculptured with several axial ribs crossed by numerous spiral cords. The aperture is elongate and pointed above.
Size: Height to 0.75" (19 mm)
Habitat/Ecology: On rocks, shells, and among eelgrass; from just below low intertidal zone to water 300' (91 m) deep
Geographic Range: Maine to Texas and Yucatán, Mexico
Notes: The female chooses any hard surface to lay her volcano-shaped eggs, which display many concentric ridges. The young are pelagic and swim away to begin the aquatic part of their lives.

Greedy Dovesnail

Costoanachis avara

Authority: (Say, 1822)
Other Names: Also known as greedy dove shell, greedy dove-shell, greedy dove snail; formerly classified as *Anachis avara*
Description: The shell's exterior is brownish yellow with a pattern of irregular, large, white dots. The shell is thick and moderately elongate, with the aperture approximately half the length of the shell. Four to twelve weak teeth are present inside the inner lip. The body whorl has seven to twenty-one ribs (on apical half only). The next whorls are graced with several axial riblets.
Size: Height to 0.5" (13 mm); width to 0.25" (6 mm)

Habitat/Ecology: On rocks or eelgrass; low intertidal zone to depths of 150' (46 m)

Geographic Range: Massachusetts to Brazil

Notes: The shell of this species varies over its geographic range. The greedy dovesnail is an opportunist and feeds upon a variety of marine life. It can increase its size dramatically in a few weeks in the presence of abundant carrion. Females lay their pyramid-shaped eggs on a variety of seaweeds. Once the young hatch, they are free-swimming.

Similar Species: Well-ribbed Dovesnail (see p. 106) has a thinner shell with flattened whorls.

Lunar Dovesnail

Astyris lunata

Authority: (Say, 1826)

Other Names: Also known as crescent mitrella, lunar dove shell, lunar dove snail

Description: The exterior shell is cream-colored to grayish, with zigzag axial rays or markings on the whorls and a glossy finish. The early whorls are translucent. The shell is spindle-shaped, with a tall spire. The whorls are smooth and flat-sided, without ribs or cords. The aperture is narrow, with the siphonal canal open at the bottom.

Size: Height to 0.25" (6 mm); width to 0.1" (3 mm)

Habitat/Ecology: On seaweeds, sand, or gravel; low intertidal zone

Geographic Range: Massachusetts to Brazil

Notes: The lunar dovesnail is a carnivore that dines on a variety of small invertebrates attached to the substrate.

Waved Whelk

Buccinum undatum

Authority: Linnaeus, 1758

Other Names: Also known as common northern buccinum, common northern whelk, edible whelk

Description: The shell's exterior color varies from pale yellowish brown to reddish. Its mantle is light yellow with dark brown blotches. A thin light brown periostracum may be present on live animals and fresh shells. The shell is broadly ovate, with five to six whorls

and a conical spire. The whorls
are sculptured with wavy vertical folds
and revolving lines.

The aperture is oval, with a flaring
outer lip.

Size: Height to 4" (102 mm); width to 2"
(51 mm)

Habitat/Ecology: On rocks, sand, or
gravel; low intertidal zone to water
600' (183 m) deep

Geographic Range: Arctic to New Jersey; Scotland; Ireland

Notes: The waved whelk is primarily a scavenger that is attracted to its next meal
from a distance away. Its long proboscis is used in feeding upon the fish bait left in
lobster pots as well. Its food includes: fish eggs, green sea urchins, and crabs.
Females deposit their eggs in an egg case that is the size of a fist. The waved whelks
in Europe grow to a much larger size.

Stimpson Whelk

Colus stimpsoni

Authority: (Mörch, 1868)

Other Names: Also known as Stimpson's colus, Stimpson's whelk

Description: The shell's exterior is
chalky white to yellowish. A thin,
yellowish brown to dark brown periostracum is present as well. The shell is
spindle-shaped, with seven to eight flat
whorls and little sculpture. The aperture is oval, with an elongated, straight,
open canal.

Size: Height to 4" (102 mm); width to
1.5" (38 mm)

Habitat/Ecology: On rocks, clay, or mud and in tidepools; low intertidal zone to
water 2800' (853 m) deep

Geographic Range: Labrador to Cape Hatteras

Notes: The Stimpson whelk is found in subtidal waters throughout much of its range,
and its shell is often found washed up on the shore. It seems to prefer the colder
temperatures of deeper water. In the northern portion of its range, north of Maine, it
may also be found in tidepools.

Ten-ridged Whelk

Neptunea decemcostata

Authority: (Say, 1826)

Other Names: Also known as corded neptune, New England neptune, New England ten-ridge whelk, wrinkle whelk; formerly classified as *Neptunea lyrata decemcostata*

Description: The shell's exterior is grayish white, with ten bold, reddish brown cords on the body whorl. The shell's interior is white. The whorls have several strong spiral cords. The shell is spindle-shaped, with a conical spire.

The whorls are sculptured with wavy vertical folds and revolving lines.

Size: Height to 5" (127 mm); width to 2.25" (57 mm)

Habitat/Ecology: On sand, rock, or mud; low intertidal zone to water 300' (91 m) deep

Geographic Range: Nova Scotia to Cape Cod

Notes: The distinctive shell of the ten-ridged whelk makes it an easy shell to identify. This species is sometimes found in lobster traps, like some of our other whelks. Females deposit a distinctive egg case that has a pillar shape to it, with overlapping scales.

Tinted Cantharus

Gemophos tinctus

Authority: (Conrad, 1846)

Other Names: Also known as gaudy lesser whelk; formerly classified as *Cantharus tinctus*, *Pisania tincta*, *Pollia tincta*

Description: The shell's exterior is reddish brown to dark brown, mottled with white. The shell is broadly ovate with five to six whorls and a conical spire. The whorls are sculptured with several revolving cords crossed by weak axial ribs.

The aperture is oval with broad and open canal.

Size: Height to 1.25" (32 mm)

Habitat/Ecology: On rocks, seaweed, and on rock jetties; low intertidal zone to water 10' (3 m) deep

Geographic Range: North Carolina to Brazil

Notes: The tinted cantharus is a predator that feeds upon smaller prey, including worms, small snails, and barnacles. Females use crevices to deposit their eggs, which have been described as "oval toadstools with a hollow top and a slender stem." The young emerge as larvae that begin their free-swimming stage in life.

False Drill

Cantharus multangulus

Authority: (Philippi, 1848)

Other Names: Also known as ribbed cantharus; formerly classified as *Pisania multangula*

Description: The shell's exterior varies from solid orange or brown to creamy with flecks of brown. The shell is spindle-shaped, with six whorls and a conical spire. The whorls are sculptured with seven to ten strong axial ribs and crossed by spiral cords. The aperture is ovate, with an open canal.

Size: Height to 1.5" (38 mm)

Habitat/Ecology: In sand or rubble; in shallow subtidal depths

Geographic Range: North Carolina to the West Indies; Texas

Notes: The genus for this species, *Cantharus*, is believed to originate from a double-handled drinking vessel that was made by the artisan Cantharus. A vessel of this type was made for Bacchus, the Roman god of wine.

Crown Conch

Melongena corona

Authority: (Gmelin, 1791)

Other Names: Also known as common crown conch, Florida crown conch

Description: The shell's exterior is dark brown to black with cream-colored, spiral bands. The shell is broadly ovate with convex whorls with a conical spire. The whorls and shoulder are sculptured with outward or upward spines.

The aperture is ovate with a very wide and open siphonal canal and a simple outer lip.

Size: Height to 5" (127 mm); width to 3" (76 mm)

Habitat/Ecology: In mud or mud and sand mixture; low intertidal zone to water 6' (1.8 m) deep

Geographic Range: Florida to Mexico

Notes: The crown conch is a highly variable species. Some individuals have shells that lack spines while others have elaborate spines. The spines, when present, often project upward giving the appearance of a crown. This species is a scavenger that feeds upon a variety of invertebrates including: fish, other mollusks, and crabs. The female deposits her eggs in egg capsules that are attached to hard objects in long strings.

Eggs

Knobbed Whelk

Busycon carica

Authority: (Gmelin, 1791)

Description: The shell's exterior varies from white to gray, with streaks of light brown to dark brown—or purple streaks in young specimens. The shell's aperture varies from bright orange to white. The shell is spindle-shaped, with approximately six whorls and a conical spire. The body whorl is large, broad, and sculptured with a series of stout spines or nodes that face outward. The aperture is oval and long, with an open, wide siphonal canal.

Size: Height to 9" (23 cm); width to 4.5" (11.4 cm)

Habitat/Ecology: On sandy shores; subtidal depths from 6–15' (1.8–4.6 m)

Geographic Range: Cape Cod to Florida

Notes: Shells of this subtidal species are often found on the beach after a storm. This species, like most whelks in the Atlantic, has a dextral (right-handed) shell, in which the body whorl curls in a clockwise direction when viewed from the front and the spire is pointed upward. Occasionally, we find sinistral (left-handed) shells. These are not common and are of great interest to collectors. Sinistral specimens of the knobbed whelk are present in the area of southern New Jersey.

Similar Species: Channeled Whelk (*Busycotypus canaliculatus*) (see p. 114)

Egg capsules

Lightning Whelk

Busycon sinistrum

Authority: Hollister, 1958

Other Name: Formerly classified as *Busycon contrarium*

Description: The shell's exterior is fawn colored with brown axial streaks. Young individuals have brighter colors. The shell is pear-shaped, with a body whorl that fills most of the shell, along with a short spire. The spiral of the body whorl turns to the left—a left-handed (sinistral) shell. The whorls are sculptured with broad triangular knobs. The aperture is wide and elongated, with a flared outer lip and an open, elongated siphonal canal.

Size: Height to 16" (41 cm); width to 7" (18 cm) but normally half this size

Habitat/Ecology: In sand, mud, or shell bottoms; low intertidal zone to water 10' (3 m) deep

Geographic Range: North Carolina to Florida and Texas; Yucatán

Notes: The graceful shell of the lightning whelk is one of the treasures found along the Atlantic Coastline. The colors of juvenile shells are also a real treat to view. The sinistral shell of this species makes it one of the easier shells to identify.

Channeled Whelk

Busycotypus canaliculatus

Authority: (Linnaeus, 1758)

Other Name: Formerly classified as *Busycon canaliculatum*

Description: The shell's exterior varies from yellowish white to gray. The shell's interior is pinkish. A thin, gray periostracum with tiny hairs is also present. The shell is pear-shaped, with the body whorl covering much of the shell, and it has a short spire. The whorls are sculptured with a beaded ridge in young individuals, but these largely disappear in older specimens. The aperture is oval, with an open, narrow siphonal canal.

Size: Height to 7" (180 mm); width to 3.5" (89 mm)

Habitat/Ecology: On sand and sand-mud bottoms; low intertidal zone to water 60' (18 m) deep

Geographic Range: Cape Cod to Florida; San Francisco Bay

Notes: The channeled whelk often dines on bivalves. It has developed a very effective method to reach the meat inside the shell of its prey. Rather than drill a hole into the shell like many other closely related mollusks, it inserts its narrow aperture canal between the valves of its victim. A clam reacts to this by closing its shell very tightly, which breaks one of its shells, enabling the channeled whelk to dine on the delicacy inside.

Similar Species: Knobbed Whelk (*Busycon carica*) (see p. 112)

Egg capsule

Pear Whelk

Busycotypus spiratus

Authority: (Lamarck, 1816)
Other Names: Also known as fig whelk; formerly classified as *Busycon pyrum*, *B. spiratum*
Description: The shell's exterior is flesh-colored, with reddish brown streaks. The shell is pear-shaped, with four to five whorls and a short, pointed spire. The whorls are sculptured with spiral threads. The aperture is oval, narrowing toward the base into a long, open siphonal canal.
Size: Height to 5.5" (14 cm)
Habitat/Ecology: On sandy shores; low intertidal zone to water 25' (7.6 m) deep
Geographic Range: North Carolina to Yucatán, Mexico
Notes: The pear whelk can be found on sand flats at low tide—often just under the surface of the sand so that the identity of the species is unknown until it is picked up. This species is a carnivore and likely a scavenger. Sinistral, or left-handed, specimens are very rare.

Bruised Nassa

Nassarius vibex

Authority: (Say, 1822)
Other Names: Also known as bruised basket shell, common eastern dog whelk, common eastern nassa, mottled dog whelk
Description: The shell's exterior varies from white to grayish brown, with reddish brown to dark brown spots or bands. The shell is broadly ovate with a

short, conical spire. There are five to seven whorls; the body whorl dominates the short, heavy shell. The whorls are sculptured with fine threads that cross about twelve transverse ribs. The sutures are well defined and shallow. The aperture is oval with a wall and lower section of body whorl covered by a broad and shiny callus.

Size: Height to 0.5" (13 mm); width to 0.25" (6 mm)
Habitat/Ecology: On sand or mudflats; shallow subtidal waters
Geographic Range: Cape Cod to Florida; West Indies; Brazil
Notes: The bruised nassa is a scavenger that has been observed feeding on many
  foods. It ingests sand and mud to remove the organic particles. It scavenges upon
  larger items, including the eggs of polychaete worms. They deposit their eggs in
  gelatinous capsules that they attach to the bottom. When the winter months
  approach, most individuals move to deeper waters.

Sharp Nassa

Nassarius acutus

Authority: (Say, 1822)
Other Name: Also known as narrow
  basket shell
Description: The shell's exterior varies
  from white to yellowish, often with a
  brown spiral thread. The shell is ovate
  with a conical spire. There are seven
  convex whorls sculptured with spiral threads that cross the transverse ribs, yielding a
  beaded appearance to the shell. The aperture is oval with a thickened outer lip and a
  narrow, open, and short siphonal canal.
Size: Height to 0.5" (13 mm)
Habitat/Ecology: On sandy shores; low intertidal zone to water 20' (6.1 m) deep
Geographic Range: North Carolina to Texas
Notes: The acute nassa is a scavenger that feeds on decaying flesh, debris, other mollusks, and their eggs. There is a symbiotic relationship of this species reported with
  young incongruous ark (see p. 143).

White Nassa

Nassarius albus

Authority: (Say, 1826)
Other Names: Also known as variable
  dog whelk, variable nassa, white
  basket shell; formerly classified as
  N. ambiguous
Description: The shell's exterior varies
  from white to yellowish white, often
  with faint brown spiral rows or spots.
  The shell's interior is white. The shell is
  stout and broadly ovate with a conical spire. There are five convex whorls that are
  sculptured with strongly angled, axial ribs, crossed by cords that vary in size. The
  aperture is circular with a thickened outer lip and narrow canals at both ends.
Size: Height to 0.5" (13 mm)

Habitat/Ecology: On sandy shores; low intertidal zone to water 100' (30 m) deep

Geographic Range: North Carolina to Brazil

Notes: The white nassa is one of several species that belong to the genus *Nassarius*, which is derived from *nassa* (a Latin word that means "wicker basket"). This originated from some species that have a surface sculpture that resembles a wicker basket.

Three-lined Basketsnail

Ilyanassa trivittata

Authority: (Say, 1822)

Other Names: Also known as New England basket whelk, New England dog whelk, New England nassa, three-lined basket shell; formerly classified as *Nassarius trivittatus*

Description: The shell's exterior varies from yellowish white to yellowish gray, often with brown spiral stripes. The shell is broadly ovate with a conical spire. There are six to seven convex whorls that are sculptured with axial ribs, crossed by ten to twelve spiral cords that are equal in size and create a beaded pattern. The aperture is ovate, with a toothed inner margin of the outer lip and a short, open siphonal canal.

Size: Height to 0.75" (19 mm); width to 0.4" (10 mm)

Habitat/Ecology: On sand, and sand-mud mix; low intertidal zone to water 300' (91 m) deep

Geographic Range: Newfoundland to Florida

Notes: The three-lined basketsnail is a delicate-looking species with an intricate shell. The living animal is white-colored with pale purplish spots. This species has been observed feeding upon the egg case of the northern moonsnail in high numbers. The three-lined basketsnail is believed to be a scavenger.

Eastern Mud Snail

Ilyanassa obsoleta

Authority: (Say, 1822)

Other Names: Also known as common mud snail, eastern mud nassa, eastern mud whelk, mud dog whelk, mud basket shell; formerly classified as *Nassarius obsoleta*

Description: The shell's exterior varies from reddish purple to light brown or black, occasionally with some banding.

The shell is stout and broadly ovate, with a rounded and worn spire. There are six convex whorls that are sculptured with numerous revolving lines crossed by minute growth lines. The aperture is ovate, with the outer lip that includes spiral ridges that originate from within and a short, wide siphonal canal.

Size: Height to 1.25" (32 mm)
Habitat/Ecology: On mudflats; low intertidal zone to very shallow subtidal waters
Geographic Range: Gulf of St. Lawrence to Florida
Notes: A dark individual of the eastern mud snail is considered by some to be one of the most unattractive snails in North America. This species is believed to live for up to five years. Their egg capsules, which feature a zigzag ridge, are deposited by females on a wide variety of substrates, including rocks, shells, and algae.

Chestnut Latirus

Leucozonia nassa

Authority: (Gmelin, 1791)
Other Names: Formerly classified as *Leucozonia caribbeana, L. jacarusoi, L. trinidadensis*
Description: The shell's exterior varies from chestnut brown to nearly black, often with a lighter band near the base and cream streaks. The shell's interior is white. The shell is solid and spindle-shaped, with a pointed spire. About seven whorls are present, and the body whorl features strong tubercles that form shoulders on the whorls. The shell sculpture features about ten axial ribs crossed by numerous spiral cords that create rather sharp shoulders. The aperture is ovate with an outer lip that is grooved from within and a short, open siphonal canal.

Size: Height to 2" (51 mm)
Habitat/Ecology: On and under rocks and in reefs; shallow subtidal depths
Geographic Range: Florida to the West Indies; Texas
Notes: This species has a long and complicated history, with at least twenty-one scientific names that have been used for it since it was first described in 1791. The chestnut latirus feeds upon various worms and barnacles.
Similar Species: **Florida Horse Conch** (*Triplofusus giganteus*) (see p. 121) juveniles are similar looking.

True Tulip

Fasciolaria tulipa

Authority: (Linne, 1758)

Other Names: Also known as true tulip shell, true tulip snail, tulip shell

Description: The shell's exterior varies from pinkish gray to cream-colored or reddish orange, with numerous broken spiral bands and brown blotches. The shell is spindle-shaped, with a conical spire. There are eight to nine convex whorls; the body whorl dominates the tall shell. The whorls are relatively smooth and the sutures are distinct. The aperture is ovate, with a thin outer lip and an open, narrow siphonal canal.

Size: Height to 10" (25 cm); width to 4" (10.2 cm)

Habitat/Ecology: On sand and muddy shores; low intertidal zone to water 30' (9 m) deep

Geographic Range: North Carolina to Brazil

Notes: The true tulip is a predator that preys upon a wide variety of mollusks. Its preference is for large gastropods, including its close relative the banded tulip (see p. 120), as well as the pear whelk (see p. 115) and young pink conch (see p. 86). The color of the living animal varies from dark red to bright red in color.

Similar Species: Banded Tulip (*Cinctura hunteria*) (see p. 120)

Eggs

Banded Tulip

Cinctura hunteria

Authority: (Perry, 1811)

Other Names: Also known as banded tulip shell, banded tulip snail; formerly classified as *Fasciolaria distans*, *F. lillium*

Description: The shell's exterior is cream-colored with orange and brown blotches and widely spaced, brown uninterrupted spiral lines. The shell is spindle-shaped, with a conical spire. There are seven to nine convex whorls; the body whorl dominates the tall shell. The whorls are smooth, lacking both noticeable ribs and cords and the sutures are distinct. The aperture is ovate, with a thin outer lip and an open siphonal canal.

Size: Height to 3" (76 mm); width to 1.4" (35 mm)

Habitat/Ecology: On sand and sand-mud shores; subtidal depths from 2–150' (0.6–46 m)

Geographic Range: North Carolina to Florida and Texas; Bahamas; West Indies; Yucatán, Mexico

Notes: The banded tulip is a predator that in turn is eaten by a large predator: the horse conch (see p. 121). This species dines upon various mollusks including the Eastern oyster (see p. 155). To reach the meat inside the shell, the banded tulip, like the true tulip (see p. 119) and horse conch, uses the thick lip of its shell to chip away at its prey's shell to create a hole to insert its proboscis, allowing it to feed on the shellfish inside.

Similar Species: True Tulip (*Fasciolaria tulipa*) (see p. 119)

Florida Horse Conch

Triplofusus giganteus

Authority: (Kiener, 1840)

Other Name: Formerly classified as *Pleuroploca gigantea*

Description: The shell's exterior varies from white to salmon with a chalky finish, and juveniles are bright orange. A thin, brown periostracum covers the shell. The shell is stout, heavy and spindle-shaped, with an elongated, conical spire. There are about ten whorls which are sculptured with axial ribs crossed by spiral cords and threads. The axial ribs are decorated with numerous knobs at regular intervals on most shells.

The aperture is ovate, with an open, narrow, and twisted siphonal canal. The operculum is thick, horny, and oval, with a pointed end. The animal's body is brick red.

Size: Height to 24" (61 cm); width to 10" (25 cm)

Habitat/Ecology: On sandy and muddy shores; low intertidal zone to water 20' (6.1 m) deep

Geographic Range: North Carolina to Florida and Texas; Mexico

Notes: The Florida horse conch is the state shell of Florida. It also is the largest shell in North American waters and the second largest in the world—behind the Australian trumpet (*Syrinx aruanus*). The Florida horse conch is a predator that feeds upon many larger mollusks including: the true tulip (see p. 119), lightning whelk (see p. 113), lace murex (see p. 102), and penshells (see pp. 150–151). For it to successfully capture its gastropod prey, it grasps its victim's operculum. This prevents the aperture from being closed so that it can insert its proboscis to dine on its prey.

Lettered Olive

Oliva sayana

Authority: Ravenel, 1834

Description: The shell's exterior varies
from cream-colored to tan, with many
chestnut or purplish brown zigzag
markings and a highly polished finish.
The shell's interior is purple. The shell
is stout and nearly cylindrical with a
conical spire.

There are five to six whorls; the body
whorl dominates the solid shell. Sutures are narrow, deep, and channeled. The aperture is long, with a thin outer lip and a wider base. The siphonal canal is simply an oblique notch at the base. There is no operculum.

Size: Height to 2.5" (64 mm); width to 0.9" (22 mm)

Habitat/Ecology: In sand; low intertidal zone to water 150' (46 m) deep

Geographic Range: North Carolina to Florida, Texas, and Brazil

Notes: The lettered olive is a common species that ploughs through the sand just below
the surface with only its siphon extended above the surface of the sand. There in the
sand, it preys upon a variety of bivalves and crustaceans. It also scavenges on
invertebrates—especially during the winter months.

Variable Dwarf Olive

Olivella mutica

Authority: (Say, 1822)

Description: The shell's exterior varies
from white to solid brown, often with a
body whorl that features a broad band
of brown or gray and a narrow band of
brown patterns. A highly polished
finish is also present. The shell is stout
and elongately ovate with a conical,
pointed spire. There are three to four
whorls of which the body whorl dom-

inates the small shell. The sutures are distinct with a deeply channeled groove. The
aperture is narrowly triangular at the upper end. There is no operculum.

Size: Height to 0.5" (13 mm); width to 0.25" (6 mm)

Habitat/Ecology: In sand; low intertidal zone to water 20' (6.1 m) deep

Geographic Range: North Carolina to Florida; Bahamas

Notes: The variable dwarf olive deposits its dome-shaped egg capsules on any hard
object it can find in its sandy environment. The young escape after about three weeks
to begin the crawling phase in their lives.

Similar Species: Rice Olive (*Olivella* cf. *prefloralia*) is a tiny, common species that is
white in color.

Caribbean Vase Snail

Vasum muricatum

Authority: (Born, 1778)

Other Name: Also known as Caribbean vase

Description: The shell's exterior is white, sometimes with brown mottlings or spots. The shell's interior is white. A tough brown periostracum may be present on the shell. The shell is stout and spindle-shaped, with a conical spire. There are six to seven whorls, which are sculptured with axial ribs featuring several knobs and crossed by cords that vary in size. The aperture is oval and elongate, with an open and wide siphonal canal. The operculum is heavy and corneous.

Size: Height to 5.75" (146 mm)

Habitat/Ecology: In sand or rubble; low intertidal zone to water 30' (9 m) deep

Geographic Range: Florida to Brazil

Notes: The Caribbean vase snail is often found living in pairs. They feed upon various worms and bivalves. Their egg capsules are elongated, slightly bent, and these are attached to various hard objects.

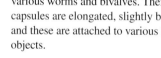

Junonia

Scaphella junonia

Authority: (Lamarck, 1804)

Description: The shell's exterior varies from white to yellowish with square brown to reddish orange spots. The shell's interior is whitish or yellowish. A thin, brown or yellowish periostracum is present on fresh shells. The shell is spindle-shaped, with a conical spire. There are five to six slightly convex whorls; the body whorl dominates the shell. The aperture is elongate and pointed at both ends, with a flaring lower outer lip and a short siphonal canal. There is no operculum.

Size: Height to 6" (152 mm); width to 2.5" (64 mm)

Habitat/Ecology: In sand; subtidal from water 6–250' (2–76 m) deep

Geographic Range: North Carolina to Florida; Mexico

Notes: The junonia is a treasured shell that occasionally washes up on the beach after a storm. This shell is the the highlight of any collection. Scallop trawlers have brought this species up in their nets. Just as the shell is covered in spots, so too is the living animal.

Common Nutmeg

Cancellaria reticulata

Authority: (Linnaeus, 1767)

Description: The shell's exterior varies from white to cream-colored, with bands or spiral splotches of reddish brown. The shell is spindle-shaped, with a conical spire. The six to seven convex whorls are sculptured with axial ribs crossed by cords that are equal in size and create a beaded pattern. Sutures are distinct. The aperture is elongated with an inner lip that features two twisted folds and a short open siphonal canal. There is no operculum.

Size: Height to 1.75" (44 mm); width to 1" (25 mm)

Habitat/Ecology: In sand; subtidal from below the low-tide line to water 50' (15 m) deep

Geographic Range: North Carolina to Brazil

Notes: Common nutmegs are not normally found at the low intertidal level; however, after a storm, many may be found there. This species feeds upon a variety of soft-bodied animals under the surface of the sand.

Common Atlantic Marginella

Prunum apicinum

Authority: (Menke, 1828)

Other Names: Also known as common Atlantic margin shell, common marginella; formerly classified as *Marginella apicina*, *M. apicinum*

Description: The shell's exterior varies from cream-colored to grayish tan, with reddish brown spots and a highly polished finish. The shell is stout and conical, with a well-rounded spire.

There are three to four smooth whorls; the body whorl dominates the entire shell. The aperture is elongated, with a thickened outer lip, an inner lip with four strong folds, and an open, wide canal. There is no operculum.

Size: Height to 0.5" (13 mm); width to 0.4" (10 mm)

Habitat/Ecology: In sand and grass beds; low intertidal zone to water 30' (9 m) deep

Geographic Range: North Carolina to the West Indies

Notes: The common Atlantic marginella deposits egg capules that are pimpled and dome-shaped. The young emerge from their egg cases as crawling individuals.

Alphabet Cone

Conus spurius

Authority: Gmelin, 1791

Other Name: Formerly classified as *Conus spurius atlanticus*

Description: The shell's exterior varies from white to creamy-white with regular, spiral rows of square yellowish orange to reddish brown spots. A thin, brown periostracum is present on fresh shells. The shell is stout and conical, with a short, concave, and stepped spire. There are nine to ten smooth whorls; the body whorl dominates the shell.

The aperture is narrow and elongated. The operculum is small and horny.

Size: Height to 3" (76 mm); width to 1.5" (38 mm)

Habitat/Ecology: In sand, near reefs and reef flats; subtidal waters from 1–50' (0.3–15 m) deep

Geographic Range: Florida to the West Indies

Notes: The alphabet cone has been designated a mildly toxic species. It is a predator that possesses a radula with detachable, dart-like teeth. In addition, this species has poison glands, which it uses to harpoon its prey. This poison can also be inflicted into a hand of an unwary collector.

Similar Species: Florida Cone (*Conus anabathrum*) (see below)

Florida Cone

Conus anabathrum

Authority: Crosse, 1865

Other Names: Also known as common spirula; formerly classified as *Conus floridanus*

Description: The shell's exterior varies from white or buff with irregular axial splotches and spiral bands of yellowish to reddish brown. A thin, brown periostracum may be present on fresh shells. The shell is stout and conical, with a pointed spire. There are seven to eight smooth whorls; the body whorl dominates the shell. The aperture is elongated with a flattened inner lip, a thin outer lip, and an open siphonal canal. The operculum is thin and narrow, with a pointed end.

Size: Height to 2" (51 mm)

Habitat/Ecology: In sand; subtidal from 5–90' (1.5–27 m) deep

Geographic Range: North Carolina to Florida

Notes: There are nearly 500 species of cone shells worldwide, and the Florida cone is one of those on our Atlantic Coast. Cone shells are popular with collectors.

The most deadly cone shell in the world comes from the Indo-Pacific, and it is called the geographic cone snail (*Conus geographus*). It is so deadly that it is nicknamed the "cigarette snail" because the amount of time it takes to smoke a cigarette is the time frame a victim has left to live, and there is no antidote!

Similar Species: Alphabet Cone (*Conus spurius*) (see p. 125)

Jasper Cone

Conus jaspideus

Authority: Gmelin, 1791

Description: The shell's exterior varies from white to purple brown, with dark yellowish brown streaks or blotches and spiral bands of tiny white and brown dashes. The shell's interior is white. The shell is stout and conical, with a pointed spire. There are eight to ten smooth, stepped whorls, and the spire whorls are sharply shouldered. The exterior is often beaded. The aperture is elongated with a thin outer lip and a wide posterior notch.

Size: Height to 1.1" (3 cm)

Habitat/Ecology: In sand; subtidal waters from 3–60' (0.9–18 m) deep

Geographic Range: North Carolina to Brazil

Notes: The Jasper cone is part of a complex of species or subspecies that has yet to be finalized. This series of species is currently believed to be subspecies of the Jasper cone. Stearns' cone, the subspecies *stearnsii* (occasionally misspelled *stearnsi*), which is darker and more slender, ranges from North Carolina to western Florida. Approximately eight other subspecies have also been named.

Eastern Auger

Terebra dislocata

Authority: (Say, 1822)

Other Names: Also known as Atlantic auger, common Atlantic auger

Description: The shell's exterior varies from pinkish gray to yellowish brown—the upper third occasionally paler—with a cream-colored band on the outer edge of body whorl and a glossy finish. The shell is sharply elongate. There are about fourteen straight whorls with about fifteen axial ribs per whorl crossed by several spiral grooves. The aperture is small and oval.

Size: Height to 2" (51 mm); width to 0.4" (10 mm)

Habitat/Ecology: In sand; low intertidal zone to water 100' (30 m) deep

Geographic Range: Maryland to Brazil

Notes: The eastern auger does not have a radula or a poison gland to obtain its food. Its diet, however, is unknown and only speculated upon. This species has been found as a Pleistocene fossil in Florida and Bermuda where it is very common.

Similar Species: Concave Auger (*Terebra concava*) (see below) with concave whorls.

Concave Auger

Terebra concava

Authority: (Say, 1826)

Description: The shell's exterior varies from white to yellowish brown, with a polished finish. The shell is sharply elongate. There are about twelve concave whorls, with several axial ribs crossed by many cords that create a beaded pattern. The aperture is small and oval.

Size: Height to 1" (25 mm); width to 0.25" (6 mm)

Habitat/Ecology: On sand; in shallow subtidal waters

Geographic Range: North Carolina to Brazil

Notes: The concave auger is one of three augers that may wash up on the beach. All augers have a polished finish, and their differences are summarized below.

Similar Species: Eastern Auger (*Terebra dislocata*) (see above)

Salle's Auger (*Impages salleana*) is purple-gray, with darkly streaked ribs and flat-sided whorls and grows to 1.5" (3.8 cm).

Shiny Atlantic Auger (*Terebra hastata*) is creamy white, with a shell that tapers much more abrubtly and grows to 1.5" (3.8 cm).

Rehder's Baby-bubble

Acteon candens

Authority: Rehder, 1939

Description: The shell's exterior is white, occasionally with caramel-colored bands on the early whorl, and with a glossy, opaque finish. The shell's interior is white. The shell is solid and broadly ovate, with a conical spire. There are about six convex whorls with a spiral sculpture.

Size: Height to 0.3" (7.5 mm); width to 0.2" (4.2 mm)

Habitat/Ecology: In muddy sand; intertidal zone to water 409' (124 m) deep

Geographic Range: North Carolina to Florida; Cuba

Notes: The Rehder's baby-bubble is a species that may be found as a shell washed up on the beach or occasionally in the mud at low tide.

Common Atlantic Bubble Snail

Bulla striata

Authority: Bruguière, 1792

Other Names: Also known as common Atlantic bubble, striate bubble; formerly classified as *Bulla umbilicata*

Description: The shell's exterior varies from cream-colored to reddish gray, with blotches or streaks of pink, red, or brown and a semi-polished finish. The shell's interior is whitish. The shell is oval and inflated, with a depressed spire.

The aperture is longer than the body whorl, with a wider base and a thin outer lip.

Size: Height to 1.1" (28 mm)

Habitat/Ecology: On sandy and muddy shores; in shallow subtidal waters

Geographic Range: North Carolina to Brazil; Bermuda; Mediterranean; West Africa

Notes: The mantle of the common Atlantic bubble snail completely covers its shell. This carnivore is photosensitive and is most active at night. It dines upon various small mollusks that it can swallow whole, crushing them inside its body with its interior calcareous plates.

Solitary Bubble Snail

Haminoea solitaria

Authority: (Say, 1822)

Other Names: Also known as solitary bubble, solitary glassy bubble, solitary paper bubble

Description: The shell's exterior varies from whitish to amber. The shell is extremely fragile and sculptured with fine spiral grooves. The shell is oval and inflated, with a depressed spire. The aperture is longer than the body whorl, with a wider base and a thin outer lip. The living animal is grayish and slug-like.

Size: Height to 0.5" (13 mm); width to 0.25" (6 mm)

Habitat/Ecology: In silty sand or mud; low intertidal zone to water 30' (9 m) deep

Geographic Range: Cape Cod to North Carolina

Notes: A living solitary bubble snail resembles a slug with a soft body that almost totally covers its shell. A flattened cephalic shield is found on the head, and it is used for burrowing in its substrate. This shield is characteristic of the order Cephalaspidea, but not all species possess it.

Eastern Melampus

Melampus bidentatus

Authority: Say, 1822

Other Names: Also known as coffee melampus, common marsh snail, salt-marsh snail

Description: The shell's exterior varies from pale brown to greenish yellow, occasionally with brown spiral bands and axial streaks. Mud often covers the colors, and fresh shells are typically richly colored. A thin, yellowish brown periostracum covers the shell. The shell is broadly ovate, with a short spire. There are about five whorls; the body whorl dominates the fragile shell. The aperture is elongated with a thin outer lip and smooth inside.

Size: Height to 0.75" (19 mm)

Habitat/Ecology: At the edges of marshes, lagoons, and mangroves; near the high intertidal zone

Geographic Range: Gulf of St. Lawrence to Gulf of Mexico

Notes: The eastern melampus is part of the family Melampidae which includes the land snails but is not closely related to the marine snails. The striped falselimpet (see p. 56) is another member of this group. The eastern melampus uses a lung to respire in air, rather than water. It is an omnivore that feeds on a wide variety of foods, including algae, detritus, and dead animals.

Similar Species: **Coffee Melampus** (*Melampus coffea*) (see p. 130) has a set of white spiral ridges inside the aperture's outer lip.

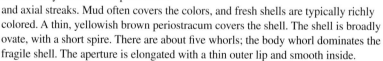

Coffee Melampus

Melampus coffea

Authority: (Linnaeus, 1758)

Other Names: Also known as coffee bean snail; occasionally misspelled *Melampus coffeus*

Description: The shell's exterior is brown with three bands of creamy white. A thin gray periostracum is also present. The shell is ovate with a tapering base. The four to five whorls are smooth on the surface. The aperture is elongated, with a thin outer lip and a set of white spiral ridges within—each ending with a tooth.

Size: Height to 0.75" (19 mm)

Habitat/Ecology: On and around mangroves; near the high intertidal zone

Geographic Range: Florida; the West Indies to Brazil

Notes: The coffee melampus deposits its jelly-like egg masses on any hard object including rocks, sticks, or similar objects. The free-swimming young emerge from the eggs approximately ten days after the highest tide waters have reached the eggs.

Similar Species: **Eastern Melampus** (*Melampus bidentatus*) (see p. 129) has an aperture with the outer lip being smooth inside.

NUDIBRANCHS AND ALLIES
(Infraclass Opisthobranchia)

Nudibranchs do not bear a shell and are well known for their striking and wild colors. This group always draws the attention of divers and beachcombers. More than 3,000 species have been described worldwide. Nudibranchs' body shapes are quite diverse, and they are placed into several groups based upon their body shape.

Sooty Sea Hare

Aplysia fasciata

The sooty sea hare swimming

Authority: Poiret, 1789

Other Names: Also known as Willcox's sea hare; formerly classified as *Aplysia brasiliana*, *Aplysia willcoxi*, *Aplysia winneba*

Description: The body is normally brownish to reddish purple or greenish in color, with a smooth, solid firmness. There is a pair of parapodia (lateral, wing-like swimming flaps) on each side of the animal. This sea hare has an internal shell that is weakly calcified and can be felt as a nut-like firmness within the body. Two pairs of rhinophores, or tentacles, are present on the head. One pair are located on top of the head just behind the eyes, and the second pair at the anterior margin of the head.

Size: Length to 9" (225 mm)

Habitat/Ecology: On rock jetties, pilings, creeks, sea walls, and grass beds; in shallow water

Geographic Range: North Carolina to Gulf of Mexico; occasional to Cape Cod

Notes: The sooty sea hare is a large species, known for its ability to swim with the slow beats of its soft "wings." It also releases a harmless purple dye when threatened by a predator or when handled. This species lays rather large strings of spaghetti-like eggs. All sea hares are hermaphrodites that can act as both a male and a female.

White Atlantic Cadlina

Cadlina laevis

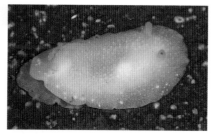

Authority: (Linnaeus, 1767)

Other Name: Formerly classified as *Doris obvelata*

Description: The body is overall translucent white, speckled with yellow, and opaque white spots are also present. The posterior end is adorned with a ring of yellow-tipped feathery gills. The coil-like rhinophores are translucent and oval. The body is flattened.

Size: Length to 1.25" (30 mm)

Habitat/Ecology: On rocks; low intertidal zone to water 2,624' (800 m) deep

Geographic Range: Arctic to Massachusetts; Russia to Spain

Notes: This beautiful nudibranch protects itself with twenty or more yellow-tipped poison glands embedded into its flattened surface. The white Atlantic cadlina feeds upon encrusting slime-sponges.

It lays rather large eggs that hatch directly into miniature nudibranchs that do not require a planktonic stage in their development. This species actually includes food inside its eggs to give its larvae a head start before they find their normal sponge foods.

Barnacle-eating Dorid

Onchidoris bilamellata

Authority: (Linnaeus, 1767)

Other Names: Also known as barnacle-eating nudibranch, barnacle-eating onchidoris, roughmantled nudibranch, rough-mantled doris; formerly classified as *Onchidoris fusca*

Description: The body is colored with a pattern of chocolate to rusty-brown mixed with a cream color. The oval-shaped body is covered with numerous rather short, knobby projections. The rhinophores are comb-like, and the sixteen to thirty-two gills are feather-like, arranged together in two partial rings.

Size: Length normally to 1.2" (30 mm), occasionally to 1.6" (40 mm)

Habitat/Ecology: In crevices; on rocks and pilings; in mud bays; high intertidal zone to water 25' (8 m) deep

Geographic Range: Arctic to Rhode Island; Alaska to Mexico; France to Russia.

Notes: The barnacle-eating dorid can be found in the high intertidal zone on rocky shorelines—where barnacles are found. Only adults dine on this prey item. Juveniles, however, feed on encrusting bryozoans. In the spring and summer, small groups of this dorid gather to mate. Here, on the underside of a rock you can often find these groups of adults along with their distinctive wavy egg masses. This nudibranch is an annual species that is often found in the presence of the hairy spiny doris (see below)

Hairy Spiny Doris

Acanthodoris pilosa

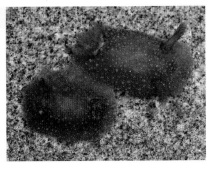

Authority: (Abildgaard in O. F. Müller, 1789)

Other Name: Also known as hairy doris

Description: The overall color varies greatly and includes: white, light yellow, tan, dark brown, or purplish brown. The body is oval and covered with slender, soft, uniform, conical projections. The rhinophores are bent backward, and seven to nine feather-like gills grace the posterior.

Size: Length normally to 1.25" (32 mm), occasionally to 2.2" (55 mm); width to 0.6" (16 mm)

Habitat/Ecology: On seaweeds, especially knotted wrack (see p. 295) and northern rockweed (see p. 293); the underside of rocks; mid intertidal zone to water 558' (170 m) deep.

Geographic Range: Arctic to Connecticut; Alaska to Puget Sound; Morocco to the Baltic Sea; Iceland; Greenland

Notes: This beautiful dorid is often found in a variety of colors at the same location. At other locations, only some colors are observed. The reason for the colors could be genetic or perhaps dietary. No one has determined the actual cause for their colors.

The hairy spiny doris is possibly our most common intertidal nudibranch. It spawns year round, laying its eggs that look like white ribbons on northern rockweed, knotted wrack, or on a rock.

Fuzzy Onchidoris

Onchidoris muricata

Authority: (O. F. Müller, 1776)

Other Names: Also known as white dorid, muricate doris; formerly classified as *Onchidoris aspera, O. hystricina,* and *O. varians*

Description: The overall body color can be either white or yellow, and a few individuals have brown speckles. Flat-topped tubercles, each on a stalk, completely cover the dorsal side of the body.

Size: Length to 0.5" (14 mm); width to 0.25" (6 mm)

Habitat/Ecology: On rocks, or on one of its foods, the white lace bryozoan (see p. 251); low intertidal zone to water 80' (18 m) deep

Geographic Range: Arctic to Connecticut; Alaska to California; France and British Isles; Russia; Iceland; Greenland

Notes: The size of fuzzy onchidoris is reported to be much smaller in late summer and autumn. Possibly this is because the individuals that are found then are the young produced earlier that year. Over 50,000 small eggs may be produced by a single individual at one time.

Similar Species: Yellow False Doris (*Adalaria proxima*) closely resembles fuzzy onchidoris except that it is often yellowish and larger (reaching 0.6" (17 mm) long). Its tubercles are also noticably pointed. The egg mass of yellow false doris is much smaller, as there are only 2,000 large eggs.

Atlantic Ancula

Ancula gibbosa

Authority: (Risso, 1818)

Other Name: Formerly classified as *Ancula cristata*

Description: The body is transparent white, and all projections have lemon-yellow tips. The body is elongated and tapered toward the rear, and a gill ring is present on the middle of its back. There are two additional projections on the front of the body.

Size: Length to 0.5" (13 mm); width to 0.1" (3 mm)

Habitat/Ecology: On rocks and seaweeds; low intertidal zone to water 330' (100 m) deep

Geographic Range: Arctic to Connecticut; Russia; Greenland.

Notes: The Atlantic ancula is more translucent than some nudibranchs, and as a result, its internal organs can be observed through its body wall. A mystery surrounds the

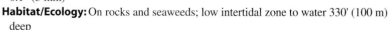

diet of this species. Various researchers believe it feeds upon: a white sponge, a colonial bryozoan, two tunicates, and algae. Once again, more research is needed to determine its real diet.

Bushy-backed Nudibranch

Dendronotus frondosus

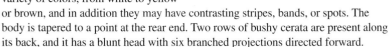

Authority: (Ascanius, 1774)
Other Names: Also known as bushy-backed sea slug; formerly classified as *Tritonia pulchella, Tritonia reynoldsii*
Description: The body occurs in a wide variety of colors, from white to yellow or brown, and in addition they may have contrasting stripes, bands, or spots. The body is tapered to a point at the rear end. Two rows of bushy cerata are present along its back, and it has a blunt head with six branched projections directed forward.
Size: Length to 1.2" (30 mm) at intertidal sites; length subtidally to 4.6" (117 mm).
Habitat/Ecology: On rocks, among seaweeds, and in tidepools; low intertidal zone to water 360' (110 m) deep
Geographic Range: Arctic to New Jersey; Alaska to California; France
Notes: The colors of this species change as the bushy-backed nudibranch changes its diet. It likely has a lifespan of two years and reproduces year-round, as its round egg masses have been found in both the cold and warm months of the year.

   Most researchers agree that this nudibranch feeds on hydroids; however, some sources list its foods to include small anemones, bryozoans, colonial tunicates, and algae. It is unlikely that this species feeds on such a wide variety of invertebrates and algae. More research is required to determine its true diet.

Sargassum Nudibranch

Scyllaea pelagica

Authority: Linnaeus, 1758
Other Names: Also known as gulfweed nudibranch, sargassum sea slug
Description: The body is yellow to orangish brown, with brown and white blotches. Small blue spots are present on the sides. Two pairs of somewhat thick and blunt projections called cerata are found on the back.
Size: Length to 2" (51 mm) and occasionally to 2.2" (55 mm)
Habitat/Ecology: Only on gulfweed
Geographic Range: Massachusetts to Brazil
Notes: This nudibranch is a wanderer originating from the Sargasso Sea. It lives on pelagic gulfweed, and it drifts to tropical and temperate land by mistake. We only

view this species as it clings to living gulfweed after it has been tossed to shore by a storm. It is perfectly camouflaged to live on gulfweed.

Graceful Aeolis

Flabellina gracilis

Authority: (Alder and Hancock, 1844)
Other Name: Formerly classified as *Coryphella gracilis*
Description: The overall color is whitish, with orange to crimson cerata with white tips. A series of white flecks makes up a streak on the tentacles. There are four to six pairs of cerata clusters. The cerata form distinctive rows on the back. It also displays a "notched" head when viewed from the side.
Size: Length to 0.5" (12 mm)
Habitat/Ecology: On rocks, in tidepools; low intertidal zone to water 108' (33 m) deep
Geographic Range: Nova Scotia to Cape Cod; France; British Isles; Denmark; Iceland
Notes: This nudibranch is one of the more common species found in the north Atlantic.
Similar Species: Red-finger Aeolis (*Flabellina verrucosa*) is similar, with cerata that are not in well-defined rows.

Dwarf Balloon Aeolis

Eubranchus pallidus

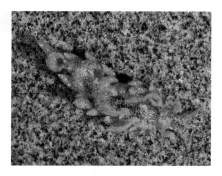

Authority: (Alder and Hancock, 1842)
Other Names: Also known as club-gilled nudibranch; formerly classified as *Eubranchus exiguus*
Description: The color of the body and cerata are translucent white, with yellowish brown to orange-brown blotches. A single row of inflated cerata is on each dorsal side of the body. The cerata do not posses the usual dark rings found in other species.
Size: Length normally to 0.4" (10 mm), occasionally to 0.8" (20 mm)
Habitat/Ecology: On rocks; low intertidal zone to shallow subtidal waters
Geographic Range: Arctic to Massachusetts; Norway to the western Mediterranean
Notes: Some think the dwarf balloon aeolis is uncommon. It is quite easy to miss; however, because it is so small. This elegant species is distinctive with its balloon-shaped cerata. Just as many other nudibranchs do, it feeds on a variety of hydroid species.

Northern Aeolis

Cratena pilata

Authority: (Gould, 1870)
Other Name: Formerly classified as
Cratena kaoruae
Description: The overall color is white
to gray for the elongated body. Long
tentacles cover the dorsal side in several lateral rows, each with a yellowish
brown to rusty brown central core. There is also a mid-dorsal row of rusty brown
patches.
Size: Length to 1.2" (30 mm)
Habitat/Ecology: On unused boats, old wharf pilings; in estuaries, tidal rivers; low
intertidal zone
Geographic Range: Massachusetts to North Carolina
Notes: The northern aeolis is a nudibranch that lives where saltwater has been diluted
with freshwater. There, it feeds upon the stinging, hydroid-like polyps (part of a life
cycle of true jellies) to obtain their nematocysts. These nematocysts are loaded into
its cerata undischarged, simply by ingesting them. These will be used as weapons in
the nudibranch's defense. It is truly amazing that each cnidosac (the tip of each
ceras) is loaded with 50 to 800 nematocysts.

Shag-rug Nudibranch

Aeolidia papillosa

Authority: (Linnaeus, 1761)
Other Names: Also known as maned
nudibranch, shag-rug aeolis; formerly
classified as *Aeolidia farinacea*
Description: The overall color varies
between light purple to gray or brown,
dusted with white, purple, or green. Its
color often reflects its diet. Numerous flattened cerata are found on the body in close
rows.
Size: Length to 4" (102 mm), occasionally to 4.7" (120 mm); width to 1.5" (38 mm)
Habitat/Ecology: On rocks, pilings, mudflats, and in tidepools of quiet waters; low
intertidal zone to water 2625' (800 m) deep
Geographic Range: Arctic to Maryland; Alaska to California; France; Japan.
Notes: The shag-rug nudibranch dines on sea anemones, especially the short plumose
anemone (see p. 16). It consumes up to 100 percent of its body weight daily on this
specialized diet. Most invertebrates become a meal if they touch an anemone. To
become immune to the anemone's nematocysts, or stinging cells, this nudibranch
first touches the anemone before retreating. This activates the production of a coating
on the nudibranch that is resistant to the stinging effects. Now the shag-rug nudibranch can feed on the anemone with immunity to the effects of the nematocysts.

When this nudibranch attacks an anemone, the anemone generates a panic phero-mone that alerts nearby anemones to the predator. When the anemone dies, the nudi-branch feeds upon the alarm pheromone, which continues to signal neighboring anemones for up to five days.

TUSK SHELLS (Class Scaphopoda)

Tusk shells are distinctive mollusks that live in deeper waters, but their shells are some-times found washed up on the shore. The organism is housed in a single shell that is long, hollow, and open at both ends.

Ivory Tuskshell

Graptacme eborea

Authority: (Conrad, 1846)
Other Names: Also known as ivory tusk; formerly classified as *Dentalium eboreum*, *Graptacme eboreum*
Description: The color of the shell is ivory-white and occasionally tinged pinkish or yellowish. Just as its name suggests, it is curved and shaped like the tusk of an elephant. The surface is polished smooth with a few raised ridges at the small end.
Size: Length to 2" (5 cm)
Habitat/Ecology: Buried in sand or mud; subtidal 15–500' (4.6–152 m) deep
Geographic Range: North Carolina to the West Indies and Texas
Notes: The wide end of a living ivory tuskshell is immersed into the sand or mud, leaving the narrow end exposed. This carnivore captures tiny bivalves and other organisms as its food with its lobed appendages. The hole in the small end is where the water enters and waste leaves. This is the most common species found along our coast; however, the others are from deeper waters.

CLAMS AND ALLIES (Class Bivalvia)

Bivalves are mollusks that have two shells, or valves, to cover the organism. Their bod-ies lack a head, and most species filter-feed microscopic plant and animal material from the water. There are even a few predatory bivalves. Globally there are about 10,000 liv-ing species—most of which live in salt water.

The two valves are normally more or less symmetrical—but not always. The two valves are recognized as the "right valve" and the "left valve." These are oriented with respect to the anterior end of the bivalve: when the pair of bivalve shells are hinged, open with the beaks uppermost, and the interiors of the shells are visible. If the pair of shells is placed in this way, the "left valve" is on the left and the "right valve" is on the right.

File Yoldia

Yoldia limatula

Authority: (Say, 1831)

Description: The exteriors of the shells are white, with a thin, shiny, greenish to chestnut periostracum and a few darker brown concentric growth lines. The interiors of the shells are white. The flat shells are ax-shaped, with small umbones positioned about halfway from the front end. The posterior end is pointed. The hinge holds thirty anterior and twenty-six posterior teeth.

Size: Length to 1.25" (32 mm); width to 2.5" (64 mm)

Habitat/Ecology: In mud or sand-mud mix; just below the low intertidal zone to water 100' (30 m) deep

Geographic Range: Gulf of St. Lawrence to North Carolina

Notes: The file yoldia is an active bivalve known to be adept at vaulting with its foot, which extends rapidly when disturbed. Several additional species may also be encountered, but not often intertidally. They can be identified by the number of teeth present on the hinge.

Atlantic Awningclam

Solemya velum

Authority: Say, 1822

Other Names: Also known as common Atlantic awning clam, swimming clam, veiled clam

Description: The shells' exteriors are covered with a thin, greenish brown, shiny and fragile periostracum, which overhangs the shells noticeably. The shells' interiors are bluish white.

Each shell is extremely fragile and oblong, with approximately fifteen "ribs"— lines that radiate from the hinge area.

The living animal has about sixteen finger-like projections around the opening of the siphon.

Size: Length to 1.5" (38 mm)

Habitat/Ecology: In mud or sand-mud mix; low intertidal zone to water 40' (12 m) deep

Geographic Range: Nova Scotia to Florida

Notes: The Atlantic awningclam is an active swimmer that moves effectively with quick, jet-propelled spurts. It is also an active and powerful burrower, with a disk-like foot that is ringed, making it difficult to remove. This species and others in its genus have symbiotic bacteria which play an important role in their nutrition.

Similar Species: Boreal Awningclam (*Solemya borealis*) has about forty fingerlike projections around the opening of the siphon. The fragile periostracum does not overhang the shells.

Turkey Wing

Arca zebra

Authority: (Swainson, 1833)
Other Name: Also known as zebra ark
Description: The shells' exteriors vary from yellowish to tan, with oblique "zebra-like" bands of reddish brown. A matted, brown periostracum is also present. Each shell is stout and oblong, with a straight hinge line. The exteriors are sculptured with several strong ribs.
Size: Length to 4" (102 mm); width to 2" (51 mm)
Habitat/Ecology: Attached to rocks, shells, mangrove roots, and in crevices; low intertidal zone to water 20' (6.1 m) deep
Geographic Range: North Carolina to Brazil
Notes: This species has been served inside a baked pie in Bermuda in past years.
Similar Species: Mossy Ark (*Arca imbricata*) (see below) lacks zebra-like brown stripes.

Mossy Ark

Arca imbricata

Authority: Bruguière, 1789
Other Name: Formerly classified as *Arca umbonata*
Description: The shells' exteriors are whitish to yellowish, marked with chestnut brown blotches. Fresh shells are covered with a shaggy periostracum. The shells are stout and rectangular-shaped, with a straight hinge. The exteriors are sculptured with weak ribs crossed with growth lines, often giving a somewhat beaded appearance.
Size: Length to 2.5" (64 mm)
Habitat/Ecology: Attached to rocks or similar hard objects; in subtidal waters from 2–15' (0.6–4.5m) deep
Geographic Range: North Carolina to Brazil

Notes: The mossy ark is a common subtidal species, and its shells often wash ashore after a storm.

Similar Species: Turkey Wing (*Arca zebra*) (see p. 139) has zebra-like brown stripes.

Red-brown Ark

Barbatia cancellaria

Authority: (Lamarck, 1819)

Description: The shells' exteriors are dark reddish brown, with a fibrous periostracum. The shells' interiors are reddish brown.

   The shells are irregular and some-what oblong-shaped. The exteriors are sculptured with weakly beaded radial ribs. The hinge line is slightly curved.

Size: Length to 1.5" (38 mm)

Habitat/Ecology: Among rocks; low intertidal zone to water 25' (7.5 m) deep

Geographic Range: Florida to Brazil

Notes: This southern species is easy to identify, with its brightly colored shells' interior coloration. Shells often wash ashore with both shells intact.

Eared Ark

Anadara notabilis

Authority: (Röding, 1798)

Description: The exteriors of the shells are white and covered with a thick, hairy periostracum which is easily rubbed off. The interiors of the shells are white. Each shell is stout and nearly round with a long hinge line that is nearly straight and a prominent posterior projection. The exteriors are sculptured with narrow radial ribs crossed with strong growth lines giving a beaded appearance.

Size: Length to 3.5" (89 mm)

Habitat/Ecology: In mud, sand, or grassy areas; in subtidal waters from 1–6' (0.3–1.8 m) deep

Geographic Range: North Carolina to Brazil

Notes: This is a common species found along much of our coastline. The youngest individuals attach their shells to small pebbles when they first settle. This byssus is lost as they begin burying themselves in the mud or sand.

Similar Species: Transverse Ark (*Anadara transversa*) (see below) lacks a prominent posterior projection.

Transverse Ark

Anadara transversa

Authority: (Say, 1822)

Description: The shells' exteriors are white with a hairy, dark brown periostracum when alive or fresh. The shells' interiors are white. Each shell is stout and oval-shaped, with a straight hinge line that lacks a prominent posterior projection. The exteriors are sculptured with approximately thirty-three strong ribs crossed with growth lines. The left valve is normally beaded.

Size: Length to 1.5" (38 mm)

Habitat/Ecology: On rocks, shells, and driftwood; low intertidal zone to water 35.6' (10.8 m) deep

Geographic Range: Cape Cod to Panama

Notes: The transverse ark, as with most arks, often washes ashore without its periostracum attached. This covering is easily lost as a shell is tossed around on our seashores.

Similar Species: Eared Ark (*Anadara notabilis*) (see p. 140) has a prominent posterior projection.

Cut-ribbed Ark

Anadara floridana

Authority: (Conrad, 1869)

Other Name: Formerly classified as *Anadara secticostata*

Description: The shells' exteriors are white, with a thick, light to dark brown periostracum. The shells' interiors are white. Each shell is heavy and obliquely rectangular, with a hinge line that is long and straight. The exteriors are sculptured with strong radial ribs— each of which has a groove running down the center.

Size: Height to 5" (127 mm)

Habitat/Ecology: In sand; in shallow to deeper subtidal waters

Geographic Range: North Carolina to Venezuela

Notes: The cut-ribbed ark is an uncommon species that is similar to the eared ark (see p. 140), except it has the distinction of having a single groove in the middle of each of its ribs.

Similar Species: Eared Ark (*Anadara notabilis*) (see p. 140)

Close-up of ribs

Blood Ark

Lunarca ovalis

Authority: (Bruguière, 1789)

Other Names: Also known as bloody clam; formerly classified as *Anadara ovalis*

Description: The shells' exteriors vary from whitish to whitish yellow and are normally covered with a thick, fibrous brown periostracum. The shells' interiors are white. Each shell is broadly oval to nearly round, with a hinge line that is slightly curved. The exteriors are sculptured with smooth, flattened, radial ribs crossed with fine growth lines.

Size: Length to 2.25" (57 mm); width to 2" (51 mm)

Habitat/Ecology: In sand or mud; in shallow subtidal waters

Geographic Range: Cape Cod to Uruguay

Notes: The blood ark gets its name from the color of its body, which is due to the presence of hemoglobin and, as a result, red blood. Few bivalves have hemoglobin in their blood. The hemoglobin of this bivalve has been used to study the properties of human hemoglobin, including fluorescence.

Incongruous Ark

Anadara brasiliana

Authority: (Lamarck, 1819)
Other Names: Formerly classified as *Anadara brasiliana*, *A. incongrua*, *Scapharca brasiliana*
Description: The exteriors are whitish and often covered with a light brown periostracum. The interiors are white or yellowish white with prominent radial grooves. Each shell is stout and trigonal with a hinge line that is short and straight. The exteriors are sculptured with wide, strongly beaded radial ribs.
Size: Length to 3" (76 mm)
Habitat/Ecology: In sand or gravel; just below low intertidal zone to water 30' (9 m) deep
Geographic Range: North Carolina to Uruguay

Notes: The common name, incongruous ark, and one of its prior scientific names, *Anadara incongrua*, both refer to the fact than the right shell, or valve, is smaller than the left.

Ponderous Ark

Eontia ponderosa

Authority: Say, 1822
Other Name: Formerly classified as *Noetia ponderosa*
Description: The exteriors of the shells vary from white to yellowish white and are often covered with a thick, mossy-like, dark brown periostracum. The interiors are yellowish white. Each shell is stout, heavy, and trigonal, with a hinge line that is narrowed in the center. The exteriors are sculptured with twenty-seven to thirty-two strong flat-topped radial ribs—each with a fine groove down the center.
Size: Length to 2.5" (64 mm); width to 2.25" (57 mm)

Habitat/Ecology: In sand or mud; the low intertidal zone to 60' (18 m) deep

Geographic Range: Virginia to Key West; Gulf of Mexico

Notes: The ponderous ark, like most arks, secretes a byssus, or series of strong filaments, to attach itself to hard surfaces. With the ponderous ark, however, the byssus disappears during the larval stages. This is because this species burrows in sand or mud instead of attaching to hard objects such as rocks.

Adams' Miniature Ark

Arcopsis adamsi

Authority: (Dall, 1886)

Other Names: Also known as cancellate ark and incorrectly as Adam's ark

Description: The exteriors of the shells vary from white to yellowish white and are covered with a thin, pale brown periostracum when fresh. The interiors are white. Each shell is small and rectangular, with a hinge line that is straight and holds many chevron-shaped teeth. The exteriors are sculptured with several fine, radial riblets crossed with equal-size concentric ridges, giving a latticed appearance.

Size: Length to 0.6" (16 mm)

Habitat/Ecology: Under rocks or coral; in water just below low intertidal zone to water 20' (6.1 m) deep

Geographic Range: North Carolina to Brazil

Notes: Adams' miniature ark is well named, since a large specimen is 0.5" (12.7 mm) long. It was named after a famous American conchologist, Charles B. Adams (1814–1853).

Giant Bittersweet

Glycymeris americana

Authority: (DeFrance, 1826)

Other Name: Also known as giant American bittersweet

Description: The exteriors of the shells vary from gray to tan and mottled with yellowish brown.

Fresh shells are covered with a velvety, dark brown periostracum. Each shell is heavy, flat, and circular, with a hinge line that is curved with nineteen to twenty-four teeth. The exteriors are sculptured with numerous radial ribs crossed with growth lines.

Size: Length to 5" (127 mm)

Habitat/Ecology: Offshore; in subtidal waters from 6–121' (1.8–36.5 m) deep

Geographic Range: North Carolina to Brazil

Notes: The giant bittersweet is a subtidal species. Its shells occasionally wash onto the beach after a storm. As its name implies, this species is bitter to the taste and as a result is not eaten.

Blue Mussel

Mytilus edulis

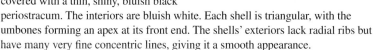

Authority: Linnaeus, 1758

Other Name: Also known as edible mussel

Description: The exteriors of the shells vary from bluish black to black and are covered with a thin, shiny, bluish black periostracum. The interiors are bluish white. Each shell is triangular, with the umbones forming an apex at its front end. The shells' exteriors lack radial ribs but have many very fine concentric lines, giving it a smooth appearance.

Size: Length to 4" (102 mm); width to 2" (51 mm)

Habitat/Ecology: On rocks, pilings, and similar hard objects; high intertidal zone to water at least 12' (3.6 m) deep

Geographic Range: Arctic to South Carolina

Notes: The blue mussel is a gourmet item often featured at seafood restaurants. These mussels are "farmed" along the Atlantic Coast at sheltered sites were they grow and increase their size. Blue mussels require seven to twelve years to reach their 2.5-inch size. Most have about a twelve-year lifespan; however, some individuals have been recorded to reach more than twenty-four years old. Intertidal specimens grow slower since they can only grow when they are feeding underwater.

Scorched Mussel

Brachidontes exustus

Authority: (Linnaeus, 1758)

Other Name: Formerly classified as *Hormomya exusta*

Description: The exteriors of the shells vary from yellowish brown to dark brown with a yellowish brown to dark brown periostracum on fresh specimens. The interiors are copper-colored or purplish gray. The shells are triangular, with the umbones forming an apex at its front end. The exteriors are sculpted with branching radial ribs.

Size: Length to 1.6" (41 mm)

Habitat/Ecology: On rocks, oysters, or other hard objects; in estuaries bays; low intertidal zone

Geographic Range: North Carolina to Venezuela

Notes: The scorched mussel can tolerate extreme fluctuations in salinity, as well as poor water quality. Its spawning also is timed with changes in water temperatures. Spawning occurs as the sea water temperature rises in the springtime.

Northern Horsemussel

Modiolus modiolus

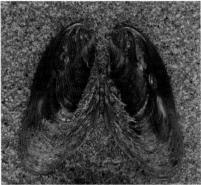

Authority: (Linnaeus, 1758)

Other Names: Also known as horse mussel; formerly classified as *Modiolus kurilensis*

Description: The exteriors of the shells vary from whitish to purplish gray, with a flaky yellowish brown to dark brown periostracum on fresh specimens. The shells' interiors are grayish white. The shells are oval and inflated, with the hinge lacking teeth and the umbones rounded and located just behind its narrowed front end. The exteriors are smooth except for concentric growth ridges.

Size: Height to 6" (15 mm); width to 3.5" (89 mm)

Habitat/Ecology: On rocks, shells, and jetties; low intertidal zone to water 500' (152 m) deep

Geographic Range: Arctic to North Carolina; Alaska to California; Europe

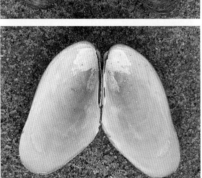

Notes: The northern horsemussel is the largest and most common mussel present in New England. Unfortunately, it is not good to eat!

Similar Species: Southern Horsemussel (*Modiolus squamosus*) is similar, with an interior that is light blue or purple and pearly. Its rough, brown periostracum clings to the posterior half of the shell. This species ranges from North Carolina to Florida to Texas and possibly Venezuela.

American Horsemussel

Modiolus americanus

Authority: (Leach, 1815)

Other Names: Also known as American horse mussel, tulip mussel; formerly classified as *M. tulipa*

Description: The exteriors of the shells vary from grayish to purple and have a brownish orange periostracum with rich reddish or purple streaks and a glossy finish. The shells' interiors are pearly white. Each shell is fragile, oblong, and inflated with the umbones forming away from the end of shell and the hinge that has no teeth. The exteriors are smooth, lacking rays, and with only faint concentric growth lines.

Size: Length to 4" (101 mm)

Habitat/Ecology: On rocks, shells, and similar hard objects; from just below the low intertidal zone to water 20' (6 m) deep

Geographic Range: North Carolina to Brazil

Notes: The colors of the shells of this species can be intense at times. In fact, the bright colors of the shells are the origin of one of its common names: the tulip mussel.

Similar Species: Northern Horsemussel (*Modiolus modiolus*) (see p. 146)

ⓘ Asian Green Mussel

Perna viridis

Authority: (Linnaeus, 1758)

Other Name: Also known as Indo-Pacific green mussel

Description: The exteriors of the shells vary from brownish black to iridescent blue or bluish green due to the periostracum. The shells' interiors are pearly white. The shells are triangular, with the beak holding a single hinge tooth on the right valve and a pair on the left. The exteriors are sculpted without radial ribs, which gives it a smooth appearance.

Size: Length normally to 3.9" (100 mm), occasionally to 6.2" (160 mm)

Habitat/Ecology: On buoys, bridges, pilings, seawalls, and intake and outfall pipes; in shallow subtidal waters

Geographic Range: South Carolina to Florida; Asia

Notes: The Asian green mussel is an exotic species, introduced from the southwest Pacific Ocean and the Indian Ocean. Its coloration makes it easily identifiable. Juveniles are typically bright green, but this color changes to brown with only the margins remaining green in adults.

    This species is an economically important one that is harvested elsewhere. Here, however, it thrives in polluted waters, and its harvesting is discouraged, as it is known to accumulate toxic substances.

Ribbed Mussel

Geukensia demissa

Authority: (Dillwyn, 1817)

Other Names: Also known as Atlantic ribbed mussel, ribbed marsh mussel; formerly classified as *Modiolus demissus, M. plicatula, M. semicostata, M. plicatulus, Mytilus demissa, Volsella demissa*

Description: The exteriors of the shells vary from dark brown to purple, with an olive-brown to dark brown periostracum on fresh specimens. The shells' interiors are whitish to bluish gray. The shells are oblong, with the hinge bearing no teeth. The exteriors are sculpted with strong radial riblets that reach the largest size at the upper portion of the hind end.

Size: Length to 4" (102 mm); width to 1.75" (44 mm)

Habitat/Ecology: Attaches to pilings or oysters in estuaries; mid to low intertidal zones

Geographic Range: Nova Scotia, Canada, to Florida; Yucatán, Mexico; introduced to California

Notes: The ribbed mussel is a common species that can be found in large colonies. At some locations their numbers exceed 1,500 per square meter (139 per square foot). This species is able to reattach itself to a substrate if it becomes detached.

    This species is somewhat sexually dimorphic. The color of the mantle in females tends to be medium brown while males produce a yellowish cream coloration.

① Charrua Mussel

Mytella charruana

Authority: (d'Orbigny, 1842)
Other Name: Also known as charru mussel
Description: The exteriors of the shells vary greatly from brown without any patterning to light brown with wavy patterns of dark brown to black. The shells' interiors are iridescent purple. The shells are triangular in shape and the exteriors are without radial ribs, which give them a smooth appearance.
Size: Length to 2.3" (60 mm)
Habitat/Ecology: Introduced habitats include: on solid intertidal objects; seawater intake pipes, boat ramps, and floating docks; in water levels at or near the low intertidal zone
Geographic Range: Georgia to Florida (introduced); Mexico to Argentina

Notes: The Charrua mussel is an introduced species that originates from Central and South America. It was first reported in 1986 when many were found clogging the seawater intake pipes of a power plant at Jacksonville, Florida. Although that introduction disappeared, other locations have been found since then. This species has now entered the waters of Georgia as it migrates northward.

Say's Chestnut Mussel

Lioberus castaneus

Authority: (Say, 1822)
Other Name: Also known as chestnut mussel
Description: The exteriors of the shells are bluish gray with a glossy, reddish brown periostracum that clings tightly to the shell. The interiors of the shells

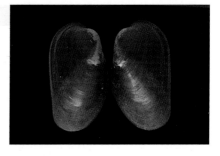

are gray. The shells are elongated and ovate, with a very shallow, oblique furrow between the front and hind ends. The exteriors are smooth, with many fine, concentric growth lines.
Size: Length to 1.5" (38 mm)
Habitat/Ecology: In sand or mud; in shallow subtidal waters to water 40' (12 m) deep
Geographic Range: South Carolina to Brazil
Notes: The light, empty valves are sometimes found in the shoreline's beach drift.

Stiff Penshell

Atrina rigida

Authority: (Lightfoot, 1786)

Other Name: Also known as stiff pen shell

Description: The exteriors of the shells vary from light to dark brown. The shells' interiors are pale brownish, with a large, pearl white section. A large muscle scar lies at or outside the edge of nacreous area (the pearly/cloudy area).

Its mantle is a distinctive orange color. The shells are wedge-shaped. The exteriors are sculpted with fifteen to twenty rough, radiating ribs that are normally armed with several tubular spines near the fan edge.

Size: Length to 12" (30 cm); width to 6.5" (17 cm)

Habitat/Ecology: In sand or sand-mud mix; low intertidal zone to water 90' (27 m) deep

Geographic Range: North Carolina to West Indies

Notes: The stiff penshell produces some rather handsome but rare black pearls, which are used in jewelry. Penshells normally bury themselves with only a small portion of the fan edge partially exposed so that they are able to feed. This exposed end is often covered with a variety of marine organisms.

Similar Species: Half-naked Penshell (*Atrina seminuda*) (see below) has a large muscle scar that lies totally inside the nacreous area.

Half-naked Penshell

Atrina seminuda

Authority: (Lamarck, 1819)

Other Name: Also known as half-naked pen shell

Description: The exteriors of the shells vary from yellowish gray to brown. The shells' interiors are pale brownish, with a large, pearl white section. A large muscle scar lies totally inside the edge of nacreous area. The mantle ranges in color from pale yellow to beige. The shells are wedge-shaped. The exteriors are sculptured with about fifteen radial ribs, and a few tubular spines may be present.

Size: Length to 10" (25 cm)

Habitat/Ecology: In sand or sand-mud mix; in shallow subtidal waters to 20' (6 m) deep

Geographic Range: North Carolina to Argentina

Notes: Penshells often have commensal organisms living inside their mantle cavities. The Atlantic pen shrimp (*Pontonia domestica*) and the blue mussel pea crab (*Tumidotheres maculates*, see p. 243) are two such examples that may be encountered when penshells wash ashore after winter storms.

Similar Species: Stiff Penshell (*Atrina rigida*) (see p. 150) has a large muscle scar that lies at or outside the edge of the nacreous area.

Sawtooth Penshell

Atrina serrata

Authority: (G. B. Sowerby I, 1825)

Other Names: Also known as saw-toothed pen shell

Description: The exteriors of the shells vary from yellowish brown to greenish brown. The shells' interiors are pale brownish, with a large, pearly white section. A large muscle scar lies totally inside the edge of nacreous area. The shell is wedge-shaped, and delicately sculptured with about thirty radiating ribs guarded with numerous tiny spines.

Size: Length to 10" (25 cm); width to 4" (10.2 cm)

Habitat/Ecology: In mud or sand-mud mix; in subtidal waters from 2–20' (0.6–6.1 m) deep

Geographic Range: North Carolina to Venezuela

Notes: At some locations around the world, penshell meat is sold as "scallop" meat. This species is fairly common on Florida beaches.

Similar Species: Amber Penshell (*Pinna carnea*) has a pale orange to amber shell that is thin-walled, with eight to twelve weak radial ribs or a smooth sculpture.

Atlantic Wing-oyster

Pteria colymbus

Authority: (Röding, 1798)

Other Names: Also known as Atlantic wing oyster, Atlantic winged oyster, winged pearl oyster; formerly classified as *Avicula atlantica*

Description: The exteriors of the shells vary from yellowish to purplish brown or black, often with lighter radial streaks. A thin, matted periostracum is often present but easily rubbed off. The shells' interiors are pearly. The shells are triangular, with a wing that is strongly notched and a hinge line that is straight, extending outward in both directions. The right valve is flat, often smaller, and the left is inflated.

Size: Length to 3.5" (89 mm)

Habitat/Ecology: On rocks, sea whips, and sea fans; in subtidal waters from 1–100' (0.3–30 m) deep

Geographic Range: North Carolina to Brazil

Notes: The Atlantic wing-oyster is a member of the pearl oyster group of bivalves. On at least one rare occasion, this species has been known to produce a pearl. Pearls are more often found in the Atlantic pearl-oyster (see below); however, it is not a common occurrence for that species, either. The Atlantic wing-oyster is sometimes found on the beach still attached to sea whips or sea fans after storms.

Similar Species: Atlantic Pearl-oyster (*Pinctada imbricata*) (see below) lacks long, wing-like projections.

Atlantic Pearl-oyster

Pinctada imbricata

Authority: (Leach, 1814)

Other Names: Also known as Atlantic pearl oyster; formerly classified as *Pinctada radiata*

Description: The exteriors of the shells vary from brownish to greenish, with white, brown, or purplish black radiating streaks.

The shells' interiors have a central pearly region and a margin of purplish brown mottled with yellow. The shells are flat and nearly circular, with a hinge line that is straight and moderately long. The right valve is flatter than the left. The exteriors are sculptured with scale-like spines that easily rub off.

Size: Length to 3" (76 mm); width to 3" (76 mm)

Habitat/Ecology: On rocks and sea fans; low intertidal zone to water 83' (25 m) deep

Geographic Range: North Carolina to Brazil

Notes: The Atlantic pearl-oyster displays beautiful mother-of-pearl lining on the central portion, inside its shell, and is the source for pearls. The frequency of this species producing pearls, however, is less than 5 percent. In Venezuela, fishermen still dive for pearls from these oysters to sell to tourists. It is no longer a commercial enterprise, since the industry has gone to cultured pearls. A cultured pearl is produced under controlled conditions by placing a small shell fragment within the oyster. The oyster then forms a pearl over top the irritant. The pearl is then harvested.

Flat Tree-oyster

Isognomon alatus

Authority: (Gmelin, 1791)

Other Name: Also known as flat tree oyster

Description: The exteriors of the shells vary from yellowish brown to purplish gray often with rays of white. The shells' interiors are pearly in the center, with a margin of yellow mottled with purple. The shells are flat, nearly circular, with a hinge line that is straight and has eight to twelve grooves. The surface of the exteriors may be smooth or scaly.

Size: Length to 3" (76 mm); width to 3" (76 mm)

Habitat/Ecology: On rocks, pilings, and seawalls; high intertidal zone to water 40' (12 m) deep

Geographic Range: Florida to Brazil; Bermuda

Notes: The flat tree-oyster is often encountered in compact clumps, especially on the roots of mangroves. These specimens are normally flatter, lighter, and larger than those found on rocks and similar objects.

Lister's Tree-oyster

Isognomon radiatus

Authority: (Anton, 1838)

Other Names: Also known as two-toned flat oyster, two-toned tree oyster; formerly classified as *Isognomon listeri*

Description: The exteriors of the shells vary from yellowish to brown, often

with radial streaks of light purplish brown. The shells are thin, irregular in shape, and often elongate, with a hinge line that is straight and has four to eight grooves. The exteriors are rough with thin, flaky layers.

Size: Length to 2.7" (70 mm)

Habitat/Ecology: On rocks; low intertidal zone to water 66' (20 m) deep

Geographic Range: Florida to Brazil; Bermuda

Notes: The shell of Lister's tree-oyster is irregular, brittle, and easily broken. Its shape is often twisted as well.

Similar Species: Two-toned Tree-oyster (*Isognomon bicolor*) is heavier, with a two-toned shell that has a hinge line with eight to twelve grooves.

Digitate Thorny Oyster

Spondylus tenuis

Authority: Schreibers, 1793
Other Names: Formerly classified as *Spondylus ictericus*
Description: The exteriors of the shells are orange and brick red, often with white mottling at the umbones. The shells are thick and circular. The exteriors are sculptured with radiating ribs that bear a few to several spines, which often digitate toward their ends.
Size: Height to 2.5" (64 mm)
Habitat/Ecology: Attached to various hard surfaces; low intertidal zone to water 100' (30 m) deep
Geographic Range: Florida to Brazil; Bermuda
Notes: This species is common; however, its shells are not often found on the beach with intact spines.
Similar Species: Atlantic Thorny Oyster (*Spondylus americanus*) is a larger species that displays erect spines and lives in subtidal depths of 30–150' (9.9–45 m).

Common Jingle

Anomia simplex

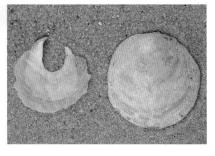

Authority: D'Orbigny, 1842
Other Names: Also known as common jingle shell, jingle shell
Description: The shells vary from translucent yellowish, coppery, or orange to silvery-white. The shells are circular but often distorted. The shell that is positioned below in life (left valve) is flat and fragile, with a large hole in the middle. The shell that is positioned above (right valve) is concave and larger, and the interior bears one round muscle scar. The inside of the left shell has an oval, dull white central area and three muscle scars.
Size: Length to 3" (75 mm)
Habitat/Ecology: Attached to rocks, shells, and coral; low intertidal zone to water 60' (18 m) deep
Geographic Range: Nova Scotia to Brazil
Notes: The shells of this species are familiar to most beachgoers. They often have a wide range of colors, including black. Some authorities consider this species to be the same as the northern European species the European jingle (*Anomia ephippium*).
Similar Species: Prickly Jingle (*Heteranomia squamula*) is a northern species that has a left valve with two muscle scars on the lower shell. It is also a species that lives deeper, from near the low intertidal zone to water 2000' (610 m) deep.

Crested Oyster

Ostrea equestris

Authority: Say, 1834
Other Name: Also known as horse
oyster
Description: The exterior of the upper
shell is grayish white or yellowish
brown, occasionally with colored rays.
A scaly periostracum, which flakes off easily, is present on fresh shells. The shells'
interiors are grayish green. The shells are circular, oval, or triangular. The right valve
has a set of small, short, teeth-like ridges that fit closely into matching pits of the left
valve. The exteriors are sculptured with a rough surface that has raised, serrated margins. The interiors of the shells have a white, centrally located muscle scar.
Size: Height to 3.25" (8.3 mm)
Habitat/Ecology: On rocks, shells, and similar hard objects; low intertidal zone to
water 350' (107 m) deep
Geographic Range: Maryland to Brazil; Uruguay; Argentina
Notes: The crested oyster is a highly variable oyster that is more colorful and flatter
when it lives in deeper waters. As a result, beachcombers normally find rather dull-
colored oysters on the beach.
Similar Species: Eastern Oyster (*Crassostrea virginica*) (see below) has a distinctive
muscle scar that is dark and off-center.

Eastern Oyster

Crassostrea virginica

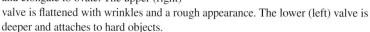

Authority: (Gmelin, 1791)
Other Names: Also known as common
Atlantic oyster, common oyster
Description: The exterior of the upper
shell is grayish. The shells' interiors are
white, with a single purple muscle scar
that is off-center. The shells are thick
and elongate to ovate. The upper (right)
valve is flattened with wrinkles and a rough appearance. The lower (left) valve is
deeper and attaches to hard objects.
Size: Length to 10" (250 mm); width to 4" (102 mm)
Habitat/Ecology: On rocks, shells, and other similar hard objects; in quiet waters
with reduced salinities; low intertidal zone to water 40' (12 m) deep
Geographic Range: Gulf of St. Lawrence to the West Indies
Notes: The eastern oyster is an important commercial fishery in North America.
Thousands of tons are produced annually. Mature female eastern oysters produce
up to 100 million eggs per year. These amazing numbers are vital to enable this
resource to continue. Native peoples have also harvested these oysters in the past as

their middens testify to. The predators of the eastern oyster include various sea stars and various snails, such as the Atlantic oyster drill, which bores a neat, round hole to dine on its prey.

Frond Oyster

Dendostrea frons

Authority: (Linnaeus, 1758)
Other Names: Also known as coon oyster, frons oyster, leafy oyster
Description: The exteriors of the shells vary from yellowish white to deep brown, often with violet edges. The shells are elongated ovate, with hinge area curved backward. The exterior of the upper (right) valve is sculptured with irregular radial ridges that often are wrinkled. The lower (left) valve develops clasping spines to attach to slender twig-like substrates.
Size: Length to 2.75" (70 mm); width to 2.25" (57 mm)
Habitat/Ecology: On sea whips, gorgonians, corals; low intertidal zone to water 15' (4.6 m) deep
Geographic Range: North Carolina to the West Indies
Notes: The frond oyster is a distinctive species often found attached to sea fans or other slender objects at the low tide level or washed up on the beach. Raccoons like to feed on them—thus the common name coon oyster.

Zigzag Scallop

Euvola ziczac

Authority: (Linnaeus, 1758)
Other Names: Also known as Bermuda sand scallop; formerly classified as *Pecten ziczac*
Description: The exterior of the convex lower (right) valve varies from reddish brown to tan, with dark zigzag markings dispersed along the lighter ribs. The exterior of the flat upper (left) valve is reddish mottled with white and brown.

The shells' interiors are white. Both valves are nearly circular with two nearly equal ears that are smooth or weakly ridged. The flat upper valve features a central concave area and is sculptured with twenty-nine to thirty-five radial ribs flattened near the side edges. The concave lower valve has eighteen to twenty-two broad, low ribs.
Size: Length to 4" (10.2 mm)
Habitat/Ecology: In sand or mud; low intertidal zone to water 200' (61 m) deep
Geographic Range: North Carolina to Brazil

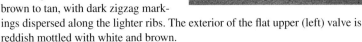

Notes: The zigzag scallop is a species that is grown for harvest in aquaculture. Their smooth and convex lower valves make them well suited for this use because they are easy to handle and slide smoothly along the bottoms of nets and cages. This is a hermaphroditic species which reproduces via broadcast spawning into the surrounding ocean.

Round-rib Scallop

Euvola raveneli

Authority: (Dall, 1898)
Other Names: Also known as Ravenel's scallop; formerly classified as *Pecten raveneli*
Description: The exterior of the convex lower (right) shell varies from whitish to tan or pinkish grooves. The exterior of the flat upper (left) shell is darker reddish brown with irregular dark markings. The shells' interiors are white. Both valves are nearly circular with two near equal ears that are ridged. The flat upper valve features a central concavity and is sculptured with twenty-one to twenty-five rounded radial ribs and visible concentric threads in the interspaces. The concave lower valve has twenty-five strong, grooved ribs with wide interspaces.

Size: Length to 2.5" (64 mm)
Habitat/Ecology: In subtidal waters from 30' (9 m) to very deep waters
Geographic Range: North Carolina to Colombia
Notes: This subtidal species is only found on the beach after a storm. Rarely does it make it to the shore as a hinged pair. Commercial fishing operations also encounter it.

Scaly Scallop

Caribachlamys sentis

Authority: (Reeve, 1853)
Other Name: Also known as sentis scallop
Description: The exteriors of the shells normally include brilliant purple, red, vermilion, or orange-red, mottled with white near the beaks. The valves are

flat, fan-shaped, with a flat hinge, and one ear is twice as large as the other. The shells are sculptured with approximately fifty radial ribs—with two to four minor ribs between the major ribs. All ribs have a scaly finish.

Size: Length to 1.6" (41 mm)
Habitat/Ecology: Under rocks; in subtidal waters below the low intertidal zone
Geographic Range: North Carolina to Brazil
Notes: Striking is the best description for this colorful species! Its impressive valves are eye candy to a photographer.

Rough Scallop

Lindapecten muscosus

Authority: (W. Wood, 1828)
Other Names: Formerly classified as *Aequipecten muscosus, Pecten exasperatus*
Description: The exteriors of the shells are reddish brown, orange, yellow, or pink with white flecks. The interiors of the shells are white. The valves are inflated, fan-shaped, with unequal ears that are strongly ribbed. The shells are sculptured with approximately twenty radial ribs—each of which is comprised of several small ribs. The ends of the major ribs are armed with sharp, erect scales, giving the shells a rough appearance.
Size: Length to 2" (51 mm)
Habitat/Ecology: In shallow subtidal waters to water 541' (164 m) deep
Geographic Range: North Carolina to Brazil
Notes: Many collectors seek out scallop shells. The famous "lemon-yellow pecten"—a rare color phase of the species—is very desirable for them.

Atlantic Bay Scallop

Argopecten irradians

Authority: (Lamarck, 1819)
Other Name: Also known as bay scallop
Description: The exterior of the shells' upper valve varies from white to yellowish brown, bluish, or reddish, occasionally with concentric bands. The valves are flat, nearly circular, with

a flat hinge and two equal-size ears. The exterior of the shell's lower valve is white. The shells are sculptured with approximately twelve to eighteen rounded radial ribs that have a smooth finish.

Size: Length to 2.8" (73 mm); width to 3" (76 mm)

Habitat/Ecology: On sand-mud mix and at eelgrass sites; low intertidal zone to water 60' (18 m) deep

Geographic Range: Arctic Ocean to Florida and Texas

Notes: This species is the famous "blue-eyed scallop." It gets its name from the thirty to forty bright blue eyes found on its mantle margin. These eyes are able to detect movement nearby. Young Atlantic bay scallops attach themselves with tiny threads to eelgrass (see p. 307) on muddy shores to escape the

Shell detail

suffocating mud. There, they grow and eventually move to deeper waters. They breed when they are one year old and rarely live to reach two years of age.

Similar Species: Atlantic Calico Scallop (*Argopecten gibbus*) (see below) has seventeen to twenty-three squarish radial ribs.

Atlantic Calico Scallop

Argopecten gibbus

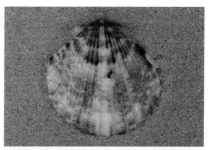

Authority: (Linnaeus, 1758)

Other Name: Also known as calico scallop

Description: The exterior of the upper (right) shell is creamy white with patterns of rose, brown, purple, or yellowish orange. The exterior of the lower (left) shell is much less colorful. The valves are inflated, nearly circular, with a flat hinge and two nearly equal ears. The shells are sculptured with approximately seventeen to twenty-three squarish radial ribs that have a smooth finish.

Size: Length to 2.75" (70 mm)

Habitat/Ecology: In sand; in subtidal waters from 5–1300' (1.5–390 m) deep

Geographic Range: Maryland to Brazil; Bermuda

Notes: The Atlantic calico scallop was once the focus of a large commercial fishery. Sadly, this fishery was over-fished, and the scallop beds have been depleted. The shells of this scallop are often found washed up on shore as the shells of the Atlantic bay scallop do.

Shell detail

Similar Species: Atlantic Bay Scallop (*Argopecten irradians*) (see p. 158) has twelve to eighteen rounded radial ribs.

Atlantic Sea Scallop

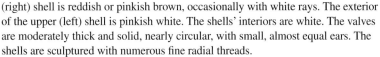

Placopecten magellanicus

Authority: (Gmelin, 1791)

Other Names: Also known as Atlantic deep-sea scallop, deep-sea scallop, giant scallop, sea scallop; formerly classified as *Pecten tenuicostatus*

Description: The exterior of the lower (right) shell is reddish or pinkish brown, occasionally with white rays. The exterior of the upper (left) shell is pinkish white. The shells' interiors are white. The valves are moderately thick and solid, nearly circular, with small, almost equal ears. The shells are sculptured with numerous fine radial threads.

Size: Length to 8" (20 cm); width to 8" (20 cm)

Habitat/Ecology: On sand, gravel, or rubble; in subtidal waters from 12–600' (4–180 m) deep

Geographic Range: Labrador to Cape Hatteras

Notes: Unlike the blue eyes of the Atlantic calico scallop, this scallop has steely gray eyes. The shells of the Atlantic sea scallop were often used as dishes by the native people along the coast. The age of this scallop can be estimated by counting the number of rings on its shell—just as the rings of a tree. The Atlantic sea scallop matures at four years and lives six to eight years on average. This species can be observed at snorkeling depths in Maine. This species is the focus of an important commercial fishery. Their shells are sometimes found on the beach after a storm.

Lions-paw Scallop

Nodipecten nodosus

Authority: (Linnaeus, 1758)

Other Names: Also known as lion's paw; formerly classified as *Pecten fragosus*

Description: The exteriors of the shells are bright red, deep orange, or maroon red and occasionally mottled with white or yellow bands. The valves are heavy and fan-shaped, with a flat hinge, and the front ear is 1.5 times larger than the hind ear. The shells are sculptured with approximately seven to nine major raised ribs that feature large hollow nodules. In addition, numerous cord-like riblets radiate from the hinge.

Size: Length to 6" (15 cm); width to 6" (15 cm)

Habitat/Ecology: In sand or rubble; in subtidal waters from at least 50–150' (15–45 m) deep

Geographic Range: Cape Hatteras to Brazil; Bermuda

Notes: The distinctive shells of the lion's paw scallop are truly striking. Single shells occasionally wash up on the beach after a storm. Despite its size and weight, the shell is usually found broken. It is believed that older individuals are found in deeper waters.

Atlantic Kittenpaw

Plicatula gibbosa

Authority: Lamarck, 1801

Other Names: Also known as Atlantic kitten's paw, kitten paw, kitten's paw

Description: The exteriors of the shells vary from white to gray with reddish brown radiating lines. The interiors of the shells are whitish. The valves are triangular, with a narrow umbonal area. The shells are sculptured with approximately five to seven radial ribs with a smooth finish. The lower (right) valve is cemented to a solid base, such as rock.

Size: Length to 1" (25 mm); width to 1" (25 mm)

Habitat/Ecology: Attached to rocks, shells, and similar hard objects; low intertidal zone to water 300' (91 m) deep

Geographic Range: North Carolina to Brazil

Notes: Unlike most scallops, the Atlantic kittenpaw attaches itself to a rock or similar hard object. If this attachment is broken, the shells simply wash up on the shore with the next storm.

Thick Lucina

Phacoides pectinata

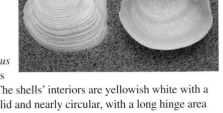

Authority: (Gmelin, 1791)
Other Names: Also known as comb
  lucine, Jamaica lucine; formerly
  classified as *Lucina jamaicensis,
  Lucina pectinata, Phacoides pectinatus*
Description: The exteriors of the shells
are white, often tinged with orange. The shells' interiors are yellowish white with a
pale orange margin. The shells are solid and nearly circular, with a long hinge area
that bears teeth. The exteriors are sculptured with several unequally spaced
concentric ridges. A deep groove runs from the umbones to the posterior margin, and
another runs from the umbones to the mid anterior margin.
Size: Length to 2.25" (70 mm)
Habitat/Ecology: In sand or sand-mud mix; in subtidal waters from 3–20' (0.9–6.1 m)
  deep
Geographic Range: North Carolina to Brazil
Notes: The thick lucina is a heavy and solid species that prefers mud to sand, and is
  most frequently found in mangrove swamps.

Buttercup Lucine

Anodontia alba

Authority: Link, 1807
Other Names: Formerly classified as
  *Lucina chrysostoma, Loripinus
  chrysostoma*
Description: The exteriors of the shells
  vary from dull white to gray. The
  shells' interiors are bright yellow to
  orange. The shells are strong, almost
  circular, and inflated with a hinge
  bearing weak teeth. The exteriors are
  semi-smooth and sculptured with
  weak, irregular, concentric growth
  lines. A groove runs from the umbones
  to the anterior margin.

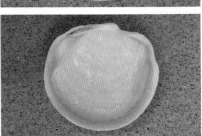

Size: Length to 2.5" (64 mm)
Habitat/Ecology: In sand; in subtidal waters from 3–300' (0.9–91 m) deep
Geographic Range: North Carolina to Costa Rica
Notes: The buttercup lucine is the most common lucine found washed up on our
  beaches.
Similar Species: Thick Lucina (*Phacoides pectinata*, see above) also has a yellow
  interior; however, it has a pronounced groove that runs from the umbones to the
  posterior margin.

Tiger Lucina

Codakia orbicularis

Authority: (Linnaeus, 1758)

Other Names: Also known as great white lucine; formerly confused with *C. tigerina*

Description: The exteriors of the shells are white. The shells' interiors are white, occasionally with a tinge of pink or lavender. The shells are solid and nearly circular, with large hinge teeth. The exteriors are sculptured with numerous radial riblets crossed with numerous concentric ridges, giving it a scale-like cross-ribbed appearance.

Size: Length to 3.5" (95 mm); height to 3" (76 mm)

Habitat/Ecology: In sand or mud; low intertidal zone to water 100' (30 m) deep

Geographic Range: Florida to Brazil

Notes: This species is the largest lucine in North America's Atlantic waters. The tiger lucina has been confused with another species, *C. tigerina*, which is found in the Pacific and Indian oceans. This is the origin of its common name.

Cross-hatched Lucine

Divalinga quadrisulcata

Authority: (d'Orbigny, 1846)

Other Name: Also known as crosshatched lucine

Description: The exteriors of the shells are ivory-white. The shells' interiors are white. The shells are circular and moderately inflated, with fine teeth along the inside of each shell's edge. The exteriors are sculptured with numerous curved radial grooves crossed with numerous concentric ridges, creating a chevron-like pattern.

Size: Length to 1" (25 mm); height to 0.9" (22 mm)

Habitat/Ecology: In sand; in subtidal waters from 6–300' (1.8–91 m) deep

Geographic Range: Massachusetts to Brazil

Notes: The distinctive shells of the cross-hatched lucine commonly wash up on the beach. Their pattern makes them some of the easier shells to identify.

Leafy Jewelbox

Chama macerophylla

Authority: Gmelin, 1791
Other Name: Also known as leafy jewel box
Description: The brilliant colors of the shells vary widely from white to yellow, orange, or purple. The thick shells

are oyster-like in shape with the lower (left) valve larger, cup-shaped, and deeper than the flat upper (right) valve. The exteriors are adorned with flattened spines, arranged in radiating rows
Size: Length to 3.5" (89 mm); height to 3" (76 mm)
Habitat/Ecology: On rocks, shells, or other solid objects; low intertidal zone to water 46' (14 m) deep
Geographic Range: North Carolina to Brazil
Notes: Specimens found growing in deeper, quiet waters often have longer, more elaborate and delicate spines. The leafy jewelbox is attached so well to its substrate that a hammer and chisel are often required to remove it. The shells of this jewelbox rarely wash ashore.

Florida Spiny Jewelbox

Arcinella cornuta

Authority: Conrad, 1866
Other Names: Also known as Florida spiny jewel box, spiny jewel box, true spiny jewel box; formerly included with *E. arcinella* (a Caribbean species)
Description: The exteriors of the shells are white. The shells' interiors are white and tinted with purplish pink. The heavy shell is inflated, irregular, and circular in shape. The exteriors are sculptured with seven to nine radial rows of heavy, short, tubular spines of varying lengths and a coarse, granular finish between ribs.
Size: Length to 1.5" (38 mm); height to 1.25" (32 mm)
Habitat/Ecology: On gravel or rubble; in subtidal waters from 16–270' (4.9–82 m) deep
Geographic Range: North Carolina to the Yucatán
Notes: This jewelbox shell commonly washes up on the beach. Young individuals attach themselves at the front of the umbo on the right valve to hard objects, such as rubble. Later, they detach to lie on the ocean's bottom. When they are unattached, their shells are more likely to wash ashore—unlike the leafy jewelbox (see above).

Broad-ribbed Cardita

Cardites floridanus

Authority: (Conrad, 1838)
Other Names: Formerly classified as *Cardita Floridana, Carditamera floridana*
Description: The exteriors of the shells are yellowish white, with a chestnut brown band arranged concentrically on the ribs. The shells' interiors are white. The heavy shell is wing-shaped, with a hinge bearing a single tooth. The exteriors are sculptured with about twenty flattened, radial ribs crossed with numerous light, concentric ridges.

Size: Length to 1.5" (38 mm)
Habitat/Ecology: In sand or mud; in subtidal waters from 3–25' (0.9–7.6 m) deep
Geographic Range: Florida to Mexico
Notes: The broad-ribbed cardita deposits its eggs in jelly-like blobs. This likely protects the eggs until the larvae are able to crawl out.

Northern Cyclocardia

Cyclocardia borealis

Authority: (Conrad, 1832)
Other Names: Also known as northern cardita, northern heart shell; formerly classified as *Venericardia borealis*
Description: The exteriors of the shells are white, with a velvet-like light to dark brown periostracum. The shells' interiors are glossy white. The heavy shell is broadly ovate. The exteriors are sculptured with fifteen to twenty rounded radial ribs and a regular, beaded finish.
Size: Length to 1.5" (38 mm)
Habitat/Ecology: In sand or under stones; low intertidal zone to water 750' (229 m) deep
Geographic Range: Arctic to Cape Hatteras
Notes: The northern cyclocardia is a common bivalve that is an important food source for several bottom-feeding fish.

Wavy Astarte

Astarte undata

Authority: Gould, 1841

Other Name: Also known as waved astarte

Description: The exteriors of the shells are white, with a thick yellowish brown to dark brown periostracum. The interiors of the shells are white. The stout shell is triangular, with the umbones

slightly forward. The exteriors are sculptured with several smooth, wave-like concentric ridges.

Size: Height to 1.5" (38 mm)

Habitat/Ecology: On sand, mud, or gravel; low intertidal zone to water 630' (191 m) deep

Geographic Range: Labrador to New Jersey

Notes: The unique sculpture of this species makes it relatively easy to identify. It is also the most common astarte found on the north Atlantic shores. Adults have a dark brown periostracum, which in the young is light brown.

Smooth Astarte

Astarte castanea

Authority: (Say, 1822)

Other Name: Also known as chestnut astarte

Description: The exteriors of the shells are white with a tough, yellowish brown to dark brown periostracum. The shells' interiors are white. The solid shells are triangular, with pointed beaks. The exteriors are smooth, with several concentric growth lines.

Size: Length to 1.25" (32 mm)

Habitat/Ecology: In mud or sand-mud mix; low intertidal zone to water 100' (30 m) deep

Geographic Range: Nova Scotia to New Jersey

Notes: If you happen to find a live smooth astarte freshly washed up on the beach, you will immediately notice its striking, scarlet red soft tissues.

Florida Pricklycockle

Trachycardium egmontianum

Authority: (Shuttleworth, 1856)
Other Names: Also known as Florida prickly cockle, prickly cockle; formerly classified as *Trachycardium isocardia*
Description: The exteriors of the shells are white occasionally with splashes of brown or purple. The shells' interiors are colorful, with pink, salmon, and purple. The fragile shell is oval and inflated, with the beaks nearly central. The exteriors are sculptured with numerous radial ribs that are studded with sharp, regular scales.
Size: Length to 2.75" (70 mm)
Habitat/Ecology: In sand; in subtidal waters from 1–25' (0.3–7.6 m) deep
Geographic Range: North Carolina to Florida
Notes: The Florida pricklycockle is a bivalve that lives in shallow offshore waters, especially in the mouths of estuaries. Its fragile shells are occasionally found on our ocean and sound beaches.

Yellow Pricklycockle

Dallocardia muricata

Authority: (Linnaeus, 1758)
Other Names: Formerly classified as *Cardium muricatum, C. islandicum, Trachycardium muricatum*
Description: The exteriors of the shells are cream-colored to yellowish and often speckled with brownish red. The shells' interiors are white to yellow. The shells are inflated and broadly ovate to almost round. The exteriors are sculptured with thirty to forty radial ribs that bear small scales at the ends of the front and rear parts of the shell.
Size: Length to 2.5" (64 mm)

Habitat/Ecology: In sand or mud; in subtidal waters from 1–30' (0.3–9 m) deep

Geographic Range: North Carolina to Brazil

Notes: The yellow pricklycockle, like most species of our cockles, remain close to the surface of the substrate it is burried in because it has short siphons for feeding, respiration, and so on. Other clams have enormous siphons that allow them to burrow deep into their substrate.

Spiny Papercockle

Papyridea soleniformis

Authority: (Bruguière, 1789)

Other Name: Also known as spiny paper cockle

Description: The exteriors of the shells are white with markings of yellow, pink or orange. The shells' interiors have a similar coloration. The shell is thin, elliptical, and bears prominent lateral teeth on the hinge. The exteriors are sculptured with about fifty radiating ribs armed with tiny spines near the ends and crossed with many fine, concentric growth lines.

Size: Length to 1.75" (44 mm)

Habitat/Ecology: In sand; low intertidal zone to water 320' (97 m) deep

Geographic Range: North Carolina to Brazil

Notes: The fragile valves of the spiny papercockle are occasionally found along our beaches. Living animals have a long and muscular foot that helps them dig effectively.

Atlantic Strawberry-cockle

Americardia media

Authority: (Linnaeus, 1758)

Other Names: Also known as American cockle, Antillean strawberry cockle; formerly classified as *Trigoniocardia media*

Description: The exteriors of the shells are yellowish white with transverse, oblique bands of reddish brown. The shell is inflated and triangular. The exteriors are sculptured with thirty-three to thirty-six rounded radiating ribs originating from the umbones toward the hind end. A few concentric growth lines are also present.

Size: Length to 2" (51 mm); height to 2" (51 mm)

Habitat/Ecology: In sand; low intertidal zone to water 18' (5.5 m) deep
Geographic Range: Cape Hatteras to Brazil
Notes: This is one of the few members of the cockle clan found in the low intertidal zone. Its shells are also found washed up on the beach.

Common Eggcockle

Fulvia laevigata

Authority: (Linnaeus, 1758)
Other Names: Also known as common egg cockle, egg cockle; formerly classified as *Laevicardium laevigatum*
Description: The exteriors of the shells are ivory white, with outer bands or tinges of brownish orange, purple, or rose. A thin, brown periostracum is often present on fresh shells. The interiors of the shells are white with tinges of yellow, red, orange, or purple. The shell is inflated and broadly ovate. The exteriors are smooth, often with numerous barely noticeable radiating ribs that run from the umbones to the shell's margin.
Size: Length to 2.75" (70 mm); height to 3" (76 mm)
Habitat/Ecology: In sand or mud; low intertidal zone to water 65' (20 m) deep
Geographic Range: North Carolina to Brazil
Notes: The common eggcockle has a reputation for being very active for a mollusk. A collector once placed a recently captured specimen in his boat only to find that his captive made a hasty retreat using its muscular foot to "leap" from the boat and escape.

Morton's Egg Cockle

Laevicardium mortoni

Authority: (Conrad, 1830)
Description: The exteriors of the shells are yellowish white, with streaks or irregular patterns of brown or orange. The interiors of the shells are yellowish, often with blotches of purple toward the hind side. The thin shell is almost circular. The exteriors are smooth, lacking ribs but with numerous fine, concentric growth lines, which can be difficult to detect.
Size: Length to 1" (25 mm); height to 1" (25 mm)
Habitat/Ecology: In sand or mud-sand mix; low intertidal zone to water 15' (5 m) deep
Geographic Range: Nova Scotia to Brazil
Notes: Morton's egg cockle is a favorite food of waterfowl. This is an active species that is reported to be able to hop on the ground and to swim.

Atlantic Giant Cockle

Dinocardium robustum

Authority: (Lightfoot, 1786)

Other Names: Also known as giant Atlantic cockle, giant heart cockle

Description: The exteriors of the shells are tan, mottled with irregular reddish brown or purplish brown spots, and with a mahogany brown hind end. The interiors of the shells are white with a reddish brown hind half. The shell is inflated and oblique, with the umbones high and rounded. The exteriors are sculptured with thirty-two to thirty-six rounded radiating ribs with scale-like ridges.

Size: Height to 5.25" (133 mm); width to 5" (127 mm)

Habitat/Ecology: In sand or mud; low intertidal zone to water 100' (30 m) deep

Geographic Range: Virginia to Mexico

Notes: The Atlantic giant cockle is the largest cockle found on our coast. It can also be made into one exquisite chowder!

Fragile Surfclam

Mactrotoma fragilis

Authority: (Gmelin, 1791)

Other Names: Also known as fragile Atlantic macera, fragile surf clam; formerly classified as *Mactra fragilis*

Description: The exteriors of the shells are white, with a thin yellowish or brownish periostracum. The thin shells are somewhat fragile and ovate in shape. The exteriors are smooth and sculptured with a low ridge that starts from the umbones and stretches to the hind margin. Fine, concentric growth lines are also present.

Size: Length to 4" (10.2 mm)

Habitat/Ecology: In sand; in subtidal waters from 30–150' (9–46 m) deep

Geographic Range: North Carolina to Brazil

Notes: The light shells of this species are often found stranded on our beaches.

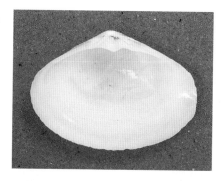

Atlantic Surfclam

Spisula solidissima

Authority: (Dillwyn, 1817)

Other Names: Also known as Atlantic surf clam, beach clam, skimmer clam, hen clam, bar clam, surf clam

Description: The exteriors of the shells are yellowish white with a thin, yellowish brown periostracum. The heavy shells are triangular, with a gape for its siphons and a bulbous beak. Umbones are shifted and turned forward. The exteriors are smooth except for many fine, concentric growth lines.

Size: Height to 5.5" (140 mm); width to 7" (180 mm)

Habitat/Ecology: In sand, as well as mud or gravel; on wave-swept beaches; low intertidal zone to water 140' (42 m) deep

Geographic Range: Nova Scotia to South Carolina

Notes: The Atlantic surfclam is a northern species that is eaten by some but often considered tough. This species often washes ashore during winter storms, where gulls dine upon it. It is also sold as fish bait.

Similar Species: Southern Surfclam (*Spisula raveneli*) (see p. 172) has central umbones and lacks the bulbous beak.

Southern Surfclam

Spisula raveneli

Authority: (Conrad, 1832)

Other Names: Also known as ravenel surfclam, southern surf clam; formerly classified as *Spisula solidissima raveneli*

Description: The exteriors of the shells are yellowish white, with a thin, yellowish brown periostracum. The heavy shells are triangular, with a gape for its siphons and lacks a bulbous beak. Umbones are positioned centrally. The exteriors are smooth except for many fine, concentric growth lines.

Size: Width to 5" (127 mm)

Habitat/Ecology: In sand or mud; low intertidal zone to water 100' (30 m) deep

Geographic Range: Cape Cod to Gulf of Mexico

Notes: The southern surfclam was formerly considered a subspecies of the Atlantic surfclam. Its range begins where the Atlantic surfclam's range ends.

Similar Species: Atlantic Surfclam (*Spisula solidissima*) (see p. 171)

Dwarf Surfclam

Mulinia lateralis

Authority: (Say, 1822)

Other Names: Also known as coot clam, duck clam

Description: The exteriors of the shells vary from cream-colored to light brown, often with banding. A thin, yellowish periostracum is also present. The shells are triangular, with a rounded ridge running from the umbones to the hind end. The exteriors are sculptured with several concentric growth lines.

Size: Width to 0.75" (19 mm)

Habitat/Ecology: In sand or mud; in subtidal waters from 2–180' (0.6–55 m) deep

Geographic Range: Maine to Mexico

Notes: The dwarf surfclam is a small clam that is an important food source for many fish and sea ducks. This is why it has the alternate common names duck clam and coot clam. These birds eat dwarf surfclams whole.

Atlantic Rangia

Rangia cuneata

Authority: (G. B. Sowerby I, 1832)
Other Names: Also known as common rangia, wedge rangia
Description: The exteriors of the shells are yellowish white, with a tough, greenish gray to grayish brown periostracum. The interiors of the shells are white. The heavy, thick shells are triangular and inflated. The umbones are pushed forward significantly. The exteriors are smooth, with many fine, concentric lines giving it a smooth appearance.
Size: Width to 2.75" (7 cm)
Habitat/Ecology: In sand, mud, or sand-mud mix; at creek mouths, river mouths, or similar locations; low intertidal zone to water 7' (2.1 m) deep
Geographic Range: Maryland to Mexico
Notes: This species is common where freshwater courses meet salt water. It has been living since Pleistocene times—more than 1 million years ago. These abundant, heavy shells were once used in the preparation of our roads as a substitute for gravel. The clam can also be eaten.

Smooth Duckclam

Anatina anatina

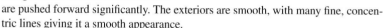

Authority: (Spengler, 1802)
Other Names: Also known as smooth duck clam; formerly classified as *Labiosa lineate*
Description: The exteriors of the shells are off-white with thin, light, yellowish periostracum. The interiors of the shells are white. The thin shells are ovate with high umbones. A cord-like ridge radiates from the beaks toward the anterior end. The exteriors are smooth, with numerous fine, concentric lines.
Size: Width to 3" (76 mm)
Habitat/Ecology: In sand or mud; surf zone to water 240' (72 m) deep
Geographic Range: North Carolina to Brazil
Notes: The smooth duckclam burrows close to the surface since its united siphons are short. There are separate sexes in this species, and they produce free-swimming young.

Channeled Duckclam

Raeta plicatella

Authority: (Lamarck, 1818)
Other Names: Also known as channeled
duck clam; formerly classified as
Labiosa plicatella
Description: The exteriors of the shells
are white, with a light yellowish periostracum. The interiors of the shells are
white to pale yellow. The thin shells
are broadly ovate. The exteriors are decorated with numerous smooth, wave-like
concentric ridges, giving it a distinctive appearance.
Size: Width to 3.25" (83 mm)
Habitat/Ecology: In sand; in subtidal waters from 10–18' (3–5.5 m) deep
Geographic Range: North Carolina to Brazil
Notes: The shells of the channeled duckclam are quite thin, yet they are normally
found intact when washed up on the beach. This species is rarely observed live,
however.

Arctic Wedgeclam

Mesodesma arctatum

Authority: (Conrad, 1830)
Description: The exteriors of the shells
are whitish, with a yellowish periostracum that frequently reflects a
metallic-like luster. The interiors of the
shells are white. The shells are wedge-
shaped, with a short posterior end, and
the hinge features a deep chondrophore
and strong lateral teeth. The exteriors are sculptured with several wide concentric
ridges.
Size: Width to 2.25" (57 mm)
Habitat/Ecology: In sand; low intertidal zone to water 300' (89 m) deep
Geographic Range: Greenland to northern New Jersey
Notes: The Arctic wedgeclam is an important food item for several ducks, especially
the white-winged scoter, surf scoter, and common scoter.

Atlantic Razor-clam

Siliqua costata

Authority: (Say, 1822)

Other Names: Also known as Atlantic razor, Atlantic razor clam, ribbed pod

Description: The exteriors of the shells are white to purplish white. A thin, shiny, yellowish brown to greenish brown periostracum covers the shell. The interiors of the shells are white. The shells are elongated, oblong, with a strong internal rib extending from the beaks downward. The exteriors are smooth without sculpture.

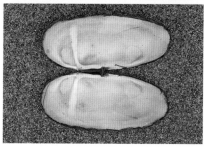

Size: Length to 2.5" (64 mm); height to 1.25" (32 mm)

Habitat/Ecology: In sand or mud; in shallow subtidal waters

Geographic Range: Gulf of St. Lawrence to Cape Hatteras

Notes: This species burrows vertically in sand or mud flats. Its shells commonly wash up on the beach, but the animal is rarely found.

Atlantic Jackknife-clam

Ensis directus

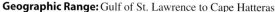

Authority: (Conrad, 1843)

Other Names: Also known as Atlantic jackknife, Atlantic jackknife clam, common straight-razor, common razor clam, straight razor clam

Description: The exteriors of the shells are whitish, with a shiny, thin, olive-green periostracum. The interiors of the shells are bluish white. The shells are elongated oblong with the ends squared off. The shells are approximately five to six times longer than it is wide. An internal ridge runs from the umbones to the hind end. The exteriors are smooth.

Size: Length to 10" (254 mm)

Habitat/Ecology: In sand or sand-mud mix; low intertidal zone to water 120' (36 m) deep

Geographic Range: Labrador to Florida; introduced to Europe

Notes: The Atlantic jackknife-clam digs deep burrows and stands upright with a foot that is almost as long as its shell. It is also able to swim using its foot with a "jet pro-pulsion" technique. It often lives in colonies, and its main predators include moon-snails and milky ribbon worms (see p. 32)

Similar Species: Minor Jackknife-clam (*Ensis megistus*) (see p. 176) has a proportionally narrower shell.

Minor Jackknife-clam

Ensis megistus

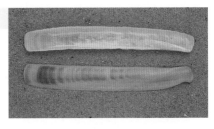

Authority: Pilsbry and McGinty, 1943
Other Names: Also known as dwarf razor clam, jackknife clam, minor jackknife clam; formerly classified as *Ensis minor*

Description: The exteriors of the shells are whitish with a shiny, thin, greenish brown periostracum. The interiors of the shells are purplish white. The fragile shells are elongated and oblong, with both ends squared off. The shells are about six to eight times longer than they are wide. An internal ridge runs from the umbones to the hind end. The exteriors are smooth.

Size: Length to 4.5" (115 mm); height to 0.6" (16 mm)

Habitat/Ecology: In sand or mud; in lagoons and bays; mid to low intertidal zones

Geographic Range: Florida to Texas

Notes: The fragile, single shells of this razor-clam often wash up on the shore. This species was formerly believed to be a subspecies of the Atlantic jackknife-clam.

Similar Species: Atlantic Jackknife-clam (*Ensis directus*) (see p. 175) has a proportionally wider shell.

Speckled Tellin

Tellina listeri

Authority: Röding, 1798
Other Names: Formerly classified as *Tellina interrupta, Tellina listeri*

Description: The exteriors of the shells are white, often tinged with yellow near the umbones and not polished. Rays of brown or purple irregular streaks radiate from the umbones to the ventral margin. The interiors of the shells are white with the umbone area yellow or occasionally purple. The shells are elongated and ovate, with an angular ridge present on the right valve, running from the umbone to the hind end. The exteriors are decorated with numerous concentric, equidistant ridges.

Size: Length to 3.75" (95 mm)

Habitat/Ecology: In sand; in subtidal waters from 3–300' (0.9–91 m) deep

Geographic Range: North Carolina to Brazil; Bermuda

Notes: The scientific name for this species, *listeri*, was named in honor of Martin Lister (1638–1712). Martin Lister was an English naturalist who wrote of one of the earliest books on marine shells.

Faust Tellin

Arcopagia fausta

Authority: (Pulteney, 1799)

Description: The exteriors of the shells are off-white, often flushed with yellow. A thin, brown periostracum is sometimes present on the shells' margins. The interiors of the shells are off-white, with tinges of yellow. The heavy shells are thick, broadly ovate, moderately inflated with a central umbo. The exteriors are sculptured with numerous concentric ridges.

Size: Length to 4" (102 mm)

Habitat/Ecology: In sand; in subtidal waters from 1–90' (0.3–27 m) deep

Geographic Range: North Carolina to Brazil

Notes: The Faust tellin does not look similar to other tellins. This heavy species buries itself deep in sand. The common Atlantic octopus (see p. 196) likes to dine upon this species.

Rose Petal Tellin

Tellina lineata

Authority: Turton, 1819

Other Name: Formerly classified as *Eurytellina lineata*

Description: The exteriors of the shells vary from rose pink to off-white. The interiors of the shells are pink or white with tinges of pink or yellow. The shells are elongated ovate, with a rounded front end and a pointed hind end. The exteriors are sculptured with numerous fine, equidistant, concentric growth lines, giving it a smooth appearance.

Size: Length to 1.5" (38 mm)

Habitat/Ecology: In sand; low intertidal zone to water 60' (18 m) deep

Geographic Range: North Carolina to Brazil

Notes: The bright, colorful shells of the rose petal tellin are gathered and used extensively in shellcrafts. They are especially common in bays.

Alternate Tellin

Tellina alternata

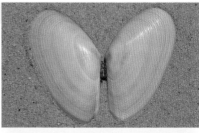

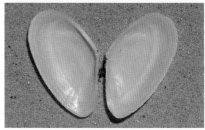

Authority: Say, 1822

Other Name: Formerly classified as *Eurytellina alternata*

Description: The exteriors of the shells are white or occasionally pink or yellow. A shiny, thin, yellowish periostracum covers the shells. The interiors of the shells are shiny, white with a flush of light yellow or orange. The shells are elongated, with a rounded anterior end and a narrowed posterior end. The exteriors are patterned with many fine, flattened, equidistant, concentric growth lines.

Size: Length to 3" (77 mm)

Habitat/Ecology: In sand; in subtidal waters from 6–420' (1.8–128 m) deep

Geographic Range: North Carolina to Gulf of Mexico

Notes: The delicate concentric growth lines on the shells of this species are quite graceful and add to the distinctiveness of this species. It is one of the more common tellins found on our beaches.

Northern Dwarf-tellin

Tellina agilis

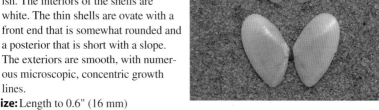

Authority: Stimpson, 1857

Other Names: Also known as northern dwarf tellin; formerly classified as *Tellina tenera*

Description: The exteriors of the shells vary from white to creamy white or pinkish with a shiny or iridescent finish. The interiors of the shells are white. The thin shells are ovate with a front end that is somewhat rounded and a posterior that is short with a slope. The exteriors are smooth, with numerous microscopic, concentric growth lines.

Size: Length to 0.6" (16 mm)

Habitat/Ecology: In mud flats; in subtidal waters from 2–150' (0.6–46 m) deep

Geographic Range: Gulf of St. Lawrence to Georgia

Notes: Tellins dine by deposit feeding—a technique of ingesting sand and mud unselectively along with various organic materials for food.

Tampa Tellin

Tellina tampaensis

Authority: Conrad, 1866
Other Name: Formerly classified as
  Angulus tampaensis
Description: The exteriors of the shells
  are shiny, white, and occasionally
  tinged with pinkish orange. The inte-
  riors of the shells are white. The shells
are broadly ovate with a rounded front end and a somewhat pointed hind end. The
exteriors are patterned with numerous fine, concentric growth lines.
Size: Length to 1" (25 mm)
Habitat/Ecology: In sand; in subtidal waters from 1–50' (0.3–15 m) deep
Geographic Range: Florida to Panama
Notes: Shells of the Tampa tellin are more abundant in sheltered bays than on beaches
  found on the open ocean.

Rainbow Tellin

Tellina iris

Authority: Say, 1822
Other Names: Also known as Iris tellin;
  formerly classified as *Scissula iris*
Description: The exteriors of the shells
  are translucent, saturated with pink
  toward the margin, and two white rays
  are often present at the hind end. The
  interiors of the shells are translucent.
The thin shells are elongate. The exteriors are patterned with concentric ridges and
microscopic lines (often called sissulations) that meet the ridges at acute angles.
Size: Length to 0.6" (15.3 mm)
Habitat/Ecology: In sand; low intertidal zone to water 120' (36.5 m) deep
Geographic Range: North Carolina to Gulf of Mexico
Notes: The shells of this species are amazingly thin and fragile. It is a wonder this
  organism can function with such a thin shell.
Similar Species: Many-colored Tellin (*Tellina versicolor*) displays the shells' con-
  centric ridges without microscopic lines cutting the ridges at acute angles.

White Crested Tellin

Tellidora cristata

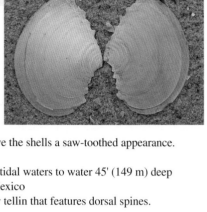

Authority: (Récluz, 1842)

Other Name: Also known as white-crested tellin

Description: The exteriors and interiors of the shells are white. The shells are triangular-shaped, with light, concentric ridges that form teeth on the anterior and posterior dorsal margins and give the shells a saw-toothed appearance.

Size: Length to 1.4" (37 mm)

Habitat/Ecology: In sand; in shallow subtidal waters to water 45' (149 m) deep

Geographic Range: North Carolina to Mexico

Notes: The white-crested tellin is the only tellin that features dorsal spines.

Baltic Macoma

Macoma balthica

Authority: (Linnaeus, 1758)

Description: The exteriors of the shells are white, often with a pink flush. The interiors of the shells are white or pink. A thin, brown periostracum is present on fresh shells. The thin, chalky shells are broadly ovate, with the front end rounded and the hind end slightly pointed. The exteriors have many fine, concentric growth lines.

Size: Length to 1.5" (38 mm); height to 1.25" (32 mm)

Habitat/Ecology: In mud, sand-mud mix or gravel; mid intertidal zone to water 33' (10 m) deep

Geographic Range: Arctic to Georgia; Bering Sea to California; Europe

Notes: The Baltic macoma, like other macomas, lies buried in the mud on its left side. It is often buried nearly 12" (30 cm) deep, with its siphons extended to the mud's surface to feed, breathe, and remove wastes. The siphons are able to reach ten times this small bivalve's shell length.

Constricted Macoma

Macoma constricta

Authority: (Bruguière, 1792)
Description: The exteriors of the shells
are white, with a light yellowish brown
to grayish brown periostracum. The
interiors of the shells are white. The
shells are ovate and slightly inflated.
The exteriors are smooth, with fine,
concentric growth lines. A fold in the shells extends from the beaks to the ventral
margin, and the hind end curves to the right.
Size: Length to 2.5" (64 mm)
Habitat/Ecology: In sand or mud; in subtidal waters from 1–6' (0.3–1.8 m) deep
Geographic Range: North Carolina to Brazil
Notes: The constricted macoma is more tolerant of extreme salinities and temperatures
than many Atlantic macomas.

Variable Coquina

Donax variabilis

Authority: Say, 1822
Other Names: Also known as butterfly
shell, coquina, coquina shell, southern
coquina, pompano wedge shell
Description: The exteriors of the shells
are glossy and vary widely from white
to yellow, orange, pink, red, mauve,
purple, or blue, often with darker rays.
The interiors of the shells are also
brightly colored.

　The thin shells are elongated and triangular wedge-shaped. The exteriors
are patterned with numerous radiating
riblets crossed with many concentric
ridges.
Size: Length to 0.75" (19 mm)
Habitat/Ecology: In sand; mid intertidal
zone to shallow subtidal waters
Geographic Range: New Jersey to the
Gulf of Mexico
Notes: The variable coquina is an abundant and very active clam that migrates up and
down the sandy beach with the tides. It remains at the same location at slack tide for
about two hours. It has a long history of use in broth and chowder.
Similar Species: Little Coquina (*Donax fossor*) (see p. 182)

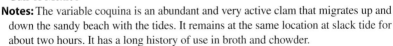

Little Coquina

Donax fossor

Authority: Say, 1822
Other Names: Also known as poor little coquina; formerly classified as *Donax parvulus*
Description: The exteriors of the shells are glossy and vary primarily from white to yellow or orange, without colored rays. The interiors of the shells are also colored with a variety of colors. The shells are inflated and are triangular wedge-shaped. The exteriors are smooth and patterned with numerous radiating riblets crossed with many concentric ridges.
Size: Length to 0.5" (13 mm)
Habitat/Ecology: In sand; low intertidal zone to subtidal waters
Geographic Range: New York to Florida
Notes: The little coquina is similar to the variable coquina—in fact they are often found on the same beaches during the summer months. During winter, however, the little coquina is not found on our beaches, as it has moved to deeper waters offshore.
Similar Species: Variable Coquina (*Donax variabilis*) (see p. 181)

Stout Tagelus

Tagelus plebeius

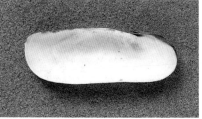

Authority: (Lightfoot, 1786)
Other Names: Also known as jackknife clam; formerly classified as *T. gibbus*
Description: The exteriors of the shells are chalky white, with a thin, yellowish brown periostracum that covers the shells. The interiors of the shells are white. The shells are elongate, and both ends are rounded with a gape. The length is approximately three times the width. The exteriors are smooth with fine, concentric growth lines.
Size: Length to 4" (102 mm); height to 1.5" (38 mm)
Habitat/Ecology: In sand-mud mix; low intertidal zone to water 1.5' (0.45 m) deep
Geographic Range: Cape Cod to Brazil
Notes: The stout tagelus is a common species, and its shells often wash up on the beach.

Purplish Tagelus

Tagelus divisus

Authority: (Spengler, 1794)

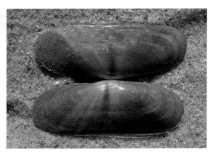

Description: The exteriors of the shells are white and light purple, with rays of white or purple that run from the umbones to the ventral margin on the hind end of the shell. A thin, yellowish brown periostracum covers the shells. The interiors of the shells are white, light purple, or occasionally deep purple. The thin shells are oblong and quite fragile. The umbones are centrally located. A rib-like structure on the shells' interiors runs from the umbones toward the ventral margin. The exteriors are smooth, with many fine, concentric growth lines.

Size: Length to 1.6" (41 mm)

Habitat/Ecology: In sand, mud, or sand-mud mix; low intertidal zone to water 6' (1.8 m) deep

Geographic Range: Cape Cod to Brazil

Notes: The purplish tagelus lives inside vertical burrows in which it extends the tip of its inhalant siphon to feed on foods suspended in the surrounding water. Single shells of this species occasionally wash up at the beach.

Queen Quahog

Arctica islandica

Authority: (Linnaeus, 1767)

Other Names: Also known as black clam, mahogany clam; formerly classified as *Cyprina islandica*

Description: The exteriors of the shells are white, covered with a thick, coarse dark brown to black periostracum. The interiors of the shells are white. The heavy shells are thick and broadly ovate, with the large umbones curved forward. The exteriors of the chalky shells are lightly sculptured with numerous concentric growth lines.

Size: Length to 5" (127 mm)

Habitat/Ecology: In sand; low intertidal zone to water 840' (256 m) deep

Geographic Range: Newfoundland to North Carolina; Iceland; Europe

Notes: This species has been commercially harvested for many years. Various restaurants and hotels often sell it.

Northern Quahog

Mercenaria mercenaria

Authority: (Linnaeus, 1758)

Other Names: Also known as cherry-stone clam, edible hardshell clam, hard-shelled clam, littleneck clam, round clam

Description: The exteriors of the shells are grayish yellow to pale brownish. The interiors of the shells are white, often with a characteristic purple tinge at the hind end. The thick shells are inflated and broadly ovate, with the umbones elevated and facing forward. The exteriors are patterned with numerous concentric growth lines. The central portions of both valves have a large, smooth surface. The bottom inside edge of the shells is crenulated.

Size: Length to 5" (127 mm); height to 4.25" (108 mm)

Habitat/Ecology: In sand or mud; in bays or inlets; low intertidal zone to water 50' (15 m) deep

Geographic Range: Gulf of St. Lawrence to Texas; introduced into California

Notes: Native peoples used beads from the northern quahog's shell linings as wampum, or shell money. They also used the shells as tools and ornaments and ate the meat.

Today this species is recognized as an important seafood and harvested commercially. If refrigerated, this species is easily kept alive, out of water for weeks because it closes its valves and keeps them closed.

Similar Species: Southern Quahog (*Mercenaria campechiensis*) (see below)

Southern Quahog

Mercenaria campechiensis

Authority: (Gmelin, 1791)

Description: The exteriors of the shells are grayish yellow to pale brownish. The interiors of the shells are white, normally with no purple coloration present. The thick, heavy shells are very inflated and broadly ovate, with the umbones elevated and facing forward. The exteriors are patterned with numerous concentric growth lines across the entire shells. The bottom inside edge of the shells is crenulated.

Size: Length to 6" (150 mm); height to 5" (127 mm)

Habitat/Ecology: In sand or mud; low intertidal zone to water 120' (36 m) deep
Geographic Range: New Jersey to Mexico; Cuba
Notes: Both the southern quahog and northern quahog are marketable clams that can live longer than twenty years. The southern quahog is not as plentiful as it once was, likely due to overfishing and lower water quality.
Similar Species: Northern Quahog (*Mercenaria mercenaria*) (see p. 184)

Cross-barred Venus

Chione cancellata

Authority: (Linnaeus, 1767)
Description: The exteriors of the shells are cream-colored to yellowish white, often with patches or rays of brown from the umbones to the ventral margin. The interiors of the shells are purple or white tinged with purple. The shells are solid and triangular; the beaks are elevated and positioned forward. The exteriors are patterned with numerous elevated, radiating ribs crossed with several similar-size, concentric ridges, giving it a cancellate (crisscrossed) appearance.
Size: Length and height to 1.75" (44 mm)
Habitat/Ecology: In sand; in shallow subtidal waters
Geographic Range: North Carolina to Brazil

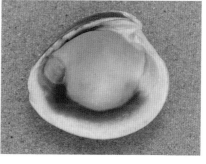

Notes: Beachcombers commonly find shells of the cross-barred venus. Their distinctive shells make identification easy.

Lady-in-waiting Venus

Puberella intapurpurea

Authority: (Conrad, 1849)
Other Name: Incorrectly spelled *Puberella interpurpurea*
Description: The exteriors of the shells are white to cream-colored, often with irregular brownish markings. The interiors of the shells are white, with or without a purplish flush in the hind portion. The thick shells are ovate, with prominent beaks that are elevated. The

exteriors are sculptured with several concentric ridges that are rounded centrally but crenulated at both ends.

Size: Length and height to 1.5" (38 mm)

Habitat/Ecology: In sand; in shallow subtidal waters to water 300' (91 m) deep

Geographic Range: Chesapeake Bay to Brazil

Notes: Shells of the lady-in-waiting venus are occasionally found on beaches after a storm.

Imperial Venus

Lirophora latilirata

Authority: (Conrad, 1841)

Description: The exteriors of the shells are white to cream-colored, with irregular markings and rays of lilac and brown. The interiors of the shells are white, with purple markings at the posterior end. The thick shells are inflated and triangular with rounded edges. The exteriors are sculptured with five to eleven broadly rounded concentric ribs and deep furrows lying between.

Size: Length and height to 1.5" (38 mm)

Habitat/Ecology: In sand; in subtidal waters from 60–200' (18–60 m) deep

Geographic Range: North Carolina to Brazil

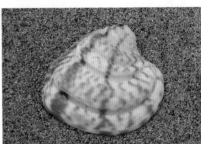

Notes: The imperial venus is a distinctive species that burrows just below the surface of the sand. It is often a bycatch of the Atlantic calico scallop fishery.

Pointed Venus

Anomalocardia cuneimeris

Authority: (Conrad, 1846)

Other Name: Formerly classified as *Anomalocardia auberiana*

Description: The exteriors of the shells are white to tan, with rays or mottlings of brown. The interiors of the shells are white and purplish brown. The shells

A discolored beach shell

are wedge-shaped, with a pointed posterior end and the slope rostrate (curved beak). The exteriors are sculptured with several rounded concentric ridges.

Size: Length to 0.75" (19 mm)

Habitat/Ecology: In sand or mud; in shallow subtidal waters to water 10' (3 m) deep

Geographic Range: Florida to Uruguay

Notes: The shells of this distinctive bivalve occasionally wash up on the beach.

Lightning Venus

Pitar fulminatus

Authority: (Menke, 1828)

Other Name: Also known as lightning pitar

Description: The exteriors of the shells are white, with interrupted rays of brown radiating from the umbones to the ventral margin. The interiors of the shells are polished white to yellowish. The shells are moderately inflated and ovate. The exteriors are smooth, with several concentric ridges.

Size: Length to 2" (51 mm)

Habitat/Ecology: In sand or mud; in subtidal waters from 10–400' (3–120 m) deep

Geographic Range: North Carolina to Brazil; Bermuda

Specimen with periostracum

Notes: The common name of the lightning venus was derived from its scientific name. The word *fulmen* in Latin means "a flash of lightning," which refers to the interrupted rays or zigzag markings.

False Quahog

Pitar morrhuanus

Authority: (Dall, 1902)

Other Name: Also known as *Morrhua venus*

Description: The exteriors of the shells are gray to brownish red. The interiors of the shells are whitish. The thin shells are broadly ovate, and the beaks are elevated and positioned forward. The exteriors are smooth, with numerous concentric growth ridges. The bottom inside edge of the shells are not crenulated.

Size: Length to 2" (51 mm)
Habitat/Ecology: In sand and mud; low intertidal zone to shallow subtidal waters
Geographic Range: Prince Edward Island to North Carolina
Notes: As its common name suggests, the false quahog closely resembles the northern quahog and southern quahog (see p. 184). The bottom inside edges of both species' shells are crenulated. The false quahog does not display purple on the inside of its shells.

Sunray Venus

Macrocallista nimbosa

Authority: (Lightfoot, 1786)
Description: The exteriors of the shells are pale salmon or pinkish gray, with interrupted radial rays of brown extending to the ventral margin. A thin, glossy, varnish-like brown periostracum covers the shells. The interiors of the shells are white, often with a yellowish flush. The shells are elongated and ovate. The exteriors are smooth, with numerous irregular, concentric growth lines.
Size: Length to 5" (127 mm); height to 2.5" (64 mm)
Habitat/Ecology: In sand or mud; low intertidal zone to water 130' (39 m) deep
Geographic Range: North Carolina to Brazil
Notes: The large, distinctive shells of this species are some of the most beautiful found on Western Atlantic shores. Single shells occasionally wash up on the shore.

Calico Clam

Callista maculata

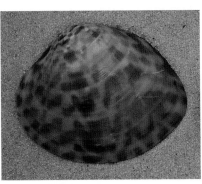

Authority: (Linnaeus, 1758)
Other Names: Also known as checkerboard clam, spotted venus
Description: The exteriors of the shells are yellowish buff or tan, with a brown checkerboard pattern and normally one to two light or dark radiating bands. They also have a high-gloss finish. The interiors of the shells are white, possibly with a pinkish or yellowish blush. The shells are sturdy and ovate. The exteriors are smooth with numerous fine, concentric growth lines.
Size: Length to 3.5" (89 mm)
Habitat/Ecology: In sand; in subtidal waters from just below the low intertidal zone to water 180' (54 m) deep
Geographic Range: North Carolina to Brazil; introduced to Bermuda

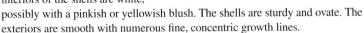

Notes: Single shells of the calico clam often wash up on Florida's western shorelines. Its checkerboard-like shells are popular with shell collectors. This species is known for its delicious taste.

Elegant Dosinia

Dosinia elegans

Authority: (Conrad, 1843)
Other Name: Formerly classified as *Dosinia concentrica*
Description: The exteriors of the shells are ivory with a thin, straw yellow periostracum covering. The interiors of the shells are white. The shells are flat and circular with a small beak. The exteriors are patterned with numerous equidistant, concentric ridges—twenty-five per inch in adults (eight to ten per centimeter).
Size: Length to 3" (76 mm); height to 3" (76 mm)
Habitat/Ecology: In sand; low intertidal zone to subtidal waters
Geographic Range: North Carolina to Brazil
Notes: The elegant dosinia closely resembles the disc dosinia. To identify a shell there are two points that will assist the collector. The number of concentric ridges on the shell is twenty-five per inch in the elegant dosinia and fifty in the disc dosinia. There is also a prominent beak in the disc dosinia that is not present in the elegant dosinia.
Similar Species: Disc Dosinia (*Dosinia discus*) (see below)

Disc Dosinia

Dosinia discus

Authority: (Reeve, 1850)
Description: The exteriors of the shells are ivory with a thin, straw yellow periostracum covering. The interiors of the shells are white. The shells are flat and circular, with a prominent beak. The exteriors are patterned with numerous equidistant, concentric ridges—fifty per inch in adults (twenty per centimeter).
Size: Length to 3" (76 mm); height to 3" (76 mm)
Habitat/Ecology: In sand and sand-mud mix; from just below the low intertidal zone to water 70' (21 m) deep
Geographic Range: Virginia to Mexico
Notes: The disc dosinia burrows on shores with loose sand and lives within protected bays and estuaries. On rare occasions, specimens may wash up on the beach in large numbers.
Similar Species: Elegant Dosinia (*Dosinia elegans*) (see above)

False Angelwing

Petricolaria pholadiformis

Authority: (Lamarck, 1818)

Other Names: Also known as American piddock, false angel wing

Description: The exteriors of the shells are chalky white, with a brown periostracum. The interiors of the shells are white. The shells are fragile and elongated, with the umbones at a fifth of the shell length from the front end. The exteriors are decorated with about forty radial ribs, which are spiny and wide-spaced at the anterior third of the shell, and which become closer spaced, without spines toward the anterior side of the shell. The ribs are crossed with several less-prominent concentric ridges.

Size: Length to 2" (51 mm); height to 0.75" (19 mm)

Habitat/Ecology: Bores into peat, mud, clay, soft rock, and occasionally waterlogged wood; low intertidal zone to shallow subtidal waters

Geographic Range: Gulf of St. Lawrence to Mexico; introduced to Washington to California

Notes: This common species bears a close resemblance to the much larger angelwing, hence its name. Live specimens of the false angelwing have large separate tubular gray siphons. Its shells often wash up on the shore.

Similar Species: Angelwing (*Cyrtopleura costata*) (see p. 193)

Softshell-clam

Mya arenaria

Authority: Linnaeus, 1758

Other Names: Also known as soft-shelled clam, long clam, longnecked clam, steamer clam

Description: The exteriors of the shells are grayish white, with a light brown or gray periostracum on fresh specimens. The interiors of the shells are white. The thin and fragile shells are ovate, with the umbones near the center. A chondrophore, or erect spoonlike tooth,

A chondrophore visible on the inside of the shell

is located under the beak of the left valve. The exteriors are slightly rough, with several irregular, concentric growth lines.

Size: Length to 6" (150 mm); height to 3.5" (89 mm)

Habitat/Ecology: In sand, mud, or gravel-mud mix; low intertidal zone to water 240' (73 m) deep

Geographic Range: Labrador to North Carolina; introduced to British Columbia to California; Europe

Notes: The softshell clam is a well-known edible species that is widely harvested. This species tunnels inside its vertical burrow near the surface of the substrate. This clam often reveals its presence by shooting a jet of water from its siphons as they retreat back into its shell.

Truncated Softshell-clam

Mya truncata

Authority: Linnaeus, 1758
Other Names: Also known as gaper, long clam, nannynose steamer
Description: The exteriors of the shells are an off-white, with a thin, yellowish brown periostracum. The interiors of the shells are white. The thin but sturdy shells are oblong, with the anterior end rounded, the hind end truncated, and a wide gape. The exteriors are slightly rough, with several irregular, concentric growth lines.
Size: Length to 3" (75 mm)
Habitat/Ecology: In sand or mud; low intertidal zone to water 300' (91 m) deep
Geographic Range: Arctic to South Carolina; Arctic to Washington (state); Japan; Norway
Notes: Although the truncated softshell-clam is found as far south as South Carolina, it is not common south of Maine. This species is considered a delicacy in Greenland and Iceland. It is also an important food for the codfish, king eider, diving ducks, and walrus.
Similar Species: Softshell-clam (*Mya arenaria*) (see p. 190)

Arctic Hiatella

Hiatella arctica

Authority: (Linnaeus, 1767)
Other Names: Also known as Arctic saxicave, arctic rock borer, red nose; formerly classified as *Hiatella striata*
Description: The exteriors of the shells are chalky white, with a thin, yellowish brown periostracum. The interiors of the shells are grayish white. The shells are ovate, with both ends rounded and the umbones near the hind end. The surface is irregular and sculptured with many concentric lines.
Size: Length to 2" (51 mm); height to 0.75" (19 mm)
Habitat/Ecology: In cracks and crevices; low intertidal zone to water 600' (183 m) deep
Geographic Range: Arctic to Panama; Alaska to Panama; Europe
Notes: The Arctic hiatella is a species that nests in various crevices, which gives it an irregular and often misshapen shell. After it burrows into its substrate, it makes that

site its permanent home by attaching a byssal cord to keep it in place for its entire life.

Atlantic Geoduck

Panopea bitruncata

Authority: (Conrad, 1872)
Other Name: Also known as geoduck
Description: The exteriors of the shells are white to cream-colored, with a grayish periostracum. The interiors of the shells are white. The sturdy shells are rectangular, with a rounded front end and a concave rear end. The exteriors are irregular, with several coarse, concentric ridges.
Size: Length to 8.25" (210 mm)
Habitat/Ecology: In sand or mud; low intertidal zone to water 158' (47.5 m) deep
Geographic Range: North Carolina to Texas
Notes: The Atlantic geoduck was once believed to be extinct. Its fossil remains are often found, but live specimens are not common. Its shells do occasionally wash up on our shores, revealing their presence in deeper waters. This species burrows up to 4 feet deep, so it is no wonder it is rare to encounter!

Atlantic Mud Piddock

Barnea truncata

Authority: (Say, 1822)
Other Names: Also known as fallen angelwing, Atlantic mud-piddock, truncated borer
Description: The exteriors of the shells are grayish white. The interiors of the shells are white. The thin shells are oblong, with gapes at both ends. The exteriors are patterned with several radiating wrinkles with scales; however, these ribs do not continue to the upper portion of the hind end. Several concentric wrinkles give the ridges a scale-like, cross-ribbed appearance in the front end and central part of the shell. In addition, one narrow auxiliary plate covers the upper margin.
Size: Length to 2.75" (7 cm)
Habitat/Ecology: Burrows in mud, clay, peat, or rarely in soft shale; low intertidal zone to water 32' (10 m) deep
Geographic Range: Maine to Brazil
Notes: The Atlantic mud piddock is a deposit or suspension feeder that dines on planktonic food suspended in the water. They have separate sexes, and their young are born as pelagic larvae.
Similar Species: **False Angelwing** (*Petricolaria pholadiformis*) (see p. 190)

Angelwing

Cyrtopleura costata

Authority: (Linnaeus, 1758)
Other Name: Also known as angel wing
Description: The exteriors of the shells are chalky white, with a grayish periostracum. The interiors of the shells are white. The shells are fragile and elongated with the prominent umbones at one-fifth of shell's length from the front end. The exteriors are decorated with about thirty spiny, radial ribs, which have wider spaces at the anterior end. These wrinkles are crossed with several concentric ridges of equal strength, giving it a scale-like, cross-ribbed appearance.
Size: Length to 8" (20 cm); height to 2.3" (6 cm)
Habitat/Ecology: Burrows into sandy mud, clay, or peat; mid intertidal zone to water 60' (18 m) deep
Geographic Range: Cape Cod to Brazil
Notes: The angelwing burrows deep into its substrates, in some cases reaching distances of approximately 3' (1 m) when burrowing into mud or sandy mud.
Similar Species: False Angelwing (*Petricolaria pholadiformis*) (see p. 190), Campeche Angelwing (*Pholas campechiensis*) (see below)

Campeche Angelwing

Pholas campechiensis

Authority: Gmelin, 1791
Other Name: Also known as campeche angel wing
Description: The exteriors and interiors of the shells are white. The thin shells are greatly elongated with gapes at both ends. The umbones are positioned approximately a quarter of the way from the front end. The exteriors are decorated with several slightly spiny radiating ribs, which are stronger at the anterior end, crossed with several concentric ridges, giving it a scale-like appearance. There are also three accessory plates over the upper margin.
Size: Length to 4.75" (121 mm)
Habitat/Ecology: Burrows in mud or clay; in subtidal waters
Geographic Range: North Carolina to Brazil
Notes: This species is rarely found live, likely because it prefers deep subtidal waters where it bores into hard substrates.
Similar Species: Angelwing (*Cyrtopleura costata*) (see above) is larger, not as elongated, and displays coarser spines.

Great Piddock

Zirfaea crispata

Authority: (Linnaeus, 1758)

Other Names: Also known as common piddock, oval piddock

Description: The exteriors of the shells are grayish white with a brown periostracum that is often worn off. The interiors of the shells are white. The sturdy shells are oblong, with a wide hind end, a pointed front end, and wide gapes at both ends. The exteriors of the shells have a groove that runs from the umbones to the middle of the lower margin. In front of the groove, radial ribs intersect several concentric ridges, giving it a somewhat scalloped finish with a saw-toothed margin. Behind the groove, irregular concentric ridges give it a somewhat smooth surface.

Size: Length to 3" (76 mm); height to 1.4" (35 mm)

Habitat/Ecology: In peat, mud, clay, or soft rock; low intertidal zone to water 240' (73 m) deep

Geographic Range: Labrador to Maryland; Europe; introduced to California

Notes: The great piddock burrows in a variety of substrates, which have a large influence in the shape of its valves. In hard substrates like soft rock, this species grows much smaller and slower than if it were burrowing in peat.

Striate Piddock

Martesia striata

Authority: (Linnaeus, 1758)

Other Name: Also known as striate martesia

Description: The exteriors of the shells are grayish white, with a thin yellowish brown periostracum. The fragile shells are wedge-shaped or pear-shaped, with a gape at both ends. The exteriors are divided into two sections by a diagonal groove that extends from the umbones to the ventral margin. Before the groove, the concentric lines are crenulated, and after the groove, the concentric lines are wrinkled and irregular. A single broad accessory plate is present.

Size: Length to 2" (51 mm); height to 1" (25 mm)

Habitat/Ecology: Bores into wood; at or below the low intertidal zone

Geographic Range: North Carolina to Brazil: Mexico to Peru

Notes: The striate piddock bores into submerged wood or other materials (including underwater lead cables, which has caused problems). This species destroys wood in a way similar to the common shipworm (see p. 195).

Common Shipworm

Teredo navalis

Authority: Linnaeus, 1758

Other Names: Also known as Atlantic shipworm, great shipworm, naval shipworm

Description: The exteriors of the shells are white with a thin yellowish brown periostracum. The fragile shells are globular, with the exteriors' anterior section armed with sharp-edged ribs for boring; the posterior section is smooth. The interiors include a long, slender rib attached to the umbo. Two simple pallets, or paddle-like appendages, are found at the rear end of the animal.

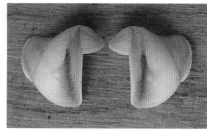

Valves only

Size: Shell length to 0.25" (6 mm); height to 0.25" (6 mm); Animal length to 12" (30 cm) or more

Habitat/Ecology: Bores into wood; at or below the low intertidal zone

Geographic Range: Arctic to the tropics on both coasts; worldwide

Notes: The common shipworm was once a serious pest for boats and docks. Today, metal and other materials have replaced wooden structures, and so most of the problems caused by this widespread organism have disappeared.

The small shells of this organism are vestigial. It produces a thin, calcareous tube that lines the burrow the shipworm has created in wood. This is where it lives since its enormous body cannot retract into its tiny shells.

Glassy Lyonsia

Lyonsia hyalina

Authority: (Conrad, 1831)

Description: The exteriors of the shells are grayish white, with a thin, translucent, shiny periostracum that covers the shells. The fragile shells are elongated oblong, with a spread-out and upturned posterior end; and the front end is

rounded. The exteriors are smooth, with numerous delicate radiating riblets crossed with several lighter, concentric ridges.

Size: Length to 1" (25 mm)

Habitat/Ecology: In sand or sand-mud mix; low intertidal zone to water 200' (61 m) deep

Geographic Range: Nova Scotia to South Carolina

Notes: The glassy lyonsia is a small, fragile bivalve with a translucent periostracum that has a surface that clings to sand. As a result, the shell is often covered with grains of sand.

Gould's Pandora

Pandora gouldiana

Authority: Dall, 1886
Other Name: Also known as Gould pandora
Description: The exteriors of the shells are white to rusty brown. The interiors of the shells are pearly white. The flat shells are wedge-shaped, and upturned at the anterior end. The valves are asymmetrical: the right is flat and the left is convex. The exteriors are smooth, with a few concentric growth lines.
Size: Length to 1.5" (38 mm)
Habitat/Ecology: In sand and mud; low intertidal zone to water 480' (146 m) deep
Geographic Range: Gulf of St. Lawrence to North Carolina
Notes: Gould's pandora is the largest of the pandoras found on our Atlantic shores. It is our most common species of pandora, often discovered at the low intertidal zone.
Similar Species: Say's Pandora (*Pandora trilineata*) is a smaller species that lives from North Carolina to Texas, with a shorter posterior end.

OCTOPODS AND SQUIDS
(Class Cephalopoda)

The creatures in this group have several remarkable characteristics. Each species has a total of eight or more arms positioned around the mouth, in addition to two gills, two kidneys, and three hearts. Some species release a dark fluid to aid in defense against predators.

Common Atlantic Octopus

Octopus vulgaris

Authority: Cuvier, 1797
Other Name: Also known as common octopus
Description: The color varies greatly, from bluish green mottled with white to reddish brown overall. Four pairs of thick arms are four times the mantle's length. The front and rear arms are shorter than side arms, however, and the skin is smooth.

Size: Average arm span to 3' (90 cm); however, 10' (3 m) giants have been found in deep waters
Habitat/Ecology: In rocky crevices; low intertidal zone to 1320' (400 m) deep
Geographic Range: Connecticut to West Indies
Notes: The common Atlantic octopus is a secretive species that typically hides under rocks during daylight hours. At night it emerges to hunt for food. The individuals found at low tide levels are normally small. It is believed that this octopus has a one-year lifespan.

Ram's Horn Squid

Spirula spirula

Authority: (Linnaeus, 1758)
Other Names: Also known as common spirula, spirula
Description: The shell is air-filled and chambered, with a coiled, circular shape that is not fused.
Size: Shell diameter to 1" (25 mm)
Habitat/Ecology: Shells found on the beach; the organism lives in subtidal waters 180–3,000' (54–900 m) deep
Geographic Range: North Carolina to Caribbean; globally in the warm and temperate seas
Notes: The ram's horn squid is a small, deep-water squid that is seldom observed alive. Its air-filled shell, however, commonly washes up on the beach. This species has been found as far north as Nantucket, but that is unusual.

Common Paper Nautilus

Argonauta argo

Authority: Linnaeus, 1758
Other Names: Also known as common paper argonaut, pelagic paper nautilus, paper nautilus
Description: The color is whitish, with brownish shading at the keels. It is double-keeled with an empty center. The shell is extremely fragile, with a series of swollen ridges. There are no chambers.
Size: Shell to 12" (30 cm)
Habitat/Ecology: Pelagic
Geographic Range: Cape Cod to Florida; global tropical and temperate waters
Notes: The common paper nautilus is a cephalopod—a member of the octopus clan. Larger females brooding their young produce a shell to protect them, which can be released at any time. These are the shells that are occasionally found on the beach. The male is tiny, reaching only 0.5" (12 mm) long without a shell since these shells are made only by females with young.

Lampshells
(Phylum Brachiopoda)

Brachiopoda—or lampshells as they are often called—is a phylum composed of organisms with two shells that are positioned above and below each other. Although they resemble mollusks, they are unrelated. Mollusks have left and right valves. Brachiopods also have a stalk that they use to attach to a substrate. They obtained their common name "lampshells" because their lower bowl-shaped shell resembles the oil lamp used by ancient Romans.

Northern Lampshell

Terebratulina septentrionalis

Authority: (Couthouy, 1838)

Other Name: Also known as northern lamp shell

Description: The shells are yellowish white in color. The valves are oval-shaped, with numerous fine riblets. The upper shell is smaller than the lower shell. A hole in a narrowed portion of the lower shell allows the attachment stalk to pass through.

Size: Length to 1.35" (32 mm); width to 0.85" (22 mm)

Habitat/Ecology: On rocks, or similar hard objects; low intertidal zone to water 12500' (3810 m) deep

Geographic Range: Labrador to New Jersey

Notes: The relatives of today's lampshell date back millions of years. Perhaps the ability of this species to live at such a wide range of depths has contributed to its survival. This is the most common species of lampshell found in the North Atlantic waters and the only one to reach intertidal depths.

Arthropods
(Phylum Arthropoda)

Arthropods are invertebrates with jointed legs, an exoskeleton made of chitin that is shed as the animal grows, and a segmented body often made up of a cephalothorax and an abdomen. *Arthropoda* means "jointed foot," a feature present in all species. Arthropods are perhaps the most widespread phylum of animals on the planet. They comprise over 900,000 living species—more than three-quarters of all that are known.

ARACHNIDS (Class Arachnida)

This class contains spiders, mites, ticks, and closely related species. Most adult members have eight legs. Additional appendages are used for feeding, reproduction, and so on. Their bodies are divided into two sections, and all species have an exoskeleton.

Red Velvet Mite

Neomolgus littoralis

Authority: (Linnaeus, 1758)
Other Names: Also known as red mite, intertidal mite
Description: Color is red overall. The abdomen has several ridges on its dorsal side, and the legs have numerous hairs. The snout is noticeably elongated.
Size: Length to 0.1" (2 mm)
Habitat/Ecology: On various shorelines; high intertidal to splash zone
Geographic Range: Circumpolar; Arctic to Maine; Alaska to Gulf of California; Japan; Europe
Notes: Although the red velvet mite is small, it is an interesting arthropod to observe. With a hand lens, you will discover it is covered with tiny white hairs. It is one of the most widely distributed of all intertidal mites. This species does not avoid bright light. In fact, it is actively wandering about both day and night. It feeds on kelp flies, midges, and occasionally dead insects. When the tide goes out, males deposit their stalked spermatophores on rock surfaces, which females later pick up.

Intertidal Wolf Spider

Pardosa lapidicina

Authority: Emerton, 1885
Description: The carapace (upper part of the thorax) is dark reddish brown, while the eye area of the head is darker, with pale indistinct bands. The legs are also dark reddish brown to blackish. Small hairs cover the whole spider.
Size: Total length to 0.3" (7.5 mm); width to 0.1" (2.9 mm)
Habitat/Ecology: On rocks, cobble beach, and seashore; above the high intertidal zone
Geographic Range: Newfoundland and Nova Scotia to Georgia
Notes: The intertidal wolf spider lives in many habitats, and its range goes into the interior of the continent. Those living along the coast have adapted well, taking advantage of a large territory that is largely unused by other spiders. Females are larger than males—as with most spiders. This species is found at the beach for much of the year. Some individuals move back and forth from neighboring coastal scrubs or cordgrass (see p. 306) areas. Egg sacs have been found from April to July, and females with young on their backs can be observed in June and July.

   During courtship, the male rapidly drums his palpi (antenna-like structures that hang from the mouth area) on the ground, and then shakes his body rapidly forward and back while standing on the tips of his legs and extending his front legs forward. During the last step, he vibrates his front legs on the female's body. The males of many spider species lose their lives to the female after reproduction. Spider reproduction can be tricky!

BARNACLES (Class Cirripedia)

Most barnacles are covered with calcareous shells for protection. Gooseneck barnacles attach to a substrate with long flexible stalks. They have a variety of lifestyles; some are parasitic to crabs, while some attach to whales or simply to any hard object. Globally there are approximately 900 species.

Fragile Barnacle

Chthamalus fragilis

Authority: Darwin, 1854
Other Names: Also known as fragile star barnacle, little gray barnacle
Description: Color of the plates are gray overall. The shape is generally circular or oval with a smooth outer finish. The rostrum (beak) is narrow and no calcareous base is present.

Size: Height to 0.25" (6 mm); width to 0.4" (10 mm)
Habitat/Ecology: On rocks; high intertidal zone
Geographic Range: Cape Cod to Florida and Texas; West Indies
Notes: This small barnacle is normally the species present highest on a rocky shoreline, often reaching as high as the spray zone. It is commonly found in small, uncrowded groups—normally above the northern rock barnacle (see below), which effectively outcompetes it at lower elevations.
Similar Species: Starred barnacle (*Chthamalus stellatus*) looks similar, with a star-shaped shell.

Northern Rock Barnacle

Semibalanus balanoides

Authority: (Linnaeus, 1767)
Other Names: Also known as rock barnacle; formerly classified as *Balanus balanoides*
Description: The plates are grayish white, and the outer surface is rough, with much folding. The shells are tubiferous (meaning hollow chambers are present in a cross-section.) The rostrum is much broader than the carina, and no calcareous base is present.
Size: Height to 1" (25 mm); width to 0.5" (11 mm)
Habitat/Ecology: On rocks and similar hard objects; low intertidal zone to shallow subtidal waters
Geographic Range: Arctic to Cape Hatteras; Alaska to Washington State
Notes: Larvae of this species frequently encounter freezing conditions along the northwest Atlantic Coast. Researchers have discovered that significant numbers of young can survive embedded in sea ice for more than two weeks. Some even survived four weeks, but the percentage decreased. This enables northern rock barnacles to survive one of the most challenging obstacles to living in the north. This species often grows under such crowded conditions that it can only increase its height, which drastically distorts its shape.
Similar Species: Rough Barnacle (*Balanus balanus*) also has a rough shell, but it has a calcareous base. This species is larger, reaching 2" (50 mm) in height, and it is found at lower levels, from the low intertidal zone to subtidal depths of 544' (165 m).
Crenate Barnacle (*Balanus crenatus*) has a calcified base; however, it is not tubiferous. This is primarily a subtidal species that is found to 100' (30 m).

Bay Barnacle

Amphibalanus improvisus

Authority: (Darwin, 1854)
Other Name: Formerly classified as
Balanus improvisus
Description: The color of the plates is
whitish, and the soft tissues are white
with pink to purple speckles. This spe-
cies has smooth plates, a low profile,
shells that are tubiferous, and a calcareous base.
Size: Height to 0.25" (6 mm); width 0.5" (13 mm)
Habitat/Ecology: On rocks, shells, pilings, and similar hard objects; low intertidal
zone to water 120' (37 m) deep
Geographic Range: Nova Scotia to Florida and Texas; Mexico; West Indies to Brazil;
Oregon to Ecuador
Notes: Unlike many species, this barnacle is tolerant of fresh water. The bay barnacle
is a common fouling species that often attaches to the bottoms of boats. To determine
if a species has a calcareous base, simply find an unattached specimen and view the
bottom. A calcareous base will totally cover the bottom.

Ivory Barnacle

Amphibalanus eburneus

Authority: (Gould, 1841)
Other Names: Also known as white
ivory barnacle; formerly classified as
Balanus eburneus
Description: The shell is ivory-white.
The soft tissue often displays purple or
yellow stripes. The shell is conical,
with a flat top and smooth sides. The
base is calcareous and tubiferous.

Size: Height to 1" (25 mm); width to 1" (25 mm)
Habitat/Ecology: On rocks, shells, and pilings; in bays and estuaries; low intertidal
zone to shallow subtidal waters
Geographic Range: Maine to South America
Notes: Shells from this common barnacle often wash ashore with rocks or shells. The
ivory barnacle occurs in brackish sites, ranging to nearly fresh water, and is often
found attached to the bottom of boats.

Striped Acorn Barnacle

Amphibalanus amphitrite

Authority: (Darwin, 1854)

Other Names: Also known as little striped barnacle, striped barnacle; formerly classified as *Balanus amphitrite*

Description: The color varies with its range. In the north, it is striped vertically with gray and white; south of Cape Hatteras, it is striped purple and white.

Size: Height to 0.75" (19 mm); width to 0.75" (19 mm)

Habitat/Ecology: On shells of mollusks and crustaceans, rocks, and pilings; in estuaries; low intertidal zone to water 60' (18 m) deep

Geographic Range: Maine to South America; Bahamas; West Indies; California to Panama

Notes: This species is commonly found in a wide variety of habitats, including estuaries, the bottoms of ships, and a wide variety of hard objects (such as the shells of both mollusks and crustaceans).

Similar Species: **Titan Acorn Barnacle** (*Megabalanus coccopoma*) (see below) is a much larger pink-colored species.

ⓘ Titan Acorn Barnacle

Megabalanus coccopoma

Authority: (Darwin, 1854)

Description: The color is pink overall. Its size dwarfs all other species found in this area.

Size: Height to 2" (50 mm); width to 2" (50 mm)

Habitat/Ecology: On solid objects, such as wood pilings and cement structures; mid intertidal zone to subtidal waters

Geographic Range: North Carolina to Florida; Brazil; Baja California, Mexico to Ecuador

Notes: The Titan acorn barnacle is an exotic species that likely arrived in this area by attaching to the hulls of ships. It is a native to the Pacific coast of the Americas, from southern California to Ecuador. The body mass of this barnacle reaches a hundred times that of native species.

Similar Species: **Striped Acorn Barnacle** (*Amphibalanus amphitrite*) (see above) is reddish in color but much smaller.

Ribbed Barnacle

Tetraclita stalactifera

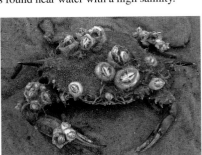

Authority: (Lamarck, 1818)

Other Names: Also known as west Indian volcano barnacle, volcano barnacle; formerly classified as *Tetraclita squamosa stalactifera*

Description: The color of the shell is creamy gray to dark gray. The shell is volcano-shaped, with numerous ribs running the entire length of the plates to the base.

Size: Height to 1.6" (40 mm); width to 1.6" (40 mm)

Habitat/Ecology: On rocks, wharfs, and similar solid objects, and in tidepools at sheltered locations; mid to low intertidal zone

Geographic Range: Florida to the West Indies

Notes: This species is often found as a solitary barnacle—unlike many other species that cluster. The ribbed barnacle is always found near water with a high salinity.

Crab Barnacle

Chelonibia patula

Authority: (Ranzani, 1818)

Other Name: Formerly classified as *Balanus ehclytrypetes*

Description: The color is nearly white or buff. The shape is flattened overall, with a small opening and a fleshy membrane. The shell is light and fragile.

Size: Height to 0.3" (8 mm); width to 0.9" (22 mm)

Habitat/Ecology: Attached to the shell of crabs, especially the blue crab (see p. 236) and horseshoe crab (see p. 225)

Geographic Range: Chesapeake Bay to Brazil; West Indies; Australia; Japan

Notes: Little is known about the natural history of the crab barnacle. Several individuals are often found on the carapace of a crab. The range of this species is nearly worldwide but only in warm seas.

Turtle Barnacle

Chelonibia testudinaria

Authority: (Linnaeus, 1758)

Other Name: Formerly classified as *Chelonobia testudinaria*

Description: The color is white overall. It has flattened shape with distinct radii that are transversely notched or grooved.

Size: Normally height to 0.7" (18 mm); width to 2" (48 mm); larger in tropical areas
Habitat/Ecology: On the shell of the loggerhead sea turtle
Geographic Range: Common from North Carolina southward; occasional records as far north as Delaware Bay; all tropical and warm temperate seas
Notes: The turtle barnacle is widely distributed in tropical and temperate seas and is likely present wherever its usual host, the loggerhead turtle, occurs. You'll only encounter this barnacle when loggerhead sea turtles come ashore to lay their eggs. It is truly amazing that a barnacle can base its whole life on the attachment to the shell of sea turtles. This species rarely attaches to other host species.

Smooth Pelagic Goose Barnacle

Lepas anatifera

Authority: Linnaeus, 1758
Other Names: Also known as common goose barnacle, goose barnacle, pelagic goose barnacle
Description: The color of the plates varies from white to pale blue, edged with a wide, bright orange band, and the stalk is dark purplish brown. The plates are smooth without ridges. The stalk is long, dark, flexible, and rubber-like, and able to attach to hard surfaces.
Size: Height to 1.75" (44 mm)
Habitat/Ecology: On floating objects, including bottles, boards, buoys, and similar objects
Geographic Range: Cosmopolitan
Notes: This pelagic species lives in the open seas and is only observed when it is washed ashore after storms. It is sometimes found attached to the shells of the common purple sea-snail (see p. 75).

This barnacle was always considered as a filter feeder; however, it has been found that it also feeds on small fishes and small floating pelagic jellies, as well as microscopic plankton. Be sure to check colonies of barnacles when they wash ashore, as they sometimes contain a barnacle predator: the caterpillar fireworm (see p. 43).

Spiny Pelagic Goose Barnacle

Lepas pectinata

Authority: Spengler, 1793
Other Names: Also known as duck barnacle, goose barnacle, pelagic goose barnacle, scaled goose barnacle
Description: The color of the plates is white to pale blue, lightly edged with orange, and the stalk is orange. The plates are smooth, with radial striations and scales, dark ridges, and spines at the edge of their plates. The stalk is short, flexible, and able to attach to hard surfaces.
Size: Height to 1" (2.5 cm)
Habitat/Ecology: On floating objects, including bottles, boards, buoys, and similar objects
Geographic Range: Cosmopolitan

Notes: The common name "goose barnacle" probably refers to the long neck of this genus and the old myth that they gave rise to geese. Small specimens often cling to the floating shells of the ram's horn squid (see p. 197).

Sea Whip Barnacle

Conopea galeata

Authority: (Linnaeus, 1771)
Other Name: Also known as seawhip barnacle
Description: The color is brown but often not visible, as the sea whip's polyps are embedded in the barnacle's tissue. The barnacle has a diamond-shaped profile.
Size: Width to 0.6" (15 mm)
Habitat/Ecology: Embedded in sea whips; shallow subtidal depths to 100' (30 m) deep
Geographic Range: New Jersey to Florida; more common south of Cape Hatteras

Notes: This barnacle is often discovered when sea whips (see p. 10) wash ashore after a storm. The sea whip tissue often grows over the barnacle, covering it. As a result, the sea whip barnacle simply looks like a bump on the sea whip rather than a separate organism.

SHRIMPS, CRABS, ISOPODS, AMPHIPODS, AND ALLIES (Class Malacostraca)

All members of this large class have three body parts: head, thorax, and abdomen. They also have compound stalked or sessile eyes, a two-chambered stomach, and normally eight legs (the first pair of which are often used as pincers). In addition, there are also appendages called pleopods, or swimmerets, that hang from the abdomen (swimming legs for brooding the eggs, capturing food, or using as gills).

Tide-pool Scud

Gammarus oceanicus

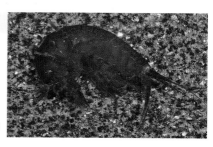

Authority: Segerstråle, 1947
Other Name: Also known as scud
Description: Color varies considerably from olive-green to reddish. Its shape is flattened—higher than it is wide. The telson (the last abdomen segment) is normally longer than it is wide and noticeably split. Two pairs of antennae are equal in length.
Size: Length normally to 1" (25 mm); width to 0.25" (6 mm)
Habitat/Ecology: In tidepools or on rocks and algae; low intertidal zone to water 100' (30 m) deep
Geographic Range: Arctic to Chesapeake Bay
Notes: This scud is a large species with kidney-shaped eyes and seven pairs of legs. It is one of the more common species found at the high intertidal zone. At deeper levels, it is one of numerous similar species that requires a microscope to identify.

The tide-pool scud is a predator that feeds on worms, small crustaceans, and other invertebrates. It is easy to observe in a shallow tidepool because of its large size.

Pink Beach Hopper

Maera danae

Authority: (Stimpson, 1853)
Other Names: Also known as beach hopper; formerly classified as *Leptothoe danae*
Description: Color is pink overall, with small black eyes. The first antennae are noticeably longer than the second antennae and nearly half the body length. The telson is deeply bilobed—each lobe bears many setae (bristles).
Size: Length to 0.75" (18 mm)
Habitat/Ecology: Among rocks and gravel, often when mud has accumulated; low intertidal zone to water 328' (100 m) deep

Geographic Range: Gulf of St. Lawrence to Cape Cod; Alaska to Monterey Bay, California

Notes: This colorful amphipod is one of the more common species found in the low intertidal zone. Female pink beach hoppers carry their eggs from March to May along the Atlantic Coast of the United States. Their lifespan is likely one or two years.

Bigclaw Skeleton Shrimp

Caprella equilibra

Authority: Say, 1818
Other Name: Formerly classified as *Caprella esmarckii*
Description: Color overall is relatively clear, with red-brown spots. Shaped like an aquatic praying mantis. No spines present on the body or cephalon (head region). Males have elongated body segments.
Size: Length to 0.9" (23 mm)
Habitat/Ecology: On a variety of substrates, including algae, seagrass, bryozoans, bivalves, and sponges—often attached to floating docks and pilings; shallow subtidal depths
Geographic Range: Mississippi to Florida, Gulf of Mexico; Europe; nearly cosmopolitan
Notes: Numerous species of skeleton shrimp are present along our Atlantic shores. This is one of the more common skeleton shrimp found at docks and similar locations. It was originally described in 1818 when it was collected from Sullivan's Island near Charleston, South Carolina.

   Two oval appendages are attached to the body segments of a skeleton shrimp below its gnathopods (leg-like appendages) that hold its large dactyli (claws). These oval appendages are its gills. The cephalon also has two pairs of antennae. Male skeleton shrimp often appear much different than females of the same species.

Smooth Skeleton Shrimp

Paracaprella tenuis

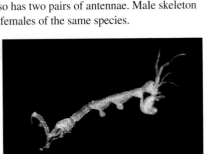

Authority: Mayer, 1903
Other Names: Also known as skeleton shrimp; formerly classified as *Paracaprella simplex*
Description: Body color is reddish brown overall. The body is smooth, lacking spines and often described as "nondescript" with no noteworthy setae on its antennae; it lacks a rostrum.
Size: Length to 0.4" (10 mm)

Habitat/Ecology: On algae, sea grasses, hydroids, sponges, and bryozoan colonies; low intertidal zone to water 72' (21.6 m) deep

Geographic Range: Gulf of St. Lawrence to Florida; Gulf of Mexico

Notes: This is one of three skeleton shrimp most commonly encountered along the Atlantic Coast of the United States. The bigclaw skeleton shrimp (see p. 208) and the long-horn skeleton shrimp (see below) are the other two. The males of most skeleton shrimp are larger and often look quite different than the female.

Similar Species: Long-horn Skeleton Shrimp (*Aeginina longicornis*) is a large, distinctive species with elongated antennae. It reaches 2.1" (54 mm) in length and is commonly encountered from Arctic to North Carolina.

Northern Gribble

Limnoria lignorum

Authority: (Rathke, 1799)

Other Names: Also known as gribble, termite of the sea

Description: The coloration is grayish overall. Its body is slender, with seven pairs of legs. The dorsal surface of the last segment is smooth. The holes it drills reach a maximum of 0.06" (1.6 mm) in diameter.

Size: Length to 0.2" (5 mm)

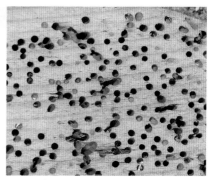

Wood destroyed by the northern gribble

Habitat/Ecology: Burrowing into submerged, untreated wood; low intertidal zone to shallow subtidal depths

Geographic Range: Newfoundland to Rhode Island

Notes: In earlier times this species and others caused great destruction along our shorelines—especially to wooden boats. With current practices of using preservatives and concrete, this species is not as destructive. As with all isopods, this species carries its eggs in a pouch under the body after fertilization. Once the twenty to thirty eggs hatch, the young begin to bore their own tunnels from the sides of their parents' burrow. As a result, the infestation spreads rapidly. Under optimum conditions, you may encounter up to 400 individuals in a square inch of wood. Normally, both a male and female are present in each burrow, with the female at the end of the burrow doing all the boring. This species feeds upon wood fibers, but the fungus that lives in wet wood is its main food.

Similar Species: Southern Gribble (*Limnoria tripunctata*) is similar-looking, with a row of tiny bumps along the edge of its telson. Its range is restricted, however, from Rhode Island to Venezuela.

Common Shipworm (*Teredo navalis*) (see p. 195) bores larger holes up to 0.33" (0.8 cm) in diameter.

Baltic Isopod

Idotea baltica

Authority: (Pallas, 1772)
Other Name: Also known as smooth seaweed isopod
Description: Color varies widely from tannish green to dark green, mottled red, brown, or patterned with black and white, etc. The long body is slender with smooth sides and seven thoracic segments, each bearing a pair of walking legs, along with a tailpiece which is a quarter of the body length. The tailpiece has a squarish end with a point in the middle.
Size: Length to 1" (25 mm); width to 0.25" (6 mm)
Habitat/Ecology: On exposed rocky shores, rock jetties, and pools, as well as on seaweeds and eelgrass beds; low intertidal zone to shallow subtidal waters
Geographic Range: Gulf of St. Lawrence to North Carolina
Notes: The Baltic isopod is the largest isopod present along the northeastern coast of North America.

It feeds on decaying vegetation, especially northern rockweed (see p. 293). If you venture to intertidal and shallow waters at night, you may come across this species.

Sharp-tailed Isopod

Idotea phosphorea

Authority: Harger, 1873
Other Name: Also known as sharp-tail isopod
Description: Color is quite variable, including brown, white, red, yellow, greenish, gray—in solid colors, banded, or mottled. The long body is slender, with smooth sides and an arrowhead-shaped tailpiece.
Size: Length to 0.5" (13 mm); width to 0.02" (5 mm)
Habitat/Ecology: On rocky shores, rock jetties, gravel bottoms, algae, tidepools; low intertidal zone to shallow subtidal waters
Geographic Range: Gulf of St. Lawrence to Cape Cod
Notes: Sharp-tailed isopods feed on vegetation, including dead eelgrass leaves and associated diatoms and detritus.

Sea Pill Bug

Sphaeroma quadridentatum

Authority: Say, 1818

Other Names: Also known as marine
roly-poly; formerly classified as
Sphaeroma quadridentata

Description: Color is dark, often with
tiny mottled white spots. Overall body
shape is round, with numerous narrow
plates covering the dorsal surface.

Size: Length to 0.43" (11 mm)

Habitat/Ecology: On barnacles, pilings, seaweeds, and similar locations; low intertidal zone

Geographic Range: Cape Cod to Florida

Notes: This pill bug of the sea or "marine roly-poly" rolls itself up into a ball when it
is disturbed, using its outer plates to protect itself.

 Exotic Sea Roach

Ligia exotica

Authority: Roux, 1828

Other Names: Also known as sea roach,
boat roach, wharf roach, wharf roach
isopod

Description: Color of the body varies
from brown to nearly black. The shape
is ovoid, and its large eyes are kidney-
shaped. The last pair of appendages (uropods) are about half the length of the body.

Size: Length to 1.25" (32 mm); width to 0.6" (16 mm)

Habitat/Ecology: On rocks, sea walls, dock pilings, and even small boats; splash
intertidal zone

Geographic Range: New Jersey to Florida and the West Indies

Notes: The exotic sea roach is a swift species that can become extremely abundant
with the right conditions.

Similar Species: Northern Sea Roach (*Ligia oceanica*) is a similar-looking but
smaller species with a pair of much shorter uropods reaching only a quarter of the
body length. They are forked, extending backward from the sides of the tailpiece.

MANTIS SHRIMPS (Order Stomatopoda)

Common Mantis Shrimp

Squilla empusa

Authority: Say, 1818
Other Names: Also known as mantis shrimp, mud shrimp
Description: Color varies from pale white to green. The shrimp-like body is flattened. This large species has mantis-like claws and three weak pairs of walking legs.
Size: Length to 10" (25 cm)
Habitat/Ecology: In sand or mud; low intertidal zone to water 508' (154 m) deep
Geographic Range: Maine to Florida and Gulf
Notes: This common species is often caught in fishing trawls. It is not actually a shrimp, although it looks very much like a flattened shrimp. Several species of invertebrates have been found living in burrows with the common mantis shrimp, including a flatworm, polychaete worm, shrimp, copepod, and crab. This species is also sometimes parasitized by the isopod *Pseudione upogebiae*, which forms a large bump on one side of the mantis shrimp's carapace.
Similar Species: **Flat-browed Mud Shrimp** (*Upogebia affinis*) is a similar-looking, but unrelated shrimp that builds its burrows in sand and mud. The front of its carapace is flat and covered with tufts of short bristles, and its second pair of legs lacks claws.

Small Mantis Shrimp

Coronis scolopendra

Authority: Latreille, 1828
Other Names: Also known as mantis shrimp; formerly classified as *Coronis excavatrix*, *Lysiosquilla excavatrix*
Description: Color of the males is translucent pale yellow, while the females are dark brown. This species is small, with an elongated body that has six equal segments on the abdomen.
Size: Length to 2.75" (70 mm)
Habitat/Ecology: In clean, coarse sand at sheltered locations; low intertidal zone to water 5' (1.5 m) deep
Geographic Range: North Carolina to Brazil
Notes: The small mantis shrimp lives in burrows that often have more than one entrance. These burrows can reach as deep as 10" (25 cm). This mantis shrimp feeds on a variety of small fishes.

SHRIMP AND CRABS (Order Decopoda)

Brown Shrimp

Farfantepenaeus aztecus

Authority: (Ives, 1891)
Other Name: Formerly classified as
   Penaeus aztecus
Description: Color normally varies
   from brown to grayish brown, but on
   occasion, red and green specimens are
   found. The first three pairs of legs are
armed with small, nearly equal-size pincers. The abdomen features long grooves
without a spot on the abdomen (see similar species below). Their antennae are also
much longer than their body.
Size: Length to 10" (25 cm)
Habitat/Ecology: On muddy sand and mud bottoms of estuaries and littoral locations;
   low intertidal zone to water 363' (110 m) deep and on occasion to 545' (165 m)
Geographic Range: Cape Cod to Caribbean
Notes: This is a one of our largest shrimps, reaching up to an amazing 10" (25 cm) in
   length. Average specimens, however, are smaller. Other species may also be encountered, however, they are not as common.
Similar Species: Pink Shrimp (*Penaeus duorarum*) is a similar species that has a
   groove running the entire length of the carapace on both sides of midline with a dark
   abdominal spot.

Peppermint Shrimp

Lysmata wurdemanni

Authority: (Gibbes, 1850)
Other Names: Also known as red
   cleaning shrimp, veined shrimp
Description: Color is translucent white
   overall, with bright red stripes.
Size: Length to 2.8" (70 mm)
Habitat/Ecology: On wharf pilings and
   around various sponges, hydroids, and tunicates; low intertidal zone to water 122'
   (37 m) deep
Geographic Range: Egg Harbor, New Jersey, to Florida, Texas, and Caribbean; Brazil
Notes: The peppermint shrimp is a fast and visually striking species that is aptly
   named—it looks like peppermint candy. Peppermint shrimps, and others in the genus
   Lysmata, work as cleaning shrimps, removing tissue debris, loose skin, and parasites
   off the surface of fishes, as well as large crustaceans. They actually actively seek the
   shrimp out for this function. The peppermint shrimp will approach fish rocking back
   and forth rhythmically, perhaps to assess the potential client and determine if it's a
   friend or foe.

Sevenspine Bay Shrimp

Crangon septemspinosa

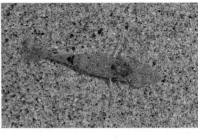

Authority: Say, 1818
Other Names: Also known as sand
shrimp, bay shrimp; occasionally listed
as *C. septemspinosus*
Description: Body is transparent, buff to
gray, with many irregular, tiny, black
spots. The rostrum is short and lacks teeth. This shrimp has claws (which is unusual
for a shrimp) on its first pair of walking legs.
Size: Length to 2.75" (70 mm); height to 0.5" (13 mm)
Habitat/Ecology: On sandy shores and eelgrass beds; low intertidal zone to water
300' (91 m) deep and occasionally to 1485' (450 m)
Geographic Range: Arctic to Florida; Alaska; Japan
Notes: Members of the *Crangon* clan are well known for living in sand and being able
to bury themselves under its surface in mere seconds. The eyes of this species are
positioned on the top of its head, allowing it to see potential prey while being nearly
completely buried in the sand. The sevenspine bay shrimp favors both open shores
and inside bays.

Brown Rock Shrimp

Sicyonia brevirostris

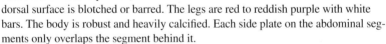

Authority: Stimpson, 1871
Other Names: Also known as rock
shrimp; formerly classified as
Eusicyonia brevirostris, *Pontophilus
brevirostris*
Description: The color of the carapace
varies from white to pinkish, and the
dorsal surface is blotched or barred. The legs are red to reddish purple with white
bars. The body is robust and heavily calcified. Each side plate on the abdominal segments only overlaps the segment behind it.
Size: Length to 4" (10 cm)
Habitat/Ecology: On rock jetties, among rubble, or on protected sand beaches; low
intertidal zone to subtidal waters 1406' (426 m) deep
Geographic Range: Gulf of Maine to Gulf of Mexico; Cuba
Notes: The brown rock shrimp is a carnivore that dines on a variety of foods, including bivalves, gastropods, worms, and crustaceans. Fish are their main predators.
Their maximum lifespan is about twenty-two months. This species has been har-
vested commercially in the Gulf of Mexico.

Marsh Grass Shrimp

Palaemonetes vulgaris

Authority: (Say, 1818)

Other Names: Also known as common shore shrimp, grass shrimp

Description: The color of the translucent carapace is light tan or white, with a few red, yellow, and blue spots; the eyestalks more red-brown. The body is slender and elongated, with the last abdominal segment having no dorsolateral grooves on the rear portion of the carapace. There is no hepatic spine, and the first half of the body is widest, with a distinct bend in middle. The rostrum tip is pointed upward, displaying numerous teeth along the top of the beak.

Ovigerous (egg carrying) female

Size: Length to 1.75" (44 mm); height to 0.25" (6 mm)

Habitat/Ecology: In tidal creeks and salt marshes, docks, oyster reefs, and pilings; often among submerged seaweeds; low intertidal zone to water 45' (14 m) deep

Geographic Range: Gaspé Peninsula to Yucatán Peninsula

Notes: The marsh grass shrimp, along with the daggerblade grass shrimp (see below), is considered to be the most common shrimp you'll encounter at the seashore. The body of marsh grass shrimp has cells that contain red, yellow, blue, or white pigments that can be expanded independently, allowing the shrimp to actually change its coloration according to the colors of its environment.

Similar Species: **Daggerblade Grass Shrimp** (*Palaemonetes pugio*) have more yellow on their eyestalks. A distinctive rostrum bears several dorsal teeth, as well as three distinct ventral teeth.

Slender Shrimps

Hippolyte spp.

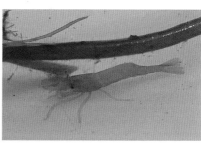

Authority: Leach, 1814

Other Name: Also known as grass shrimps

Description: Colors vary widely, from mottled brown-red to bright green, often resembling the vegetation these shrimps live with. The rostrum is long, and the abdomen is sharply bent. The first and second legs bear claws—the first is stronger and short; the second has a carpus (wrist) that is divided into three joints.

Size: Length 0.75" (19 mm)

Habitat/Ecology: On seaweeds and eelgrass in shallow estuaries; low intertidal zone to shallow subtidal waters

Geographic Range: Connecticut to Brazil

Notes: The shrimps in this group are quite small, especially when compared with some of the other species found in our area. They are adept at hiding among seaweeds and eelgrass (see p. 307). The best location to observe this group of shrimps is at a dock located near eelgrasses.

Similar Species: Eelgrass Broken-back Shrimp (*Hippolyte zostericola*) is commonly found among eelgrasses (*Zostera* spp., see p. 307), with its green body color making it inconspicuous. This small species only reaches a length of 0.7" (1.8 cm).

Sargassum Shrimp

Leander tenuicornis

Authority: (Say, 1818)

Other Names: Also known as brown grass shrimp; formerly classified as *Palaemon tenuicornis*

Description: Overall the body is brown to green, olive, or yellow with opaque spots. The large rostrum has numerous teeth on both the upper and lower edges.

Size: Length to 2" (47 mm)

Habitat/Ecology: On floating gulfweed as well as submerged seaweeds; on pilings and wharves

Geographic Range: Tropical and subtropical waters all over the world except for the west coast of Americas; Bay of Fundy (occasionally) to Falkland Islands

Notes: The sargassum shrimp is often found washed ashore, clinging to stranded pelagic gulfweeds. This habitat is so restricted that it eliminates most other shrimps' presence. Although this species is found on other seaweeds, it is more likely to be observed on gulfweeds by a beachcomber.

Similar Species: Slender Sargassum Shrimp (*Latreutes fucorum*) is a short, to 0.8" (2 cm) long, species that is transparent, brown, yellow, or colorless. It often has bright blue spots on its body, and its rostrum has no teeth on the upper or lower edges. As its common name suggests, it is also lives on gulfweeds.

Arrow Shrimp

Tozeuma carolinense

Authority: Kingsley, 1878

Other Name: Formerly classified as *Angasia carolinensis*

Description: Color is normally green but can also be brownish, red, purple, or transparent depending upon foods and habitat. Its body is slender and elongated. A prominent abdominal hump is present, but not a sharp bend as with broken back shrimps. The rostrum is long and slender, with a slight upturn and spines on the ventral surface only.

Size: Length to 2" (50 mm)

Habitat/Ecology: On marine grasses normally; low intertidal zone to water 247' (75 m) deep

Geographic Range: Cape Cod to Brazil

Notes: The arrow shrimp is common in shallow waters with various types of vegetation. It often swims with its body in a vertical position, then rests by clinging on the surrounding vegetation. This shrimp is also well known for its ability to remain motionless when disturbed—relying on its coloration and body shape for protection.

Spotted Bumblebee Shrimp

Gnathophyllum modestum

Authority: Hay, 1917

Other Name: Also known as bumblebee shrimp

Description: The body is transparent overall with many large, scattered brown, yellow, and orange spots and numerous dark spots. The legs are banded with brown or purple. The body is thick, with a rounded abdomen. The first two pairs of legs have claws, and the second pair are longer.

Size: Length to 0.8" (21 mm)

Habitat/Ecology: On sea urchins, coral, and sponges; near the low intertidal zone to water 89' (27 m) deep

Geographic Range: Beaufort, North Carolina, to Florida; Gulf of Mexico

Notes: The spotted bumblebee shrimp is one of the easiest shrimps to identify. Although this colorful species is never very abundant, it is always a real pleasure to view.

Bigclaw Snapping Shrimp

Alpheus heterochaelis

Authority: Say, 1818

Other Names: Also known as common snapping shrimp, tiger pistol shrimp, big-clawed snapping shrimp

Description: The color of the body is a translucent green, with purple tinges on the sides of the carapace. Claws are present on the first and second legs. One oversize claw on the first pair has a notch in both the upper and lower sides at the base.

Size: Length to 2" (50 mm).

Habitat/Ecology: In rocky shores, among shells and stones, and often on oyster beds; low intertidal zone to water 100' (30 m) deep

Geographic Range: Chesapeake Bay to Brazil

Notes: Snapping, or pistol shrimps, have a large, modified claw that is often used to make a sharp, popping noise—hence their common names. People at oyster beds and similar areas at low tide can sometimes hear these sounds. It was assumed that these snapping noises were the sound of two claws hitting together, but research has shown that is not the case. The shrimp actually shoots a jet of water at a very high velocity, which generates low pressure, creating a bubble in the jet that collapses with a loud snapping sound. Each bubble is tiny, but it holds an amazing amount of energy. The bigclaw snapping shrimp is the largest snapping shrimp found in our region.

Striped Snapping Shrimp

Alpheus formosus

Authority: Gibbes, 1850

Other Name: Formerly classified as *Crangon formosus*

Description: The overall color is yellowish or greenish brown, with fine speckles of orange. There is also a prominent narrow light stripe along the body's mid-dorsal line. The carapace is half the length of the abdomen.

Size: Length to 1.5" (40 mm)

Habitat/Ecology: On rocky shores with rubble, and mud flats, seawalls, and wrecks; low intertidal zone to water 135' (42 m) deep

Geographic Range: Beaufort, North Carolina, to Brazil; Bermuda

Notes: The striped snapping shrimp is best identified by its coloration. It is a small species that is not as common as the big-clawed shrimp.

Similar Species: Bigclaw Snapping Shrimp (*Alpheus heterochaelis*) (see p. 217)
Speckled Snapping Shrimp (*Synalpheus fritzmuelleri*) (see p. 219)

Green Snapping Shrimp

Alpheus normanni

Authority: Kingsley, 1878

Other Names: Formerly classified as *Alpheus beanie*, *Crangon beanie*

Description: Overall gray or green with a white median and lateral stripe that is often present with a mottling of dark green or brown. The large claw is normally dark green and banded with yellowish brown to yellow on the inner side.

Size: Length to 1.2" (30 mm)

Habitat/Ecology: On rocky or shelly shores, rubble, pilings, sand burrows, or eelgrass beds; low intertidal zone to water 241' (73 m) deep

Geographic Range: North Carolina to Brazil

Notes: Like all snapping shrimps, the large claw is used for protection against other snapping shrimp. The green snapping shrimp also uses the claw to crush and eat juvenile northern quahog clams (see p. 184).

Speckled Snapping Shrimp

Synalpheus fritzmuelleri

Authority: Coutiere, 1909

Description: The body is transparent overall, with numerous tiny red spots covering much of the body. Its large claw displays various shades of green.

Size: Length to 0.8" (20 mm)

Habitat/Ecology: On reefs and jetties, boulders, crevices, and in sponges; low intertidal zone to water 168' (51 m) deep

Geographic Range: North Carolina to Brazil; Bermuda; St. Helena Island, Baja California, Mexico

Notes: This species is often parasitized by the bopyrid isopod (*Hemiarthrus synalphei*).

Similar Species: Bigclaw Snapping Shrimp (*Alpheus heterochaelis*) (see p. 217)
Striped Snapping Shrimp (*Alpheus formosus*) (see p. 218)

American Lobster

Homarus americanus

Authority: H. Milne-Edwards, 1837

Other Names: Also known as northern lobster, lobster

Description: Color is generally greenish black above and paler below. Rare yellow or blue individuals have also been observed. The body is elongated with two large claws; the largest is a "crusher" claw, and the other is a smaller and sharper "cutter" claw.

Size: In deep water: length to 34" (86 cm); width to 9" (23 cm); intertidal specimens are small

Habitat/Ecology: On rocky and muddy shorelines in quiet bays; low intertidal zone to water 2000' (606 m) deep

Geographic Range: Labrador to North Carolina

Notes: The American lobster is a distinctive and well-known commercial species in the North Atlantic. Intertidal specimens, however, are small. Subtidal specimens over

60 lb. (27 kg) have been captured. Adults reach maturity at about five years and may live for over a hundred years, but few ever reach this age today.

The claws of the lobster are suited for specific feeding tasks. Its larger "crusher" claw is used to crack open hard foods like snails and clams. The smaller and sharper claw is used for dining on its food. The male's first two pairs of swimmerets are specially modified for mating by using them to transfer his sperm cells into the female.

Carolinian Ghost Shrimp

Callichirus major

Authority: (Say, 1818)
Other Name: Formerly classified as *Callianassa major*
Description: The body is transparent gray, with porcelain white claws and a hard section of the carapace. Yellowish to reddish digestive glands and gonads show through the transparent bodies as well. The abdomen is long, gradually widening from the anterior end. The largest claw has a strongly curved finger.
Size: Length of body 3.7" (95 mm)
Habitat/Ecology: In sand on open ocean beaches; low intertidal zone to water 6.6' (2 m) deep

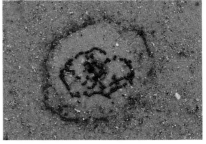

Fecal pellets at burrow entrance

Geographic Range: North Carolina to Florida; Brazil
Notes: The Carolinian ghost shrimp is our largest ghost shrimp, burrowing as deep as 6' (1.8 m) in the sand to make its home. It feeds on organic particles using hairy "brushes" on its front legs to sift through the sand. Its burrow openings are pencil sized and are often encountered with its distinctive fecal pellets (see photo above) at its burrow entrances.

Inside the burrows of the delicate Carolinian ghost shrimp, a commensal crab—the Cristate pea crab (*Pinnixa cristata*)—is often found, along with a tiny orange copepod.

Georgia Ghost Shrimp

Biffarius biformis

This female is gravid (with eggs).

Authority: (Biffar, 1971)
Other Names: Also known as biform ghost shrimp; formerly classified as *Callianassa biformis*
Description: The delicate body is transparent gray, with porcelain white claws. Females have similar sized claws on their first legs, while males have one large and one small claw. A small, smooth rostrum is found on its elongated body. The frontal portion of the carapace is flattened and covered with short bristles.
Size: Length of body to 1.2" (32 mm)
Habitat/Ecology: In protected areas with mud; low intertidal zone to water 33' (10 m) deep
Geographic Range: Massachusetts to Florida
Notes: This delicate-looking species is a very small ghost shrimp and often identified simply by its size, with burrows nearly as thin as a matchstick.
Similar Species: Flat-browed Mud Shrimp (*Upogebia affinis*) is bluish to yellowish gray overall, with a stocky build. Its first legs are hairy; its rostrum is large, flat, and spiny; and its claws are equal in size. Its body may reach 4" (100 mm) long. It is found in muddy sand, often beneath flat stones, ranging from Cape Cod to Brazil. This species makes permanent burrows on mud flats and in shallow estuaries. This mud shrimp is not actually a shrimp but more closely related to hermit crabs.

HERMIT CRABS, PORCELAIN CRABS, AND ALLIES (Family Paguridae)

Longwrist Hermit Crab

Pagurus longicarpus

Authority: Say, 1817
Other Names: Also known as long-clawed hermit crab, long-armed hermit crab, hermit crab, dwarf hermit crab
Description: Color of body varies from grayish to greenish white; pincers are tannish gray to tan, with a stripe down the middle that is edged in white. The right pincer is larger than the left.
Size: Carapace length to 0.5" (13 mm); width to 0.4" (10 mm)
Habitat/Ecology: In sand, mud, rock, and weed bottoms; along open shores and in estuaries; low intertidal zone to water 656' (200 m) deep
Geographic Range: Nova Scotia to Florida and Texas

Notes: Longwrist hermit crabs often bury themselves in mud and sediments with only their eyestalks left uncovered. They remain there most of the day to emerge at twilight. During autumn in New England, the water temperatures cool considerably, and this species begins to migrate to deeper waters. Once the temperatures reach 39° F (4° C), the crabs make a depression in the muddy bottom where they are covered by sediments and will remain for the winter.

Many hermit crabs occupy a specific species of shell. In many Atlantic areas, female longwrist hermit crabs use the shells of the eastern mud snail (see p. 117) and the Atlantic oyster drill. Adult males are always larger than females, and so they normally choose the common periwinkle's shell (see p. 65).

Acadian Hermit Crab

Pagurus acadianus

Authority: Benedict, 1901
Other Name: Also known as Acadian hermit
Description: The color of the carapace is brown, and the legs are orange or reddish brown with white at the base. The hand of the pincers displays an orange to reddish stripe down the middle. The right walking leg is much larger than the left.
Size: Carapace length to 1.25" (32 mm); width to 1" (25 mm)
Habitat/Ecology: In tidepools and among rocks; low intertidal zone to water 1600' (488 m) deep
Geographic Range: Labrador to Chesapeake Bay
Notes: Hermit crabs require discarded snail shells for their protection. Their soft bodies fit snugly into these shells. As the hermit crabs grow they require new, larger shells. If a crab is unable to locate a large enough shell, it will remain in a shell that is too small for its body. This may prevent it from completely retreating inside its shell, rendering it vulnerable to predators. It may also restrict its growth so that it cannot increase its body size as it normally would.

Hermit crabs mate when they are outside their shells at molting time.

Flat-clawed Hermit Crab

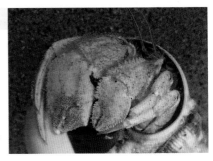

Pagurus pollicaris

Authority: Say, 1817
Other Names: Also known as flat claw hermit, thumb-clawed hermit crab
Description: The body and pincers are tan to light brown, with the pincers becoming white in the southern portion of their range. The pincers are

noticeably flattened and semicircular, and the right pincer is larger, with serrated edges.

Size: Carapace length to 1.25" (31 mm)

Habitat/Ecology: In bays and estuaries; below the low intertidal zone to shallow subtidal waters

Geographic Range: Penobscot Bay to Florida and Texas

Notes: This species is occasionally found in empty shells after they have been tossed ashore during a storm. Shells of the shark eye (see p. 92) and whelk shells make up its home of choice. They use the protection of their two pincers to close up the opening when they have retreated inside their shell. A hermit crab has five pairs of legs—three pairs of which protrude from its shell. The first pair has pincers; the second and third pairs are longer and used for walking; the fourth and fifth pairs are much smaller to brace the crab inside its shell.

Atlantic Hairy Hermit Crab

Pagurus arcuatus

Authority: Squires, 1964

Other Name: Also known as hairy hermit crab

Description: Overall color ranges from brown to reddish brown. This species is hairy overall, with pincers on the first pair of walking legs. The right pincer is larger and covered with low, rounded projections.

Size: Carapace length to 1.25" (32 mm); width to 1" (25 mm)

Habitat/Ecology: In rocky shores and in tidepools; low intertidal zone to water 900' (274 m) deep

Geographic Range: Arctic to Long Island Sound

Notes: This species, like the Acadian hermit crab (see p. 222), is a northern hermit that is easy to identify. Large individuals often use the shells of Stimpson whelk (see p. 108) or the waved whelk (see p. 107) for their homes. Small specimens are often observed in tidepools.

Striped Hermit Crab

Clibanarius vittatus

Authority: (Bosc, 1802)

Other Name: Also known as thinstripe hermit

Description: Color overall is greenish to brown; the legs are brown or greenish, striped lengthwise with white to pale orange. The first pair of walking legs are armed with pincers that are equal in size and twice as long as wide.

Size: Carapace length to 1.25" (32 mm); width to 0.5" (13 mm)

Habitat/Ecology: On beaches, mudflats, harbors, and bays of protected shores; low intertidal zone to shallow subtidal waters

Geographic Range: Virginia to Florida and Texas; West Indies to Brazil

Notes: The striped hermit crab is boldly marked with pinstripes on its legs, making it an easy hermit to identify. It commonly uses shells of large moonsnails (see pp. 93–95), whelks, and Scotch bonnets (see p. 97).

Hermit crabs dine on detritus and carrion—nature's sanitary engineers of the beach.

Giant Red Hermit Crab

Petrochirus diogenes

Authority: (Linnaeus, 1758)

Other Names: Also known as giant hermit crab, giant red hermit

Description: The color of the body is reddish overall. The pincers have white spots, the antennae are red-and-white-banded, and the eyes are blue. Both pincers are covered with heavy, irregular scales, and the right pincer is noticeably larger.

Size: Carapace length to 4.75" (121 mm); width to 2.25" (57 mm)

Habitat/Ecology: In sandy sites and seagrass flats; shallow subtidal waters to water 300' (91m) deep

Geographic Range: North Carolina to Florida and Texas; West Indies

Notes: When a hermit crab occupies the shell of the pink conch (see p. 86), you know it's large! This hermit is the giant of the Atlantic Coast. It's only found after a storm when it is thrown to the shore with the wind and waves.

Caribbean Land Hermit Crab

Coenobita clypeatus

Authority: Fabricius, 1787

Other Names: Also known as common land hermit crab, land hermit crab, purple pincher hermit crab, soldier crab; *Cenobita clypeata* (incorrect spelling)

Description: The color of the body varies widely, from light brown to reddish brown. The legs are marked with many purple dots and fine hairs. The pincers are unequal: the left pincer is larger, rounded, and bright purple.

Size: Carapace length to 1.5" (38 mm); width to 0.5" (13 mm)

Habitat/Ecology: Among plants, including in forests; above high-tide line

Geographic Range: Florida to the West Indies

Notes: The Caribbean land hermit crab is the only land hermit found on our Atlantic Coast. This hermit is an omnivore and scavenger that feeds on almost anything, from fallen fruit to rotting wood, carrion, and sea turtle eggs.

This species is normally nocturnal, but it is sometimes observed during the early hours and later during the day—just before sunset. Land hermit crabs only live on land, not in the ocean. Only females return to the ocean to release larvae during reproduction. They are also sometimes kept as pets.

Atlantic Horseshoe Crab

Limulus polyphemus

Authority: (Linnaeus, 1758)

Other Names: Also known as horseshoe crab, king crab

Description: The carapace is greenish tan in young specimens to brown in mature individuals. The carapace is horseshoe-shaped, with a dome contour that covers the crab's legs from view. A spiked tail is also present.

Size: Length to 24" (61 cm); width to 12" (30 cm)

Habitat/Ecology: In sand or mud shores; low intertidal zone to water 75' (23 m) deep

Geographic Range: Gulf of Maine to Gulf of Mexico

Notes: This primitive-looking creature is not a true crab—it is actually more closely related to the spider. During the time of their reproduction at high tide, each female digs a hole above the low intertidal zone for 200 to 300 greenish eggs. These are then fertilized by the male and buried in the sand for several weeks. Mini Atlantic horseshoe crabs will eventually hatch from there to begin their lives. Atlantic horseshoe crabs reach sexual maturity at nine to ten years and can live to reach seventeen years old. At maturity they may weigh 10 lb. (4.5 kg).

Atlantic horseshoe crabs have interesting eating habits. First, they grind up their food with the base of their legs, and then they push it into their mouth, which is located on the underside of the body, between the legs. Their food includes worms, clams, and other invertebrates.

The horseshoe crab flatworm (*Bdelloura candida*) is a very small—to 0.5" (14 mm)—flatworm that is found on the gills of the Atlantic horseshoe crab. Its color varies from yellowish to white, and it possesses a sucker on its squared rear end. Its range is the same as that of its host.

Pentagonal Porcelain Crab

Megalobrachium soriatum

Authority: (Say, 1818)

Other Name: Also known as eroded porcelain crab

Description: The color is brown to gray overall. The carapace is shaped like a hexagon with a bumpy surface. The chelipeds (legs bearing large pincers) are covered in tubercules. Antennae are approximately as long as the carapace.

Size: Carapace length to 0.3" (8 mm)

Habitat/Ecology: Among rocks, corals, and sponges; low intertidal zone to water 561' (171 m) deep

Geographic Range: Off Cape Hatteras to Texas; West Indies; Mexico; Panama

Notes: The pentagonal porcelain crab is truly an amazing species to be able to live in the low intertidal zone, as well as the depths of greater than 2.5 miles (4 km) in the ocean.

Spotted Porcelain Crab

Porcellana sayana

Authority: (Leach, 1820)

Other Name: Also known as Say's porcelain crab

Description: The overall color is reddish to rusty brown, with a widely variable pattern of yellowish or bluish white spots or stripes on the carapace. The carapace is slightly longer than it is wide.

Size: Carapace length to 0.55" (14 mm); width to 0.46" (12 mm)

Habitat/Ecology: In rubble, oyster shells, and rock crevices; low intertidal zone to water 304' (92 m) deep

Geographic Range: Cape Hatteras, to Gulf of Mexico; Brazil

Notes: The spotted porcelain crab is an uncommon species that can be found in crevices and similar locations. It sometimes lives with larger hermit crabs, including the giant red hermit crab (see p. 224) and flat-clawed hermit crab (see p. 222). The relationship of the spotted porcelain crab with these hermits is believed by many sources to be a commensal one. The large shells that these crabs live in are often large enough to house both a porcelain crab and a hermit.

Cherry-striped Porcelain Crab

Petrolisthes galathinus

Authority: (Bosc, 1802)
Other Name: Also known as lined porcelain crab
Description: The color of the body is olive overall, with impressive cherry-red, transverse stripes. The carapace is

rough, with several ridges. The walking legs are hairy and the claws have dense hairs on the outer margin. The wrist joint on each claw bears four teeth.
Size: Carapace length to 0.8" (2 cm)
Habitat/Ecology: Under rocks and in shell hash; in tidepools; low intertidal zone to water 178' (54 m) deep
Geographic Range: North Carolina to Brazil
Notes: This small crab is food for several fishes, including the dusky squirrelfish, rock hind, Nassau grouper, striped drum, Spanish hogfish, and reef scorpionfish.

Ⓘ Green Porcelain Crab

Petrolisthes armatus

Authority: (Gibbes, 1850)
Description: The overall color varies widely from green to orange-brown and mottled with dark brown or blue. The mouthparts also have a noticeable blue coloration and the pincers have an orange spot.
Size: Carapace length to 0.4" (10 mm)
Habitat/Ecology: On rocky shores, oyster reefs, and similar sites; high intertidal zone to shallow subtidal waters
Geographic Range: South Carolina to Florida; Brazil; Gulf of California to Peru; western Africa
Notes: The green porcelain crab is generally considered to be an introduced species; however, it is possible that this has been a recent natural range extension. This crab is a species native to South America that was collected from south Florida as early as the 1930s. It is having a large impact on our oyster reef communities. In some areas, densities greater than 11,000 individuals per square meter have been found during the warmer months of the year.

Eggs are often found on the undersides of females, as with most species of crabs.

Olive-pit Porcelain Crab

Euceramus praelongus

Authority: Stimpson, 1860

Other Names: Also known as long-
headed porcelain crab, olive pit porcelain crab, olivepit porcelain crab

Description: The carapace is greenish
gray to tan, with a patterning of light
and dark lines. The carapace is notice-
ably elongated—the length is greater than twice the width, and its front has three
teeth. The antennae are short—less than the length of the body. Pincers are present
on the first legs.

Size: Carapace length to 0.6" (16 mm)

Habitat/Ecology: On sandy shores with smooth and broken-shell bottoms; low intertidal zone to water 125' (38 m) deep

Geographic Range: Delaware to Gulf of Mexico; Texas

Notes: This crab resembles an olive pit, making it an easy species to identify with its
very descriptive common name. It burrows backward in the sand and in rubble.

Similar Species: Atlantic Mole Crab (*Emerita talpoida*) (see below) has a similar
body shape but does not have pincers, and it digs in the sand.

Atlantic Mole Crab

Emerita talpoida

Authority: (Say, 1817)

Other Names: Also known as Atlantic
sand crab, common mole crab, mole
crab

Description: Color ranges from tan or
beige to purplish. The carapace is
much longer than the width and shaped
like a football with a pointed abdomen. The first pair of antennae are short and hairy;
the second pair of antennae are long and feather-like.

Size: Carapace length to 1.5" (38 mm)

Habitat/Ecology: In sand on wave-swept beaches; high intertidal zone to water 11'
(3.5 m) deep

Geographic Range: Cape Cod to Florida and Texas; Mexico

Notes: The larger individuals are normally female, and males are less than half the
size of the females. This active species digs remarkably fast and is constantly on the
move to maintain its position with the changing tides. It is not at true crab and cannot
pinch when handled, so it is an easy species to view at the seashore. Atlantic mole
crabs are commonly found during the summer months but move to deeper waters for
the winter.

Catherine's Mole Crab

Albunea catherinae

Authority: Boyko, 2002
Other Names: Also known as mole crab; *Albunea paretii* is not a synonym
Description: Overall color varies from off-white to light brown. The carapace is flattened; the width is approximately the same as the length. Antennae are very long and small pincers are present.
Size: Carapace length to 0.75" (20 mm)
Habitat/Ecology: On exposed sandy beaches, especially near inlets; low intertidal zone to water 213' (64 m) deep
Geographic Range: Virginia south to Florida; Gulf of Mexico to Texas
Notes: Catherine's mole crab is not as common as the Atlantic mole crab (see p. 228). Catherine's mole crab looks like a miniature sea mole, while the Atlantic mole crab looks more like a sea football. Catherine's mole crab is also found at a lower position on the beach.
Similar Species: Atlantic Mole Crab (*Emerita talpoida*) (see p. 228)

Calico Box Crab

Hepatus epheliticus

Carapace of the calico box crab

Authority: (Linnaeus, 1763)
Other Names: Also known as Dolly Varden crab, gulf calico crab
Description: The color of the carapace is overall yellowish or grayish to brownish with several large irregular spots of light red with dark borders. The pincers are heavy and equal in size. The length of the carapace is approximately two-thirds the width, and it's shaped vaguely like a fan. A row of coarse, low, round projections are found on the outer front surface.
Size: Carapace length to 2.3" (60 mm); width to 3.4" (88 mm)
Habitat/Ecology: On sandy shores; low intertidal zone to water 300' (91 m) deep
Geographic Range: Chesapeake Bay to Mexico; Cuba; Jamaica; Dominican Republic
Notes: The calico box crab is a member of the box crabs or shame-faced crabs. These crabs place their pincers in front of their faces to keep sand out of their gill chambers. The hermit crab anemone (see p. 17) often attaches to the calico box crab.
Similar Species: Flaming Shame-faced Crab (*Calappa flammea*) (see p. 230) is a similar-looking species, with flame-like streaks on its carapace.

Flaming Shame-faced Crab

Calappa flammea

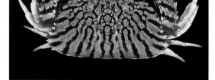

Authority: (Herbst, 1794)
Other Names: Also known as flamed box crab, flame-streaked box crab, shamefaced crab
Description: Carapace color is gray overall, marked with a purplish brown, flame-shaped pattern. The carapace has a distinctive shape, with a back edge that is straight and a front edge with numerous teeth. The pincers are unequal and heavy.
Size: Carapace length to 4" (102 mm); width to 5.5" (140 mm)
Habitat/Ecology: On sandy shores; subtidal waters to 240' (73 m) deep, occasionally to 865' (262 m)
Geographic Range: Cape Hatteras to Florida and Texas; Mexico; Bermuda; Bahamas
Notes: An empty carapace washed ashore after a storm is normally the only hint that this species is present in subtidal waters. The shells of clams, snails, and hermit crabs are chipped away to provide the foods for the flaming shame-faced crab. The shame-faced crabs all hide their face with their large claws, making themselves look somewhat bashful or ashamed. This is normally done when they bury their bodies in the sand.
Similar Species: Calico Box Crab (*Hepatus epheliticus*) (see p. 229) is a similar species that lacks the flame-like streaks on its carapace.

Mottled Purse Crab

Persephona mediterranea

Authority: (Herbst, 1794)
Other Names: Also known as purse crab; formerly classified as *Persephona punctata*, sometimes misspelled *Persephone punctata*
Description: Color varies from grayish to bluish or pinkish, with large, round, reddish brown spots. The shape of the carapace is nearly perfectly round, with a cylindrical front and three prominent spines at the rear.
Size: Carapace length to 2.7" (70 mm); width to 2.6" (67 mm)
Habitat/Ecology: On sandy shores or shelly mud; low intertidal zone to water 180' (55 m) deep
Geographic Range: New Jersey to Florida, Gulf of Mexico; West Indies to Brazil
Notes: Although the scientific name would suggest that this species is from the Mediterranean, this is not the case. This species is only found along the Atlantic Coast of the Americas. The common name of the purse crabs comes from the next to last segment on the female's abdomen. It enlarges enormously in order to allow her eggs to fit inside.

False Arrow Crab

Metoporhaphis calcarata

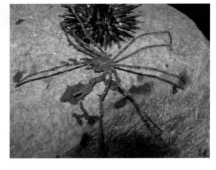

Authority: (Say, 1818)

Other Names: Also known as gulf arrow crab, hairy arrow crab; sometimes misspelled as *Metaporhaphis calcarata*

Description: The carapace color is dirty gray to lemon yellow. The triangular shape is longer than it is wide and narrower at the front. The rostrum is as long or longer than the carapace, and the eyes protrude to the sides. The legs are long and slender—each with a sharp, recurved spine from the third segment of each walking leg.

Size: Carapace length to 1" (24 mm); width to 0.2" (10 mm)

Habitat/Ecology: On hard surfaces with a variety of fouling organisms, including hydroids; low intertidal zone to water 297' (90 m) deep

Geographic Range: Cape Hatteras to Brazil

Notes: The false arrow crab is a rather easy species to identify, as there are no other intertidal species that come close to its description. The size of the carapace does not give a true picture of the size of this species due to the length of its legs.

Atlantic Lyre Crab

Hyas araneus

Authority: (Linnaeus, 1758)

Other Names: Also known as toad crab, great spider crab

Description: The overall color is purplish red, and the legs have bands of red or orange in younger specimens. The body is violin-shaped, with the widest section toward the rear. A small tooth is present behind the eye. The beak is triangular and deeply cleft along the midline

Size: Length to 3.75" (95 mm); width to 2.5" (64 mm)

Habitat/Ecology: On muddy shores, rock, or pebbles; among various kelp, in tidepools; low intertidal zone to water 170' (52 m) deep

Geographic Range: Arctic to Rhode Island

Notes: Various algae and bryozoans are often attached to the carapace of this species to aid in its camouflage. This makes this species one of the more difficult crabs for the beachcomber to find.

Similar Species: Arctic Lyre Crab (*Hyas coarctatus*) is a similar species that is smaller, with a crest-like process on the margin behind the tooth. It ranges from the Arctic to Cape Hatteras.

Six-spined Spider Crab

Libinia dubia

Authority: H. Milne-Edwards, 1834
Other Names: Also known as doubtful
 spider crab, longnose spider crab,
 portly spider crab, southern spider
 crab, spider crab
Description: Overall color is grayish
 yellow to brown. The carapace is oval
and armed with several spines over its surface, including a row of six spines along
the carapace's midline. The rostrum is deeply forked.
Size: Length to 4" (102 mm); width to 3.75" (95 mm)
Habitat/Ecology: On muddy shores and various others; low intertidal zone to water
 150' (45 m) deep
Geographic Range: Cape Cod to Texas; Bahamas; Cuba
Notes: The juveniles of this species and the nine-spined spider crab are not easily
 identified. Mature specimens have developed characteristics for their species;
 however, juveniles have not. Both species display long, thin legs and a fat body,
 giving them a "spidery" appearance.
Similar Species: Nine-spined Spider Crab (*Libinia emarginata*) (see below)

Nine-spined Spider Crab

Libinia emarginata

Authority: Leach, 1815
Other Names: Also known as common
 spider crab, nine-spine spider crab,
 portly spider crab
Description: Overall color is yellowish
 brown to dark brown. The carapace is
 oval and armed with several spines

Juvenile found living in cannonball jelly

over its surface, including a row of nine spines along the carapace's midline. In addition, seven spines form a row behind each eye. The rostrum is only slightly forked.
Size: Length to 4.9" (124 mm)
Habitat/Ecology: On muddy, sandy, or rocky shores; low intertidal zone to water 131'
 (40 m) deep; occasionally to 407' (124 m)
Geographic Range: Nova Scotia to Gulf of Mexico
Notes: Both the nine-spined spider crab and the six-spined spider crab (see above)
 may spend a portion of their juvenile lives traveling. They catch a ride on a jelly,
 especially cannonball jellies (see p. 26), traveling and feeding upon the jelly's tissues
 and tentacles while they catch a ride.

   Young of both spider crabs also decorate their outer shell with seaweed or other
organisms by carefully attaching these to the tiny setae or hook-like hairs on their
carapace. They rub these adornments across their shell to entangle them there. This
helps to camouflage the crabs in their environment. Often, the only way we can

detect them is when they move. Some other organisms that they attach include sponges, bryozoans, ascidians, and hydroids.

Similar Species: Six-spined Spider Crab (*Libinia dubia*) (see p. 232)

Red-ridged Clinging Crab

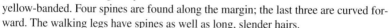

Mithraculus forceps

Authority: A. Milne-Edwards, 1875
Other Names: Also known as rock mithrax, yellow coral crab; formerly classified as *Mithrax forceps*
Description: Color varies from chestnut to yellowish brown or pale yellow, or greenish brown. The legs may be yellow-banded. Four spines are found along the margin; the last three are curved forward. The walking legs have spines as well as long, slender hairs.
Size: Carapace length to 0.8" (21 mm)
Habitat/Ecology: On rocky shores, under corals, and in coral crevices; low intertidal zone to water 180' (54 m) deep
Geographic Range: North Carolina to Gulf of Mexico; Caribbean; Brazil
Notes: The red-ridged clinging crab is a small crab that feeds upon algae among various coral species.

Jonah Crab

Cancer borealis

Authority: Stimpson, 1859
Other Name: Also known as northern crab
Description: Color of the entire crab is red mottled with white. The large teeth on the front and side margins of the carapace are serrated or saw-toothed. The shape of the carapace is fan-shaped, and the pincers are equal in size.
Size: Length to 4" (102 mm); width to 6.25" (16 mm)
Habitat/Ecology: In tidepools and on rocky shores (but their preference is for sandy bottoms); low intertidal zone to water 2620' (799 m) deep
Geographic Range: Nova Scotia to Florida
Notes: Although the Jonah crab prefers colder waters, it is found as far south as Florida. This species is similar to but not as abundant as the Atlantic rock crab (see p. 234).

The Jonah crab mates in late summer, and the female carries the developing eggs over the winter months. She carries her eggs under the abdomen, which is common for many species of crabs. The eggs hatch in early summer to begin their life swimming with the plankton.

Similar Species: Atlantic Rock Crab (*Cancer plebejus*) (see p. 234)

Atlantic Rock Crab

Cancer plebejus

Authority: Poeppig, 1836

Other Names: Also known as rock crab; formerly classified as *Cancer irroratus*

Description: Color is purplish brown, with a dull white pattern overall. The colors vary widely, with juveniles including blue and white. The large blunt teeth on the front and side margins of the carapace are smooth and rounded. The carapace is fan-shaped, and the pincers are equal in size.

Size: Carapace length to 3.5" (89 mm); width to 5.25" (133 mm)

Habitat/Ecology: On mud, rocky, and gravel shores, and in tidepools; low intertidal zone to water 2600' (780 m) deep.

Juvenile

Geographic Range: Labrador to South Carolina

Notes: The Atlantic rock crab is a common commercial species caught in northern waters and marketed throughout the area. Often their empty exoskeletons wash up on the seashore after they have shed them. All crabs shed their exoskeleton in order to grow—a process that allows a larger outer shell to form around their bodies. At this stage they are vulnerable, so they seek out a location to hide, allowing their new exoskeleton to harden.

Similar Species: Jonah Crab (*Cancer borealis*) (see p. 233)

① European Green Crab

Carcinus maenas

Authority: (Linnaeus, 1758)

Other Names: Also known as European shore crab, green crab

Description: Overall color is generally greenish on the dorsal surface, with yellow and black markings. Females are red-orange on their ventral surface, while males and juveniles are yellowish below. Adults have three frontal teeth between their eyes and five marginal teeth along their outer edges.

Size: Carapace length to 2.6" (67 mm); width to 3.1" (79 mm)

Habitat/Ecology: On muddy and rocky shores, jetties, and in tidepools; low intertidal zone to water 20' (6 m) deep; occasionally to 650' (195 m) deep

Geographic Range: Nova Scotia to New Jersey; Panama; Brazil; British Columbia to California; Japan; South Africa; Australia; Europe (native)

Notes: The European green crab is a native of Europe that has expanded its range rapidly over the last few years. This is a swimming crab, although it actually lacks the paddle-shaped hind feet that most species in this group display. Males may live to five years and females typically live to three years, laying between 185,000 to 200,000 brightly colored orange eggs at one time. The European green crab is an omnivore, consuming algae, snails, clams, worms, and a variety of small crustaceans.

Lady Crab

Ovalipes ocellatus

Authority: (Herbst, 1799)
Other Names: Also known as calico crab, ocellated crab
Description: The carapace is yellowish gray, highlighted with leopard-like, purple spots. The carapace front margin bears five similar-size teeth. The last pair of legs are shaped like paddles.

Lady crab carapace

Size: Length to 2.5" (64 mm); width to 3" (79 mm)
Habitat/Ecology: On sand, rock, or mud; low intertidal zone to water 130' (40 m) deep
Geographic Range: Cape Cod to South Carolina. Isolated populations also in Prince Edward Island and Texas
Notes: The lady crab is known for burying itself backward in sand just below the surface. The last pair of legs are paddle-like, indicating that is is a member of the family of swimming crabs (Portunidae). Handle this species with care, as it is reported to be vicious.

Speckled Crab

Arenaeus cribrarius

Authority: (Lamarck, 1818)
Description: The color of the carapace is olive to light brown or gray, decorated with numerous irregular white spots—each of which is highlighted with a dark outline. Similar white spots

are present on the claws. Each side of the carapace is armed with eight teeth and one spine. The last pair of legs are shaped like paddles.
Size: Carapace width to 6" (15 cm)
Habitat/Ecology: In sand; low intertidal zone to water 224' (68 m) deep
Geographic Range: Massachusetts to Brazil
Notes: Like many other crabs, the speckled crab often buries itself completely in sand. It accomplishes this by moving backward and using its claws to flip the surrounding sand.

Blue Crab

Callinectes sapidus

Authority: Rathbun, 1896
Other Name: Also known as common edible crab
Description: The color of the carapace is grayish or greenish, and the walking legs are blue. Males have blue fingers on the hand, and females have red. The carapace width is approximately 2½ times its length. Each side of the carapace is armed with eight teeth and one large spine. A total of four equal-size teeth are present between the eyes. The last pair of legs are shaped like paddles.
Size: Carapace width to 9.25" (23 cm); length to 4" (10.2 cm)
Habitat/Ecology: In sand; low intertidal zone to water 120' (17 m) deep
Geographic Range: Nova Scotia to Uruguay
Notes: The blue crab is a major species of commercial importance for a large area of the Atlantic Coast. As a result a great deal of scientific research has focused upon this species. It is found in nearly all types of estuarine and near shore habitats.
Similar Species: Lesser Blue Crab (*Callinectes similis*) (see below) has a total of four teeth between the eyes, and the outer teeth are much larger.

Lesser Blue Crab

Callinectes similis

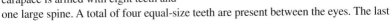

Authority: Williams, 1966
Other Name: Also known as gulf crab
Description: The dorsal side of the carapace is green on the carapace, and there are areas of iridescence at the base of the outer teeth. The claws and walking legs are tinted with vivid purplish to light blue. The carapace is smooth and uniformly granular. Each side of the carapace is armed with eight teeth and one large spine. A total of four teeth are present between the eyes—the outer pair are much larger. The last pair of legs are shaped like paddles.
Size: Carapace width to 4.8" (122 mm); length to 2.1" (55 mm)
Habitat/Ecology: In sand or mud; low intertidal zone to water 1251' (379 m) deep
Geographic Range: Delaware Bay to Yucatán, Mexico
Notes: The lesser blue crab is not an easy species to identify because it resembles the blue crab so closely. This is a smaller species that is not as common as the blue crab, but it can be plentiful at times.
Similar Species: Blue Crab (*Callinectes sapidus*) (see above)

ⓘ Bocourt Swimming Crab

Callinectes bocourti

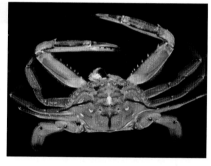

Authority: A. Milne-Edwards, 1879

Other Names: Also known as blunt-tooth swimming crab, red-blue crab

Description: The dorsal side of the cara-pace is olive to forest green, with bold, reddish marks. The walking legs and chelipeds (claws) are red and white. Each side of the carapace is armed with nine teeth. A total of four teeth are present between the eyes. The last pair of legs are shaped like paddles.

Size: Carapace width to 6" (156 mm); length to 3" (76 mm)

Habitat/Ecology: In sand and mud; low intertidal zone to shallow subtidal waters

Geographic Range: Native from Caribbean to Brazil; occasional in Florida, Mississippi, and North Carolina

Notes: This swimming crab has made its way to our coast on several occasions. These individuals have not remained and do not represent breeding populations. They appear to arrive on various types of floating debris.

Iridescent Swimming Crab

Portunus gibbesii

Authority: (Stimpson, 1859)

Other Name: Also known as swimming crab

Description: The dorsal side of the carapace is tan to greenish, with dark brown lines of differing orientations and iridescent spots close to the teeth on the outer edge. The walking legs are purple. The carapace width is approximately two times the length. The chelipeds are slender and elongated. Each side of the carapace is armed with eight teeth and one large spine. A total of eight teeth are present between the eyes. The paddle-shaped legs have a purple spot.

Size: Carapace width to 3" (76 mm); length to 1.4" (37 mm)

Habitat/Ecology: Sandy areas, mud, and estuaries; subtidal waters 1–1289' (0.3–393 m) deep

Geographic Range: Massachusetts to French Guiana

Notes: The iridescent swimming crab, as its name indicates, displays iridescence, but it is somewhat variable, as the spots next to its marginal teeth are often not distinct in older, eroded specimens. The legs are often marked with vibrant purple and irides-cent areas.

Sargassum Swimming Crab

Portunus sayi

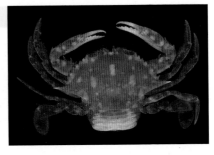

Authority: (Gibbes, 1850)
Other Names: Also known as sargassum crab, Say's portunus
Description: The dorsal side of the carapace is variable from chocolate brown to purplish, mottled with white or brownish spots, and no blue is present. The pincers are long with a spine on the outer margin of the hand, two spines on the next joint, and then four spines on the third joint. Each side of the carapace is armed with eight teeth and one large lateral spine. A total of six teeth are present between the eyes. The last pair of legs are shaped like paddles.
Size: Carapace width to 2.4" (61 mm); length to 1.2" (31 mm)
Habitat/Ecology: Pelagic on gulfweed
Geographic Range: Nova Scotia to Brazil
Notes: The sargassum swimming crab closely mimics its surrounding pelagic gulfweeds (see p. 295), rendering it nearly invisible. This pelagic species is only occasionally found washed up on our shores, clinging to gulfweed after a storm. It shares this pelagic environment with several other species that also live on gulfweed, including sargassum nudibranch (see p. 134), sargassum shrimp (see p. 216), gulfweed crab (see p. 244), and sargassum bryozoan (see p. 252).

Blotched Swimming Crab

Achelous spinimanus

Authority: (Latreille, 1819)
Other Name: Also known as spiny-handed portunus
Description: The dorsal side of the carapace is olive to brown, mottled with dark brown and white. The claws have fingers that are reddish brown with white spots. Each side of the carapace is armed with eight teeth and one slightly larger spine. A total of six teeth are present between the eyes. The last pair of legs are shaped like paddles.
Size: Carapace width to 4.3" (110 mm); length to 2.5" (65 mm)
Habitat/Ecology: In sand or mud; very low intertidal zone to water 300' (91 m) deep
Geographic Range: New Jersey to Brazil
Notes: The blotched swimming crab is best identified by its coloration. It is often found in the company of the iridescent swimming crab (see p. 237).

① Indo-Pacific Swimming Crab

Charybdis hellerii

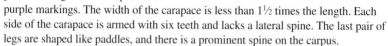

Authority: (A. Milne-Edwards, 1867)

Other Names: Also known as Pacific swimming crab; formerly classified as *Charybdis merguiensis*, occasionally misspelled *Charybdis helleri*

Description: The dorsal side of the carapace is dark green with a pattern of purple markings. The width of the carapace is less than 1½ times the length. Each side of the carapace is armed with six teeth and lacks a lateral spine. The last pair of legs are shaped like paddles, and there is a prominent spine on the carpus.

Size: Width to 0.3" (8 cm)

Habitat/Ecology: On soft bottoms and among rocks; low intertidal zone to water 165' (50 m) deep

Geographic Range: Introduced to North Carolina to Brazil; native to Australia, China, Hong Kong, India, Indonesia, Japan, Madagascar, Pakistan, Philippines, Singapore, Somalia, South Africa, and Sri Lanka

Notes: The Indo-Pacific swimming crab is an introduced species that was first discovered on the Atlantic Coast in 1987 in the Gulf of Mexico. It is native to the Indo-Pacific and has now invaded numerous areas around the world. At least one female has been discovered carrying eggs in the Indian River Lagoon, indicating that they likely breed there. The success of this species' invasions has been attributed to many factors. One factor is likely that large females can lay as many as 3,200,000 eggs per brood.

Stone Crab

Menippe mercenaria

Authority: (Say, 1818)

Other Names: Also known as Florida stone crab; formerly classified as *Cancer mercenaria*

Description: The carapace color is dark brownish red or mottled with dusky gray spots. The walking legs are dark reddish, with bands of yellow. They have a large crusher claw that includes an enlarged basal tooth.

Size: Carapace length to 3.1" (79 mm); width to 4.6" (117 mm)

Habitat/Ecology: In mud and sand beds, oyster reefs, among shell and rocky shores, and in rock crevices; low intertidal zone to water 198' (60 m) deep. Adults burrow in sandy-mud shoals.

Geographic Range: North Carolina to Florida; Texas; Bahamas; West Indies to the Yucatán

Notes: The stone crab lives in crevices and burrows in a variety of habitats. This crab is captured as a commercial and recreational species for the eating of its large claws.

Only males and females without eggs can legally be taken, with a minimum size of the pincer at 2.75" (70 mm) from the first joint to the claw's tip. The pincers are often harvested and the crabs released to grow new pincers. Regulations govern recreational crabbing by hand and traps. Details can be found at Florida's Fish and Wildlife website: http://myfwc.com/fishing/saltwater/recreational/stone-crabs/

Atlantic Mud Crab

Panopeus herbstii

Authority: H. Milne-Edwards, 1834
Description: The carapace is dark brown to gray. The fingers of the claws are brown with white tips. The claws are unequal. The major claw bears a large tooth that is visible when the fingers are closed. Males and some females bear a small red spot at their mouthparts.
Size: Carapace length to 1.7" (43 mm); width to 2.4" (62 mm)
Habitat/Ecology: On muddy shores and in estuaries; rock and shell shores; low intertidal zone to water 72.6' (22 m) deep
Geographic Range: Boston to Brazil; Bermuda
Notes: This is one of the more common mud crabs found in our Atlantic shores. Females have been found to be with eggs at every month of the year in Florida. Several species of mud crabs are present in our area.
Similar Species: Equal-clawed Mud Crab (*Neopanope sayi*) has a carapace that is brown to bluish green to buff, with reddish brown spots. Its carapace reaches 0.8" (21 mm) wide.
Flat-backed Mud Crab (*Eurypanopeus depressus*) is green to brown or buff, with spots of reddish brown. Its claws' finger tips are light colored. The marginal teeth are all dull and rounded, and the first is fused together with the orbit.

Broadback Mud Crab

Eurytium limosum

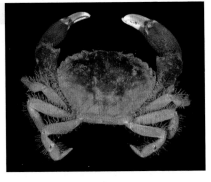

Authority: (Say, 1818)
Other Names: Also known as broad-backed mud crab, mangrove mud crab
Description: The color of the carapace is a purplish blue, gray, or black. The fingers are white, with the upper finger pink or purple near the base, white at the tip, and orange claws. The claws are massive and unequal.
Size: Carapace length to 1.1" (27 mm); width to 1.7" (43 mm)
Habitat/Ecology: On mud shores, coral reefs, and under rocks; high intertidal zone to water 234' (71 m) deep
Geographic Range: South Carolina to the West Indies; Brazil; Bermuda

Notes: The broadback mud crab is more common in Florida and the southern edge of its range than in the northern part of its range. It digs burrows in the mud banks of salt marshes. One researcher found this species to be more active in the marshes of Georgia when the skies were cloudy or during a high tide. The broadback mud crab is one of several mud crabs that are often found along the Atlantic Coast. A few other species are listed below.

Similar Species: Flat-backed Mud Crab (*Eurypanopeus depressus*) is a similar-looking species that is much smaller, reaching 0.6" (16 mm) and 0.75" (19 mm) wide. The carapace is grayish olive to olive-brown. The area between the eye sockets is nearly straight, with a notch in the middle. The pincers are unequal, and the larger pincer has nearly straight fingers with tips that are hollowed out. This crab is found from Massachusetts Bay to Florida and Texas.

    White-fingered Mud Crab (*Rhithropanopeus harrisii*) is a species that is bluish above and paler below with a square carapace that may reach to 0.6" (15 mm) long. The claws' fingers are white or lighter than the palm. It is found from the Gulf of St. Lawrence to Brazil.

Ⓘ Asian Shore Crab

Hemigrapsus sanguineus

Authority: (De Haan, 1835)
Other Names: Also known as Japanese shore crab, western Pacific shore crab, Pacific crab
Description: The color ranges from greenish to orange-brown or red, and the claws feature red spots. Three spines are present on each side of the carapace.
Size: Carapace width to 1.6" (42 mm)
Habitat/Ecology: On rocky shores; high intertidal zone to water 12.9' (3.9 m) deep
Geographic Range: Maine to North Carolina; Russia to Japan; Europe
Notes: The Asian shore crab is a small omnivore that feeds on macroalgae, salt marsh grass, amphipods, gastropods, bivalves, barnacles, polychaetes, and small fish. It was first discovered in New Jersey in 1988, and since then it has spread along our shores in both directions. It originates from Russia to Japan and was likely introduced through the release of water from the ballast of a ship. This species is capable of producing 50,000 eggs per clutch and may have up to four clutches per breeding season.

Similar Species: Chinese Mitten Crab (*Eriocheir sinensis*) is another introduced species that displays furry "mittens" on its claws—especially noticeable on males. Its overall color varies from brown to yellow and occasionally purple. This species originates from China.

❶ Tidal Spray Crab

Plagusia depressa

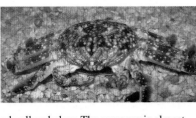

Authority: (Fabricius, 1775)
Other Names: Also known as flattened crab, flattened plagusia, spray crab
Description: The color is light reddish, patterned with dark red or purple above and yellow below. The carapace is almost circular, with four teeth present along the side margin. The body is flat and the legs have spurs visible on the anterior margin. Pincers are equal and covered with longitudinal rows of nodules surrounded by hairs; the male's pincers are as long as the carapace and the female's are shorter.
Size: Carapace length to 1.75" (44 mm); width to 1.9" (48 mm)
Habitat/Ecology: At the surf zone of rocky shores and on wharves, floating docks, and jetties, or on coral reefs; low intertidal zone to water 314' (95 m) deep
Geographic Range: North Carolina to Florida; California; Bermuda; West Indies to Brazil, Africa
Notes: The tidal spray crab does not regularly frequent the intertidal zone, but it occasionally is found on our shores. This species is believed to be introduced from Africa from a wooden sailing ship. It is also known to cling tenaciously to a wide range of objects including drifting debris, buoys, oil platforms, and ship hulls. From Africa it travels the world!

Oyster Pea Crab

Zaops ostreum

Authority: (Say, 1817)
Other Names: Also known as American oyster pea crab, oyster crab; formerly classified as *Pinnotheres ostreum*
Description: The overall color is whitish or salmon pink without any distinctive markings. The carapace is round, smooth, unmarked, and nearly hairless. Females are much larger than males.
Size: Carapace width to 0.2" (5 mm)
Habitat/Ecology: In the mantle of various bivalves; low intertidal zone
Geographic Range: Massachusetts to Brazil
Notes: The oyster pea crab is a parasitic crab that lives chiefly inside eastern oysters (see p. 155), as well as in scallops, mussels, or the tubes of the parchment tubeworm (see p. 42). Researchers have determined that the presence of this crab inside the gills of the eastern oyster is harmful to the host because it causes erosion to the gills. As a result, the oysters do not grow at the same rate as unaffected oysters do. Some eastern oysters were found that had more than 200 crabs in a single individual. Pea crabs invade their hosts at different times of the year, depending upon their latitude. In Delaware Bay, the peak of invasions takes place in September, after the oysters have grown to a size sufficient to harbor crabs. In North Carolina, invasions begin as early as June.

Blue Mussel Pea Crab

Tumidotheres maculatus

Authority: (Say, 1818)

Other Names: Also known as mussel crab, mussel pea crab

Description: Overall color of the male is dark brown. They are furry and covered with light worn spots. Females may have brown fur that can be shed or rubbed off. The shape of the carapace is nearly round—slightly longer than it is wide.

Size: Carapace length to 0.6" (16 mm); width to 0.6" (16 mm)

Habitat/Ecology: Inside the mantle cavities of living blue mussels and other bivalves; low intertidal zone to water 151' (45.7 m) deep

Geographic Range: Cape Cod to Argentina

Notes: The blue mussel pea crab lives within the mantle of the blue mussel (see p. 145). There it steals food from its host, as well as causing lesions on its gills. This reduces the mussel's growth capabilities. This crab has also been found living in pen shells, jingle shells, scallops, parchment worm tubes, colonial tunicates, and sea stars.

Researchers found that significantly more subtidal blue mussels were infected with the blue mussel pea crab than intertidal mussels. The relationship between the blue mussel pea crab and the blue mussel was formerly believed to be a symbiotic one, but now it is considered to be parasitic.

Crested Pea Crab

Austinixa cristata

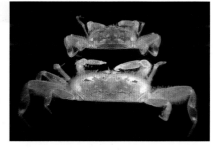

Authority: (Rathbun, 1900)

Other Name: Formerly classified as *Pinnixa cristata*

Description: Two color patterns may be found: yellowish orange to tan overall or dark gray to black overall, often with some white spots. The shape of the carapace is oval, wider than long. There is a transverse crest across the rear portion of the carapace, along with a ridge at each side.

Size: Carapace length to 0.1" (3.6 mm); width to 0.4" (10.1 mm)

Habitat/Ecology: In the burrows of ghost shrimp and worms; low intertidal zone to water at least 6.5' (2 m) deep

Geographic Range: North Carolina to Gulf of Mexico

Notes: This pea crab is one of several pea crabs found along the Atlantic Coast. It lives in the burrows of the Carolinian ghost shrimp (see p. 220) as well as various worm tubes.

Eastern Tube Crab

Polyonyx gibbesi

Pair with female and eggs on right

Authority: Haig, 1956

Other Names: Also known as parchment worm polyonyx; formerly classified as *Polyonix creplini*

Description: The carapace color varies from off-white with brownish mottling to brown. The shape of the carapace is oval but not elongated. Large fringed claws are present along with long antennae.

Size: Carapace length to 0.4" (10 mm); width to 0.5" (14 mm)

Habitat/Ecology: Inside the tube of the parchment tubeworm; low intertidal zone to shallow subtidal depths

Geographic Range: Woods Hole, Massachusetts, to Uruguay

Notes: The eastern tube crab is a porcelain crab that lives inside the tube of the parchment tubeworm (*Chaetopterus variopedatus*) (see p. 42). A pair of these small crabs is usually present together here. If eastern tube crabs are absent, the parchment-worm crab (see below) takes its place inside the tube.

Similar Species: Parchment-worm Crab (*Pinnixa chaetopterana*) is a similar-looking species that has short antennae and a large, hairless claw. The oval carapace is over twice as wide as long, and its sides are densely pubescent. Its range is from Wellfleet, Massachusetts, to Brazil.

Gulfweed Crab

Planes minutus

Authority: (Linnaeus, 1758)

Other Names: Also known as gulf weed crab, turtle crab, Columbus crab

Description: Overall color ranges from greenish yellow to reddish brown, mottled with brown and spots of white. The carapace is circular, and no teeth are found on the joints of the legs. The hind legs are not paddle-shaped.

Size: Carapace length to 0.7" (19 mm); width to 0.7" (19 mm)

Habitat/Ecology: On floating gulfweed (*Sargassum* spp.) or other floating objects

Geographic Range: Newfoundland to Brazil. There seems to be some debate, however, regarding both the northern and southern boundaries for this wanderer.

Notes: The gulfweed crab is a tropical wanderer, traveling much of the world by grabbing onto its lifeline: the pelagic gulfweeds. It ventures into the temperate climate when the ocean currents take it there. Its colors mimic gulfweeds well, and this crab may be found clinging to these gulfweeds when they wash ashore after a storm. The gulfweed crab has also been found clinging to sea turtles. The color of this species is governed by chromatophores that slowly respond to the colors of the crab's environment and extracellular pigments, which make any color changes less noticeable.

Similar Species: Sargassum Swimming Crab (*Portunus sayi*) (see p. 238)

Wharf Crab

Armases cinereum

Authority: (Bose, 1802)

Other Names: Also known as square-backed crab, wood crab, friendly crab; formerly classified as *Sesarma cinereum*

Description: The color of the carapace is dark olive to brown. The carapace is smooth, flat, and nearly square. The eyes are located at the front corners of the carapace. The immovable finger on the pincer has a large tooth. There is no small marginal notch present on its carapace.

Size: Carapace length to 0.75" (19 mm); width to 0.9" (22 mm)

Habitat/Ecology: On and around pilings, rocks, sand beaches, drift logs, and boat hulls; above the high intertidal zone

Geographic Range: Chesapeake Bay to Florida and Texas; Honduras; West Indies to Venezuela

Notes: The wharf crab is a small species that is normally observed at the seashore or on the wharf, but it actually lives in shallow burrows above the high tide mark in the supralittoral fringe. In the past, this species was often found as a stowaway on ships.

Similar Species: Purple Marsh Crab (*Sesarma reticulatum*) (see below)

Purple Marsh Crab

Sesarma reticulatum

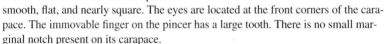

Authority: (Say, 1817)

Other Names: Also known as marsh crab; formerly classified as *Sesarma cinereum*

Description: The overall color varies from purplish black to dark brown, and its pincers are purplish. Its carapace is square, with a thick, heavy body, and the last few joints of the middle legs are covered with light hairs. A small marginal notch is present on its carapace.

Size: Carapace length to 0.9" (22 mm); width to 1.1" (28 mm)

Habitat/Ecology: In the mud of salt marshes, on sheltered shores; at the high intertidal zone

Geographic Range: Cape Cod to Florida and Texas

Notes: The purple marsh crab often shares a burrow with the Atlantic marsh fiddler in salt marshes. Here it often cuts swaths near its burrow and feeds on marsh grass. The entrance to its burrow is often surrounded by a mud chimney.

Mottled Shore Crab

Pachygrapsus transversus

Authority: (Gibbes, 1850)

Other Names: Also known as common shore crab, Gibbes' pachygrapsus

Description: The color of the carapace varies widely from black or olive to yellowish brown or gray. Striations are also present in brown, red, or dark olive. The carapace is square or trapezoidal. A single long spine can be found at the outer corner of its eyes as well as a second shorter spine next to it.

Size: Carapace length to 0.4" (10 mm); width to 0.5" (13 mm)

Habitat/Ecology: On rocks, mangrove roots, pilings, and sandy shores; high intertidal zone

Geographic Range: North Carolina to Florida and Texas; Bermuda; West Indies to Uruguay

Notes: The mottled shore crab is a tropical species that makes its way into our temperate region as far as North Carolina. In tropical regions an isopod, *Leidya bimini*, is often found on this crab.

Mangrove Tree Crab

Aratus pisonii

Authority: (H. Milne Edwards, 1837)

Other Names: Also known as mangrove crab, tree crab

Description: The color of the carapace varies from brown to olive-green mottled with black. The shape of the carapace is somewhat shield-like, with the widest portion at the anterior. The claws are graced with tufts of dark hair.

Size: Carapace length to 0.9" (22 mm); width to 1" (25 mm)

Habitat/Ecology: On and below red mangrove trees; low to above the high intertidal zone

Geographic Range: Florida to West Indies; Brazil; Nicaragua to Peru

Notes: The mangrove tree crab is able to climb mangrove trees since it has sharp tips on the end of its legs. This crab moves down from mangrove trees to venture out at low tide onto the intertidal flats.

Blue Land Crab

Cardisoma guanhumi

Authority: Latreille, 1828
Other Names: Also known as duppy, great land crab
Description: The color of the carapace in adults is pale gray or bluish and in young, blue to violet. The pincers are unequal. The carapace is globular and smooth, with a fine ridge along the sides.
Size: Carapace length to 4" (102 mm); width to 5" (127 mm)
Habitat/Ecology: In sand or mud sites; estuaries, wastelands, irrigation ditches, marshes, and inland waterways; especially close to the ocean; above high intertidal zone
Geographic Range: Florida to Texas; Bahamas; West Indies to Brazil
Notes: The blue land crab is a large species with a spread between its claws that can reach more than 2' (61 cm). The large pincer of the male often exceeds 12" (30 cm) long. This is normally a nocturnal species, but it can sometimes be observed during the day, especially in the early morning. It forages on fruit and leaves.

Atlantic Ghost Crab

Ocypode quadrata

Authority: (Fabricius, 1787)
Other Names: Also known as sand crab, ghost crab
Description: The overall color of the adult is a yellowish to straw-colored, with pincers that are white or pale lavender. Juveniles are yellowish brown, with patterns of darker brown. The pincers are unequal. The eyestalks are long, club-shaped, and slender.
Size: Carapace length to 1.75" (44 mm); width to 2" (51 mm)
Habitat/Ecology: On sandy beaches; at and above the high intertidal zone

Juvenile

Geographic Range: Rhode Island to Florida and Texas; West Indies to Brazil
Notes: The Atlantic ghost crab is a fast, active, and alert crab that is both a predator and a scavenger. It is one of very few crabs that walks on its tip toes. Normally this species remains inside its burrows in the daytime, emerging at night to feed. It often forages near the water's edge. The variable coquina (see p. 181) and Atlantic mole crab (see p. 228) are its main prey. You can sometimes watch the Atlantic ghost crab's activities under the light of a full moon.

Redjointed Fiddler

Uca minax

Authority: (Le Conte, 1855)

Other Names: Also known as brackish water fiddler, red-jointed fiddler crab

Description: The color of the carapace is chestnut-brown. The carapace has an H-shaped depression near the center. Red color is present on the joints of the male's major claw, and a diagonal row of small raised granules is present on the inside of the palm. Females are similar but with more subdued colors and two small pincers. The eyestalks are long and slender.

Size: Carapace length to 1" (25 mm); width to 1.5" (38 mm)

Habitat/Ecology: On muddy shores; often far from the ocean; above the high intertidal zone

Geographic Range: Cape Cod to Florida and Texas; West Indies to Colombia

Notes: The redjointed fiddler is the largest of the Atlantic fiddlers found along our coastline. Males wave an impressive major claw that reaches 2" (50 mm) or more in length in order to impress nearby females. This fiddler is often found in brackish waters that are nearly fresh, including along rivers a significant distance from the ocean.

Similar Species: Atlantic Marsh Fiddler (*Uca pugnax*) (see p. 249) has a dark olive to nearly black carapace and lives in muddy environments.

Atlantic Sand Fiddler (*Uca pugilator*) (see below) has a light-colored carapace with an H and lives in sandy or sandy and muddy environments.

Atlantic Sand Fiddler

Uca pugilator

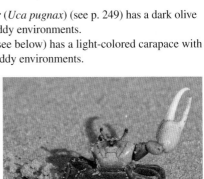

Authority: (Bosc, 1802)

Other Names: Also known as boxer fiddler crab, calico-backed fiddler, calling fiddler, sand fiddler

Description: The color of the male's carapace is light purplish to grayish blue, with an H-shaped depression positioned centrally and a purple patch in the front. The surface of the inner palm of the large pincer is smooth. Females are similar but with more subdued colors and two small pincers. The eyestalks are long and slender.

Size: Carapace length to 1" (25 mm); width to 1.5" (38 mm)

Habitat/Ecology: On protected sand beaches, sandy and mud beaches, marshes, and tidal creeks; at and above the high intertidal zone

Geographic Range: Cape Cod to Florida and Texas; (rare records as far north as Boston Harbor); West Indies

Notes: The Atlantic sand fiddler has been given the scientific name *pugilator*—an appropriate choice since it means "fist fighter," indicating the nature of its claw waving. Males use their claw, waving it and rapping it on the ground to produce vibrations, to signal females. While both are used during daylight hours to attract females, only rapping is performed during the night.

The lifespan of fiddlers in our temperate climate is normally less than two years.

Similar Species: Atlantic Marsh Fiddler (*Uca pugnax*) (see below) has a dark olive to nearly black carapace and lives in muddy environments.

Redjointed Fiddler (*Uca minax*) (see p. 248) has a light purplish to grayish blue carapace with an H and lives on muddy shores.

Atlantic Marsh Fiddler

Uca pugnax

Authority: (Smith, 1870)

Other Names: Also known as marsh fiddler, mud fiddler

Description: The color of the male's carapace is dark olive to nearly black, with a royal blue spot near the center. On the male's large claw, a diagonal row of small raised granules is present on the inside of the palm. Females are similar but lack the blue spot and have two small pincers. The eyestalks are long and slender.

Size: Carapace length to 0.6" (16 mm); width to 0.9" (22 mm)

Habitat/Ecology: On mud banks, sand and mud marshes, and along tidal marshes; at the high intertidal zone

Geographic Range: Cape Cod to Florida; Texas

Notes: The Atlantic marsh fiddler prefers to live in muddy habitats, but it is also found in sand and mud marshes where the Atlantic sand fiddler (see p. 248) lives. There is often a sharp boundary where the two live together. In some instances, however, they intermingle freely, although there is no interbreeding. The purple marsh crab (see p. 245) is also often found living in the same sites as the Atlantic marsh fiddler. This is our smallest fiddler.

Fiddlers are part of the diet to a wide range of animals, including various fishes, rails, egrets, ibises, and herons, as well as blue crabs.

Similar Species: Atlantic Sand Fiddler (*Uca pugilator*) (see p. 248) has a light-colored carapace with an H, and it lives in sandy or sand and mud environments.

Redjointed Fiddler (*Uca minax*) (see p. 248) has a light purplish to grayish blue carapace with an H and lives on muddy shores.

Moss Animals
(Phylum Bryozoa or Ectoprocta)

Bryozoans produce colonies, each consisting of hundreds or thousands of individuals, called zooids. Each zooid secretes and lives inside a zooecium. These zooecia (plural) come in many different shapes and form a certain type of colony depending upon their shape. Most bryozoans are hermaphroditic—individuals have both ovaries and testes. Some species release both eggs and sperm directly into the ocean, where they combine, but most species brood their eggs. Bryozoans feed on fine particles present in the water. Nearly 2,000 different species are known in the world.

Rubbery Bryozoan

Alcyonidium hauffi

Authority: Marcus, 1939
Other Name: Also known as Hauff's Alcyonidium
Description: The color is gray-brown. The encrusting colonies are rubbery and cover sea whips and other species. The surface of this bryozoan is covered with numerous conical projections, and the aperture of each zooid is not located on an oral prominence.
Size: Height to 15" (38 cm); width to 4" (10 cm)
Habitat/Ecology: On sea whips; low intertidal zone to shallow subtidal waters
Geographic Range: North Carolina to Florida; Brazil
Notes: The rubbery bryozoan is a distinctive species that appears to have a somewhat restricted range. It was only described as a species in 1939. Be sure to look closely on this bryozoan to find the tiny nudibranch obscure corambe (*Doridella obscura*), a species that feeds only on this bryozoan.

Leafy Bryozoan

Flustra foliacea

Authority: (Linnaeus, 1758)
Other Names: Also known as horn wrack, hornwrack, lace corals, sea mats
Description: The branches are gray or yellow to tan-colored; the shape of the branches is broad, flat, and frequently lobed.
Size: Height to 8" (20 cm)
Habitat/Ecology: On rocks and in tidepools; low intertidal zone to subtidal depths of 328' (100 m) and greater
Geographic Range: Arctic to Nova Scotia; Britain and Ireland
Notes: Resembling a plant, this northern species smells strongly of lemons when collected fresh. The light branches of this species often blow high on the seashore after a storm. Although this species is well known in Europe, it was not reported on our coast until 1960. Colonies of leafy bryozoans have been found that are more than twelve years old. Researchers have reported toxicity of extracts of this species on the larvae of other invertebrates, fish, and bacteria. Some people, including fishermen, have reported allergic reactions to it.

ⓘ White Lace Bryozoan

Membranipora membranacea

Authority: (Linnaeus, 1767)
Other Names: Also known as encrusting bryozoan, kelp encrusting bryozoan, lacycrust bryozoan, kelp lace, coffin bryozoan
Description: This species is white and shaped into flat, thin colonies comprised of small, rectangular, individuals. The overall shape is irregular, growing outward and radiating from the center.
Size: Colonies often exceed 3" (76 mm) in diameter
Habitat/Ecology: On seaweeds (especially kelp), floats, and rocks
Geographic Range: Nova Scotia to New Hampshire; Alaska to Baja California; Europe
Notes: In 1987 the white lace bryozoan was introduced from Europe into the Gulf of Maine. Within two years it had become the dominant species of bryozoan living on kelps in that area. This species has the common name kelp encrusting bryozoan in the Pacific Northwest.

Sargassum Bryozoan

Jellyella tuberculata

Authority: (Bosc, 1802)

Other Names: Also known as gulf weed
bryozoan, sargassum sea mat; formerly
classified as *Membranipora tuberculata*, *Membranipora tehuelca*

Description: The color of the zooids is
white. Each zooecium has two strong
projections at its upper corners. The
walls of the zooecia are much more heavily calcified than those of the white lace
bryozoan (see p. 251).

Size: Colonies often exceed 1" (25 mm) in diameter

Habitat/Ecology: On *Sargassum* and various other algae

Geographic Range: North Carolina to Brazil; California to Peru and the Galapagos
Islands; Japan; Indian Ocean; the East Indies

Notes: As its common name suggests, the sargassum bryozoan favors attaching itself
to gulfweed (see p. 295) and floating widely over the oceans. It can also be found on
other algae growing on the shores of warmer waters.

Lacy Crust Bryozoans

Electra spp.

Authority: Lamouroux, 1816

Other Names: Also known as sea lace,
lacy crust

Description: The color of the zooids is
white or grayish. The zooecia have a
box or coffin shape.

Size: To 12" (30 cm) in diameter

Habitat/Ecology: On rocks, shells,
seaweeds, and in tidepools; low intertidal zone to subtidal water 100' (30 m) deep
and greater

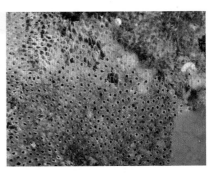

Geographic Range: Along the entire Atlantic Coast

Notes: Lacy crust bryozoans can be quite difficult to identify to a species. Some
species display sharp spines that are used for protection. These species feed upon
minute creatures that are suspended in the water. Their chief enemies include a
variety of nudibranchs.

Common Bugula

Bugula neritina

Authority: (Linnaeus, 1758)

Description: Colonies are a distinctive reddish purple to reddish brown. The zooids are arranged in two rows and alternately face the same direction.

Size: Height to 6" (15 cm)

Habitat/Ecology: On rocks, shells, mangrove roots, dock sides, buoys, dock pilings; low intertidal zone to shallow subtidal depths

Geographic Range: Massachusetts to Florida; Caribbean

Notes: The common bugula is one of our most common and recognizable bryozoans. Its color and shape are distinctive, and the zooids are hermaphroditic. Unfortunately this species has been transported to many warmer locations around the world and is now an introduced exotic at these locations. These sites include the Arabian Sea, Argentina, Australia, Belgium, Brazil, the Caribbean Sea, the Celtic Sea, Chile, the East China Sea, and Ecuador.

Spiny-skinned Animals
(Phylum Echinodermata)

Spiny-skinned animals, or echinoderms, have a soft layer of skin that covers an internal skeleton made of calcareous plates. Tentacle-like structures called tube feet are also present on all species in this phylum, and adults exhibit radial symmetry. The animals in this large group have amazing powers of regeneration.

The types of echinoderms that you may encounter on the shore include sea stars, brittle stars, sea urchins, sea cucumbers, sand dollars, and others.

SEA STARS (Class Asteroidea)

Sea stars normally have five to twenty-four arms or rays depending upon the species. Their feeding habits range from those of a filter-feeder to those of an active predator. They use their pincer-like pedicellariae for defense and cleaning. Sea stars are always a delight to view at the seashore.

Forbes' Sea Star

Asterias forbesi

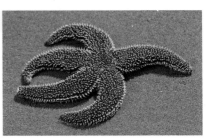

Authority: (Desor, 1848)
Other Names: Also known as common starfish, Forbes' asterias
Description: The arboral surface varies from tan or olive to red or purple. The madreporite or sieve plate is bright orange. Its spines are scattered and do not form any pattern. There are normally five rays or arms.
Size: Radius to 5" (125 mm)
Habitat/Ecology: On rocks, sand, or gravel and in tidepools; low intertidal zone to water 150' (45 m) deep
Geographic Range: Penobscot Bay to Gulf of Mexico
Notes: Forbes' sea star is a predator of several mollusks, including the eastern oyster (see p. 155), northern quahog (see p. 184), and Atlantic surfclam (see p. 171). It is a major predator, especially to the eastern oyster, but the Atlantic surfclam is often able to escape this predator by jumping away with its muscular foot. This has only been observed in juvenile surfclams, however.

Northern Sea Star

Asterias rubens

Authority: Linnaeus, 1758

Other Names: Also known as common sea star, northern starfish; formerly classified as *Asterias vulgaris*

Description: The arboral surface varies from brown or olive to red, or purple or orange. The madreporite is dull yellow.

Its spines are scattered and do not form any pattern. There are normally five rays or arms.

Size: Radius to 8" (200 mm)

Habitat/Ecology: On sand, rocks, jetties, and in tidepools; low intertidal zone to water at least 66' (20 m) deep

Geographic Range: Labrador to Cape Cod; Europe

Notes: This species grows quickly and reaches a size of 3" (75 mm) in a mere four months. This species is a keystone predator, like many sea stars, that feeds upon a variety of barnacles and bivalves, including the eastern oyster (see p. 155). Research has determined that this species migrates to deeper waters with the onset of winter.

Margined Sea Star

Astropecten articulatus

Authority: (Say, 1825)

Description: The arboral surface varies from deep purple to blue, with contrasting orange marginal plates. The underside is white. There are normally five rays.

Size: Radius to 5" (125 mm)

Habitat/Ecology: On sand; low intertidal zone to water 541' (165 m) deep

Geographic Range: New Jersey to Uruguay

Notes: In one study conducted in North Carolina, this species was described as a "voracious, nonselective predator." In this study it was found to feed upon a total of ninety-one species of invertebrates. The main prey items included gastropods, tusk shells, bivalves, small crustaceans, and juvenile sand dollars.

Netted Sea Star

Luidia clathrata

Authority: (Say, 1825)

Other Names: Also known as gray sea star, lined sea star, slender armed starfish

Description: The background color of the arboral surface is gray or tan with a central dark stripe down each ray. A series of dark lines or a net-like pattern runs parallel to the central line. Its spines are velvet-like. There are normally five tapering rays.

Size: Radius to 4" (100 mm)

Habitat/Ecology: On sandy shores; low intertidal zone to water 328' (100 m) deep

Geographic Range: New Jersey to Brazil; Bermuda

Notes: The netted sea star is able to feed upon larger prey than we often think possible. It is able to feed upon sand dollars whole by distorting its central disk. It has also been observed preying upon the Atlantic calico scallop (see p. 159). Clearly this is an active predator of the marine world. This species is more often found washed up on the beach than in the intertidal zone.

Nine-armed Sea Star

Luidia senegalensis

Authority: (Lamarck, 1816)

Description: The arboral surface varies from gray to bluish or greenish, with an outer edge of the rays that ranges from gray to orange. A dark line runs down each ray and is paired with a net-like pattern. Its spines are velvet-like. There are normally nine strap-like rays.

Size: Radius to 8" (20 cm)

Habitat/Ecology: In sand; subtidal depths from 6.5–151' (2–46 m) deep

Geographic Range: Florida to Brazil; Senegal

Notes: The nine-armed sea star dines on a wide variety of invertebrates, including bivalves, gastropods, annelid worms, and crustaceans. On rare occasions this species experiences a mass mortality when weather conditions rapidly push them to the shore.

Atlantic Blood Star

Henricia sanguinolenta

Authority: (O. F. Müller, 1776)

Other Names: Also known as blood sea star, blood starfish

Description: The arboral surface varies from red or orange to yellow or purple. Its spines are equally sized and form a granular texture. The madreporite is white. There are normally five rays or arms that are slender and cylindrical with a small disk.

Size: Radius to 4" (102 mm)

Habitat/Ecology: On rocky shores; low intertidal zone to water 7920' (2414 m) deep

Geographic Range: Arctic to Cape Hatteras

Notes: The female Atlantic blood star lays its eggs in early spring and then keeps them in a brood pouch until the young emerge. They emerge into miniature blood stars, as there is no free-swimming larval stage in this species. This species is a filter-feeder that feeds upon suspended material in the water.

Rose Star

Crossaster papposus

Authority: (Linnaeus, 1767)

Other Names: Also known as rose sea star, rose starfish, snowflake star, snowflake sea star, spiny sun star, spiny sunstar, common sun star; formerly classified as *Solaster papposus*, *Asterias papposus*

Description: The arboral surface is scarlet, with concentric banding of yellow, white, pink, or red. The pattern is net-like with raised ridges, and the central disk is large. There can be eight to fourteen rays, but normally there are eleven.

Size: Radius to 7" (18 cm)

Habitat/Ecology: On rocks; low intertidal zone to water 4000' (1200 m) deep

Geographic Range: Circumpolar; Arctic to Gulf of Maine; Alaska to Puget Sound; Britain; Arctic to China

Notes: The striking colors of the rose star make it truly beautiful. This species is a top predator, as it feeds upon other sea stars, eating them whole.

Northern Sun Star

Solaster endeca

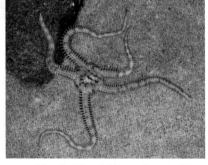

Authority: (Linnaeus, 1771)

Other Names: Also known as purple sunstar, smooth sun star

Description: The arboral surface varies from purple or red to pink or orange. The madreporite is yellowish orange. Its dorsal side is covered with short prickle-like pseudopaxillae that do not form any pattern. There are normally nine to ten rays but this can range from seven to fourteen.

Size: Radius to 8" (20 cm)

Habitat/Ecology: On rocks, wharves, pilings, and gravel; low intertidal zone to water 900' (274 m) deep

Geographic Range: Arctic to Cape Cod; Alaska to Washington (state)

Notes: The northern sun star dines mainly on smaller sea cucumbers and sea stars. There is no free-swimming larval stage in the development of this species. It is often picked up accidentally in dredges and lobster traps.

BRITTLE STARS (Class Ophiuroidea)

Most species of brittle stars have five long rays joined to a flattened central disc; however, some species have more arms. They are called brittle stars because their rays often break when being handled.

Daisy Brittle Star

Ophiopholis aculeate

Authority: (Linnaeus, 1767)

Other Names: Also known as serpent star, painted brittlestar

Description: The overall colors of this species are remarkably variable, including red, orange, yellow, white, blue, green, brown, and black. The combinations and designs are also as varied as possible, using various lines, spots, and bands. The disk is scalloped with a lobe extending from the disk between each pair of arms. The arms carry a series of blunt spines and oval plates.

Size: Disk diameter to 0.75" (19 mm); arms are 3½ to 4 times the disk diameter

Habitat/Ecology: Under rocks and in kelp holdfasts; low intertidal zone to water 5435' (1657 m) deep

Geographic Range: Arctic to Cape Cod; Bering Sea to California

Notes: On many rocky shores, these common brittle stars hide during the daylight hours. They emerge from their hiding spots at night to move around and search for food. With their wide array of colors, they are always a delight to view.

Dwarf Brittle Star

Amphipholis squamata

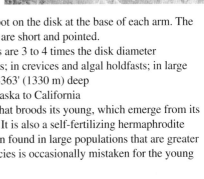

Authority: (delle Chiaje, 1828)
Other Names: Also known as brooding brittle, holdfast brittle star, small brittle star, serpent star; formerly classified as *Axiognathus squamata*, *Amphiura squamata*
Description: The color varies from brown to gray or orange, with a white spot on the disk at the base of each arm. The disk is round and the spines on the arms are short and pointed.
Size: Disk diameter to 0.25" (6 mm); arms are 3 to 4 times the disk diameter
Habitat/Ecology: Under and among rocks; in crevices and algal holdfasts; in large tidepools; high intertidal zone to water 4363' (1330 m) deep
Geographic Range: Arctic to Florida; Alaska to California
Notes: The dwarf brittle star is a species that broods its young, which emerge from its brood pouches as miniature brittle stars. It is also a self-fertilizing hermaphrodite that is luminescent. This species has been found in large populations that are greater than 500 per square meter. This tiny species is occasionally mistaken for the young of other larger species.

Short-spined Brittle Star

Ophioderma brevispina

Authority: (Say, 1825)
Other Names: Also known as green brittle star, mud brittle star, smooth brittle star
Description: The color overall is a uniform olive to brown or black with banded arms. Fine granules cover the disk. The spines on the arms are typically short and held close to the sides of the arms.
Size: Disk diameter to 0.6" (16 mm); arms are approximately 4 times the disk diameter
Habitat/Ecology: On sandy shores, among the roots of eelgrass or in tidepools; low intertidal zone to water approximately 604' (183 m) deep
Geographic Range: Cape Cod to Brazil
Notes: This brittle star is known to dine on a wide assortment of foods, including worms, small crustaceans, sponges, and algae. It is occasionally washed up on the beach during a storm.

SEA URCHINS AND SAND DOLLARS
(Class Echinoidea)

Sand dollars and sea urchins are round, with a hard, calcareous skeleton covered with spines and tube feet. They use their stalked pincers to keep the test (shell) clean from the various organisms that try to settle on their exterior.

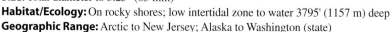

Green Sea Urchin

Strongylocentrotus droebachiensis

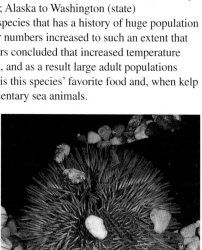

Authority: (O. F. Müller, 1776)
Other Name: Also known as sea egg
Description: The overall color is normally green but can also be brownish or reddish green. The oval test is covered with spines that are not greater than a third of the diameter of the test. The area next to the anus has several scale-like plates of varying sizes.
Size: Total diameter to 3.25" (83 mm)
Habitat/Ecology: On rocky shores; low intertidal zone to water 3795' (1157 m) deep
Geographic Range: Arctic to New Jersey; Alaska to Washington (state)
Notes: The green sea urchin is a northern species that has a history of huge population fluctuations. In the 1960s and 1970s their numbers increased to such an extent that the kelp beds were decimated. Researchers concluded that increased temperature promoted larval growth and development, and as a result large adult populations were present four to six years later. Kelp is this species' favorite food and, when kelp is not available, it will also feed upon sedentary sea animals.

Short-spined Sea Urchin

Lytechinus variegatus

Authority: (Lamarck, 1816)
Other Names: Also known as green sea urchin, variegated sea urchin, variegated urchin
Description: The overall color is variable and includes white, green, pinkish red, and brown. The oval test is curved and covered with numerous short spines.
Size: Total diameter to 3" (76 mm)
Habitat/Ecology: On sand and gravel flats; low intertidal zone to water 825' (250 m) deep
Geographic Range: North Carolina to West Indies; Bahamas

Notes: The short-spined sea urchin uses its tube feet to hold various shell and plant debris in place to help camouflage itself.

Purple-spined Sea Urchin

Arbacia punctulata

Authority: (Lamarck, 1816)
Other Names: Also known as brown rock urchin, common arbacia, purple sea urchin
Description: The color of the test and spines is normally purple or brown, but reddish gray to black individuals have also been found. The spines are long and slender—approximately half the width of the test.
Size: Total diameter to 2" (50 mm)
Habitat/Ecology: In sand or cobble; low intertidal zone to water 700' (210 m) deep
Geographic Range: Cape Cod to West Indies; Barbados

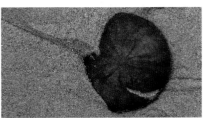

Test

Notes: The purple-spined sea urchin is a common species that is primarily an herbivore, although when algae are not available, it is known to feed on sponges, coral polyps, sand dollars, and even its own species. If a shadow is cast upon this species, it moves its spines to face the source of the shadow—as if it were protecting itself against a predator.

Common Sand Dollar

Echinarachnius parma

Authority: (Lamarck, 1816)
Other Name: Also known as sand dollar
Description: Brownish to purplish with distinct petal-like patterns made from tiny holes on the surface. Overall round, flat, and thin. Bleaches white.
Size: Height to 0.25" (6 mm); width 3.1" (79 mm)
Habitat/Ecology: On sandy and muddy bottoms; low intertidal zone to depths of 5,280' (1,613 m)
Geographic Range: Labrador to Maryland
Notes: As its name suggests, this species is the most common sand dollar found

Test

along the north Atlantic coastline. Its white test or skeleton is commonly found along the shorelines after a storm. The living animal is covered in a velvety purple jacket made up of minute spines that cover its skeleton. Tiny, hair-like cilia cover these spines which, in combination with a mucus coating, help move food to its mouth opening in the center of the grooves beneath the animal. Sand dollars feed on diatoms and other microorganisms, and in turn are predated upon by flounder, cod, haddock, and other bottom-feeding fishes. This species, like many other marine species, experiences reproductive failure in waters with low salinities.

Northern Five-slotted Keyhole Urchin

Mellita isometra

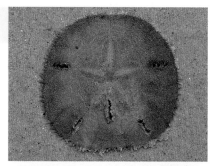

Authority: (Harold and Telford, 1990)

Other Names: Also known as keyhole urchin, five-holed keyhole urchin; formerly included with *Mellita quinquiesperforata*

Description: The test is gray and it sun-bleaches to white. Five lunules (oval slots) grace its test. The "petals" numbered 1, 3, and 5 on the dorsal side of the test are equal in length. The size of the total "daisy" pattern is approximately half the diameter of the test. For the living animal, color ranges from tan to brown or dark green. The overall shape is circular, often slightly penta-gonal. Small spines are present that move while the animal is alive. They are so short that they resemble felt.

Size: Height to .4" (1 cm); width 4" (10 cm)

Habitat/Ecology: On soft sand bottoms; low intertidal zone to water 164' (50 m) deep

Geographic Range: Nantucket to Florida and the Bahamas

Notes: The northern five-slotted keyhole urchin is often found in dense aggre-gations just beneath the sand's surface in shallow waters.

Test

Northern five-slotted keyhole urchin with an extra linule at the top

Originally the five-slotted keyhole urchin (*Mellita quinquiesperforata*) included three species that closely resemble each other. The northern five-slotted keyhole urchin is the smallest species of this group and lives in the northernmost areas. Two other very similar five-slotted keyhole urchins live in the Gulf of Mexico and south.

Similar Species: Six-slotted Sand Dollar (*Leodia sexiesperforata*) is another species that is occasionally encountered as far north as Cape Hatteras. As its common name suggests, it bears six elongated holes in its test. The size of the total "daisy" pattern is much smaller—approximately one-third the diameter of the test.

Mud Heart Urchin

Moira atropos

Authority: (Lamarck, 1816)
Other Names: Also known as heart urchin, mud urchin, sea porcupine
Description: The color of the test is greenish when fresh and bone-white when sun-bleached. It is egg or heart-shaped, with five deep grooves, and very fragile. The color of the fine spines varies from white or yellow to light brown; they are very short.
Size: To 2.5" (6 cm) long
Habitat/Ecology: On soft mud or sandy-mud bottoms; low intertidal zone to water 160' (50 m) deep; occasionally to 480' (146 m)
Geographic Range: Cape Hatteras to Brazil
Notes: As its common name suggests, this species favors mud bottoms where it burrows beneath the surface. To live in mud, this heart urchin arranges the tips of its spines into a circle and secretes mucus to plaster a tube wall. This mucus forms a continuous tube where the spines have passed as the urchin descends. In this way it is able to extend its tube feet to feed on detritus located on the top of the mud. When it moves forward, it simply produces a second mucus tube and ceases to use its first tube. This species is known to spawn in Florida, from March to April, immediately after a full moon.
Similar Species: Rock-boring Urchin (*Echinometra lucunter*) has a test to 2.5" (6.3 cm), in length with an oval shape. Fresh tests have brownish highlights and sun-bleach to white. Their thick, purple-brown spines are known to reach 1" (2.5 cm) long.

Inflated Sea biscuit

Clypeaster rosaceus

Authority: (Linnaeus, 1758)
Other Names: Also known as brown sea biscuit; formerly known as *Diplothecanthus rosaceus*, *Echinanthus rosaceus*
Description: The color is brown when fresh and white when sun-bleached. The shape is oval, flattened beneath with concave lower (oral) surface and arched on top with a five-parted, petal-

like sculpture (clearly visible when the spines are no longer present). The living animal may be reddish, yellowish, greenish brown, or brown and is covered with short spines that give it a furry appearance.

Size: Length to 6" (15 cm), occasionally to 8" (20 cm)

Habitat/Ecology: In turtle grass beds, sandy areas, and reef tracts; in subtidal waters 3–164' (1–50 m) deep; occasionally to 935' (285 m)

Geographic Range: Southern Florida to Barbados; occasionally to South Carolina; also present in Venezuela, Colombia, Panama, Belize, and Texas

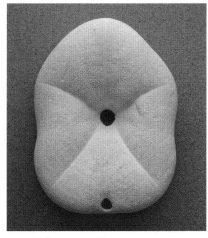

Notes: The bleached test of the inflated sea biscuit occasionally washes up on the shore. Amazingly, the large test of this species is often found intact and in good condition. This nocturnal species is believed to feed on dead turtle grass. One study found that this species likely plays an important role in producing fine sediment on reefs. A single individual can transform 5.5 kg (12 lb.) of coarse sand to fine sand in a single year. It's unlikely that you'll encounter living animals on the shoreline.

SEA CUCUMBERS (Class Holothuroidea)

A sea cucumber is often shaped like a cucumber, but that is the only similarity to a cucumber it has. Its mouth is found at one end that bears branching tentacles, which it uses to feed with, and an anus is present at the opposite end. A sea cucumber moves or attaches to substrates with five rows of tube feet that run the length of its body. Microscopic ossicles (skeletal plates) are present in the body wall—as with all echinoderms. There are approximately 700 species of sea cucumbers worldwide, and some reach an amazing 6.6' (2 m) long.

Hairy Sea Cucumber

Sclerodactyla briareus

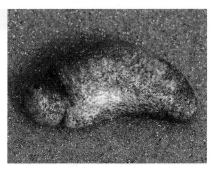

Authority: (Lesueur, 1824)

Other Names: Also known as brown sea cucumber, hairy cucumber

Description: The body color is dark brown or green. The body is barrel-shaped, with a taper at both ends, and covered with tiny tube feet that resemble hairs.

Size: Length to 4.75" (121 mm); width to 2" (51 mm)

Habitat/Ecology: On sand or mud; low intertidal zone to water 60' (18 m) deep
Geographic Range: Cape Cod to the West Indies
Notes: The hairy sea cucumber gets its name from the tiny tube feet that resemble hairs. These "hairs" are often worn off when the sea cucumber is beached. The feeding tentacles are not often visible, but when they are, they are located next to the mouth.

Orange-footed Sea Cucumber

Cucumaria frondosa

Authority: (Gunnerus, 1767)
Other Name: Also known as orange-footed cucumber
Description: The body color is reddish brown on the dorsal side and paler on the ventral side; the tube feet are tinged orange. The young are lighter colored.
The body is barrel-shaped, with variable ends. The tentacles are large, retractable, and multi-branched. The tentacles can reach half the length of the body when fully extended.
Size: Length to 19" (48 cm); width to 5" (127 mm)
Habitat/Ecology: On rocky shores; low intertidal zone to water 1208' (368 m) deep
Geographic Range: Arctic to Cape Cod
Notes: This species, like many sea cucumbers, is able to expel its inner organs from its rear end. This action is thought to foil the attack of a predator—leaving them with a pile of viscera rather than the entire animal. The sea cucumber is then able to regenerate the missing organs over time. The American lobster (see p. 219) is one of this species' predators.

Pale Sea Cucumber

Pentamera pulcherrima

Authority: Ayres, 1852
Other Names: Also known as sea cucumber; formerly classified as *Cucumaria pulcherrima*
Description: The body color is white to pinkish, with translucent skin. The body is barrel-shaped, with a taper at both ends and covered with stout little tube feet situated in five distinct rows.
Size: Length to 2" (50 mm)
Habitat/Ecology: In fine sand or mud with eelgrass; just below the low intertidal zone to water 80' (24 m) deep
Geographic Range: South Carolina to the Gulf of Mexico
Notes: The pale sea cucumber is a subtidal species that is most frequently found after it has been washed onto the beach after a storm.

Synaptas

Leptosynapta spp.

Authority: Verrill, 1867

Description: The body is transparent
with a white, yellowish, or pink color
overall. The elongated body resembles
a worm that lacks tube feet; however,
twelve pinnate (feather-like) tentacles
are found at the front end.

Size: Length to 12" (30 cm)

Habitat/Ecology: In muddy sand or under stones; low intertidal zone to shallow subtidal depths

Geographic Range: Along the entire Atlantic Coast

Notes: Synaptas are often misidentified as worms. Their elongated bodies do not
resemble any "normal" members of the sea cucumber clan. To complicate matters
further, they are not likely to extend their tentacles while being handled. They feed
much like other sea cucumbers, by bringing food to their mouth, one tentacle at a
time. A wide variety of small marine life provides food for this group. Young adult
synaptas have been observed swimming at the water's surface in the darkness of late-
summer nights. The reason for this behavior is unknown.

Tunicates
(Subphylum Tunicata [Urocordata])

Tunicates have several characteristics at one stage of their life history or other, which enable them to be included in the phylum Chordata. These include: a tubular nerve cord, a notochord (skeletal supporting rod), and others. Tunicates, sometimes referred to as Urochordates, are some of the highest developed forms of life found at the seashore. The subphylum Tunicata contains the class Ascidiacea (ascidians) as well as the class Thaliacea, (pelagic salps—jelly-like organisms) and the class Larvacea (transparent planktonic organisms). This guide includes only the ascidians, also called sea squirts. All ascidians, both larvae and adults, are covered in a tunic—a covering made up of protein, carbohydrates, and uncommonly in the animal world, cellulose.

There are two types of ascidians, solitary and colonial. These groups of ascidians have no taxonomic significance; however, they help us understand their natural history.

SOLITARY SEA SQUIRTS

Solitary sea squirts are normally large individuals. Solitary ascidians are often ovoid or irregular in shape.

Orange Sea Grape Tunicate

Molgula citrina

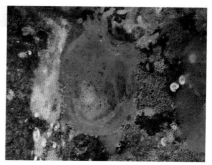

Authority: Alder and Hancock, 1848
Other Names: Also known as orange sea grape; formerly classified as *M. nuda*
Description: Translucent, greenish tunic with orange reproductive organs visible; the tunic is globular overall, with some lateral compression, and not normally covered with debris. Siphons are separated from each other by the space of one siphon or greater.
Size: Height to 0.6" (16 mm) high.
Habitat/Ecology: On rocks; normally low intertidal zone to water to 120' (36 m) and occasionally to 756' (227 m) deep
Geographic Range: Arctic to Rhode Island
Notes: The shape of this species has been likened to a grape—hence its common name. The orange sea grape tunicate is also found widely distributed in the waters of

northern Europe. This species produces large eggs but in small numbers. It is viviparous, meaning the tadpole larvae remain inside the atrium for their development—an unusual situation for an ascidian.

Several other species of the genus *Molgula* are also found along the Atlantic Coast. Positive identification may require dissection.

Similar Species: Common Sea Grape Tunicate (*Molgula manhattensis*) (see below)

Common Sea Grape Tunicate

Molgula manhattensis

Authority: (De Kay, 1843)
Other Names: Also known as sea grapes; formerly classified as *M. dentifera*
Description: The tunic is grayish green and globular overall, with some lateral compression, and normally muddy and hairy. Siphons are next to each other—with little space between siphons.
Size: Diameter to 1–2" (25–50 mm)
Habitat/Ecology: In quiet bays, on various hard surfaces, such as rocks, pilings, and floats, as well as on eelgrass (see p. 307); shallow waters and rarely to waters 96' (29 m) deep
Geographic Range: Arctic to Texas; rare in Florida
Notes: This tunicate is well known for its ability to tolerate pollution—even in New York Harbor, where it is often found living in dense clusters. It lays numerous small eggs in contrast to the orange sea grape tunicate (see p. 267), which lays fewer, larger eggs. The common sea grape tunicate spawns its gametes at night and does not retain them inside its atrium for development. It reproduces throughout the year, although reproduction is most intense during the warmer summer months.
Similar Species: Sandy-skinned Tunicate (*Molgula occidentalis*) may also be occasionally encountered at low tide. Its oval tunic is larger—to a height of 2" (5 cm)—tough, wrinkled, and tan to reddish brown. As its common name suggests, it is typically covered in sand or mud.

Translucent Sea Squirt

Ascidia interrupta

Authority: Heller, 1878
Other Name: Formerly classified as *Ascidia hygomiana*
Description: The tunic is greenish, glassy and fragile; the external shape normally elongate but quite variable.
Size: Height to 2.4" (60 mm)

Habitat/Ecology: On shells, rocks, floats, pilings, and boat bottoms; low intertidal zone to very shallow depths

Geographic Range: Beaufort, North Carolina, to northern Florida; rare in South Carolina and Georgia; also present in southern Brazil, Jamaica, the Bahamas, Cuba, Puerto Rico, St. Thomas, and Curaçao

Notes: The translucent sea squirt is normally a greenish color because there are green cells present in its blood which contain a very high concentration of vanadium. It is believed that this large species reproduces throughout the year. The translucent sea squirt is often found under crowded conditions.

Ⓘ Asian Stalked Sea Squirt

Styela clava

Authority: Herdman, 1881

Other Names: Also known as club tunicate, Asian stalked tunicate

Description: The tunic is yellowish to reddish brown, club-shaped, and thick and leathery with a warty exterior. Both siphons positioned at the top and pointed upward.

Size: To 6" (150 mm) high, 2" (51 mm) wide

Habitat/Ecology: In quiet, sheltered waters on rocks and pilings; subtidally to 80' (24m)

Geographic Range: Massachusetts to Connecticut

Notes: As its common name indicates, this large ascidian is a native of Asia that has been transported on ships' hulls to California, Europe, and Australia. It is considered a seafood in Korea. Considering the concentrations of heavy metals found in tunicates, this practice is not recommended.

Pleated Sea Squirt

Styela plicata

Authority: (Lesueur, 1823)

Other Names: Also known as leathery rough sea squirt, sea squirt, striped tunicate

Description: The tunic is thick, convoluted and tough; the siphons are four-lobed and boldly striped with red or purple lines in a + shape over the opening. Various other organisms are often encrusted on the tunic of this species.

Size: Height to 2.5–3" (6–8 cm), occasionally to 4" (10 cm)

Habitat/Ecology: On hard surfaces in quiet areas with good water movement including rocks, pilings, boat bottoms, and similar objects; from low intertidal zone to water 100' (30 m) deep

Geographic Range: North Carolina to both coasts of Florida; West Indies, southern California

Notes: This species is easy to identify due to the colorful adornments on its siphons. The pleated sea squirt is sometimes found with several individuals clumped together. In these instances, each has developed separately from different larvae. This species is occasionally found washed ashore in singles and in groups.

SOCIAL TUNICATES

Social tunicates are one type of colonial ascidian. Colonial ascidians form large collective colonies. Social ascidians are individuals (zooids) that are positioned close to each other and are joined at the base by stolons (root-like structures) but distinct from each other.

Red Colonial Tunicate

Symplegma rubra

Authority: Monniot, 1972

Other Name: Also known as red encrusting tunicate

Description: Colony color ranges from orange-yellow to cherry-red; individuals have an oval outline, with two distinct tubular siphons opening on the dorsal surface. A gelatinous transparent film covers the zooids, allowing the viewer to see the individuals inside. Four longitudinal vessels are visible on each side of the branchial sac. (A hand lens is needed to view these.)

Size: Colonies are a minimum of 0.5" (1 cm) thick; may reach 4" (10 cm) in diameter

Habitat/Ecology: In quiet waters, including harbors and seagrass beds; on hard surfaces, including, rocks, seawalls, pilings, mangrove roots, oysters, or various other organisms; low intertidal zone to water 112' (34 m) deep

Geographic Range: Florida to Brazil; Tanzania, Mozambique

Notes: The soft colonies of the red colonial tunicate grow by stolons along their outer margin. Individual zooids are produced from these stolons, which in turn expand the size of the colony. Individuals of this species are hermaphroditic; however, the entire colony is either made up of mature male or female zooids at any one time.

COMPOUND ASCIDIANS

Compound ascidians are the second type of colonial tunicates. Compound ascidians include many small individuals that are actually embedded into a continuous mass with a common tunic (covering).

① Carpet Tunicates

Didemnum spp.

Authority: Savigny, 1816
Other Name: Also known as white crusts
Description: The colors are white, yellow, reddish, and brown. Colonies are tough crusts. No arrangement of zooids is apparent; apertures may not be obvious.
Size: Diameter of colonies to 4–8" (10–20 cm); to 0.2" (5 mm) thick
Habitat/Ecology: On rocks, shells, pilings, algae, and similar objects; low intertidal zone to depths of 1350' (411 m)
Geographic Range: Along the entire Atlantic Coast

Notes: Carpet tunicates are invasive species that have invaded the entire Atlantic Coast and many other waters. Their crust-like colonies incorporate minute calcareous spicules, which require a microscope to view, so the identification of most species also requires a microscope. Some of the more common species are listed below.
Similar Species: Northern White Crust (*Didemnum albidum*) forms irregularly shaped colonies that are white, yellowish, or salmon with numerous tiny openings. Its range includes the Arctic to Cape Cod.

Glossy White Crust (*Didemnum candidum*) is a similar-looking species to northern white crust, with tiny spicules that require a microscope to view. Its range includes the area from the Bay of Fundy, Nova Scotia, to Florida, the West Indies, and Brazil.

Paintsplash Tunicate (*Didemnum duplicatum*) is likened to "a splash of thick white paint," hence its name. The colony looks smooth and glossy as well—just like a fresh coat of enamel paint.

Chocolate Tunicate (*Didemnum psammatodes*) is a distinctive chocolate brown species that is found from St. Augustine, Florida, south.

❶ Harbour Star Ascidian

Botryllus schlosseri

Authority: (Pallas, 1766)

Other Names: Also known as eyed tunicate, golden star tunicate

Description: The color is variable, including white, yellow, gold, brown, or purple. The colony is encrusting, with patterns shaped into distinctive star-shaped clusters with rows and loose circles or clusters around raised excurrent pores.

Size: Individuals to 0.06" (1.6 mm); colony to 4" (102 mm) across, 0.1" (3 mm) thick

Habitat/Ecology: On solid surfaces, including rocks, shells, pilings, boat bottoms, and algae; low intertidal zone to shallow waters

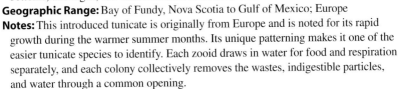

Geographic Range: Bay of Fundy, Nova Scotia to Gulf of Mexico; Europe

Notes: This introduced tunicate is originally from Europe and is noted for its rapid growth during the warmer summer months. Its unique patterning makes it one of the easier tunicate species to identify. Each zooid draws in water for food and respiration separately, and each colony collectively removes the wastes, indigestible particles, and water through a common opening.

❶ Violet Chain Ascidian

Botrylloides violaceus

Authority: Oka, 1927

Other Names: Also known as chain compound ascidian, orange sheath tunicate, violet tunicate; formerly classified as *Botrylloides aurantium*

Description: The color of the colony is quite variable, including orange, purple, yellow, or reddish; forms a thin, soft, crust. The individual zooids are arranged in twisting rows with a chain-like pattern.

Size: Colony to 6" (15 cm) across, 0.1" (3 mm) thick

Habitat/Ecology: In quiet bays and harbors on hard surfaces, including rocks, pilings, and floats; low intertidal zone to shallow subtidal waters

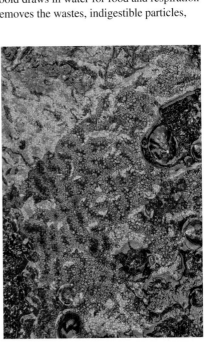

Geographic Range: The entire Atlantic Coast

Notes: The violet chain ascidian is an invader that likely originated from Asia. It has several enemies, including gastropods and nudibranchs. There is also a flatworm that ingests individuals right out of their tunic, consuming them whole. Like several other tunicates, this species reproduces by budding, which occurs at the edge of the colony.

Common Sea Pork

Aplidium stellatum

Authority: (Verrill, 1871)

Other Name: Formerly classified as *Amaroucium stellatum*

Description: Color of the colonies varies considerably when they are found stranded on the beach. There, colors include white, yellow, pink, green, red, or purple. These "rubbery lumps" or slabs are firm and solid. The zooids are visible being elongated and arranged in somewhat regular circular groups over the entire surface, and the small cloacal orifice is found in the center of each circle.

Size: Width to 12" (30 cm); thickness to 1" (25 mm)

Habitat/Ecology: On rocks or sandy bottoms; low intertidal zone to water 262' (80 m) deep

Geographic Range: Massachusetts to Florida

Notes: Numerous predators including sharks, skates, and other bottom-feeding fishes feed on common sea pork.

Similar Species: Northern Sea Pork (*Aplidium constellatum*) produces thin colonies that often have a coating of sand that adheres to the outer surfaces.

Sea Liver

Eudistoma hepaticum

Authority: (Van Name, 1921)

Other Name: Formerly classified as *Polycitor hepaticus*

Description: The overall color of the colony is deep purple. It is solid and often reaches massive sizes. It resembles sea pork except for its color.

Size: Colony length to 10.6" (27 cm); width to 9.4" (24 cm); depth to 4" (10 cm)

Habitat/Ecology: On rocky shores, boulders, and floating docks; low intertidal zone to water 66' (20 m) deep

Geographic Range: Florida to Yucatán

Notes: You'll normally encounter sea liver when storms wash it ashore. This species forms large colonies. It is present year-round and is reported to turn white in midwinter.

Fishes
(Classes Chondrichthyes and Osteichthyes)

Fishes are made up of two major groups: cartilaginous fishes (Class Chondrichthyes) and bony fishes (Class Osteichthyes). Cartilaginous fishes have a skeleton made up of cartilage rather than bones and include the skates, rays, and sharks. As their name suggests, bony fishes have a bony skeleton. Most fishes living now (approximately 21,000 species) are bony fishes. All fishes have gills to obtain oxygen from the water, a backbone surrounding the spinal cord, and single-loop blood circulation.

CARTILAGINOUS FISHES
(Class Chondrichthyes)

Cartilaginous fishes include sharks, skates, and rays. They are vertebrates with an internal skeleton that is made entirely of cartilage and contains no ossified bone.

Little Skate (Egg Case)

Leucoraja erinacea

Authority: (Mitchill, 1825)
Other Names: Also known as summer skate; hedgehog skate; tobacco box; formerly classified as *Raja erinacea*
Description: The egg case is light brown, changing to black when dry. The capsule's exterior is smooth and leathery, with long tendrils or "horns" at each corner. The length of the tendrils is greater than the length of the capsule.
Size: Fresh egg capsule (not including the tendrils): length 2.1–2.5" (53–64 mm); width 1.4–1.9" (35–48 mm)
Habitat/Ecology: Often found washed up on exposed sandy beaches
Geographic Range: Nova Scotia to Virginia
Notes: Empty egg cases are often found on the beach, where they are called "mermaid's purses." This is the most common species of egg case found washed up on the beaches of the North Atlantic. Eggs of little skate are laid year-round in pairs, buried in the sand. Eggs normally require between five and six months to hatch, but during colder months this can be extended to ten months. The adult little skate is flat

and disk-like, and it reaches a length of 20" (51 cm). The dorsal surface is gray or brown.

Winter Skate (Egg Case)

Leucoraja ocellata

Authority: (Mitchill, 1815)
Other Names: Also known as eyed skate, spotted skate, winter skate; formerly classified as *Raja ocellata*
Description: The egg case is greenish brown, changing to brown or black when dry. The capsule's exterior is smooth and leathery, with tendrils at each corner. The length of the tendrils is greater than the length of the capsule. A fibrous mat is attached to both edges of the "purse" (these may break off on the beach).
Size: Fresh egg capsule (not including the tendrils): length 2.5–3.4" (64–86 mm); width 1.4–1.9" (44–52 mm)
Habitat/Ecology: Often found washed up on exposed sandy beaches
Geographic Range: Gulf of St. Lawrence to North Carolina
Notes: Skate egg cases or purses are best identified with a combination of features rather than by size alone. This is due to the fact that the purses shrink significantly as they dry—often more than 30 percent. Female skates anchor the tendrils or "horns" of each egg case to algae to ensure that the capsule remains in place. The adult winter skate is flat and disk-like and reaches a length of 36" (91 cm); the dorsal surface is light brown, often with several eye spots. This species also has more teeth than the little skate (see p. 274).
Similar Species: Barndoor Skate (Egg Case) (*Raja laevis*) is yellowish or greenish brown, drying to black. The purse ranges from 4.7–5.1 inches (12–13 cm) long with four tendrils that are shorter than the capsule. This is the largest skate found in the Atlantic Northeast.

Clearnose Skate (Egg Case)

Raja eglanteria

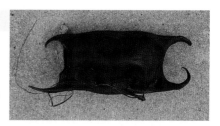

Authority: Bosc, 1800
Other Names: Also known as brier skate, clear-nose brier skate, clear-nose summer skate
Description: The egg case is blackish. The capsule's exterior is somewhat smooth and leathery, and has tendrils at each corner. The length of all tendrils is less than the width of the capsule. No fibrous mat is attached.
Size: Fresh egg capsule (not including the tendrils): length 2–3.5" (50–89 mm); width 1.5–2.25" (38–57 mm)
Habitat/Ecology: Often found washed up on exposed sandy beaches
Geographic Range: Massachusetts to the Gulf of Mexico

Notes: The clearnose skate lays its eggs in Florida from December through to May. A female lays up to sixty-six eggs in one season. Egg incubation is believed to take at least three months. The adult clearnose skate is flat and disk-like, and normally reaches a length of 24" (51 cm), with the largest on record at 37". The dorsal surface is gray or brown with darker spots, blotches, and elongated bars.

BONY FISHES (Class Osteichthyes)

Bony fishes, as their name implies, have an internal skeleton that is made of ossified bone. This group is the largest class of vertebrates, with over 29,000 species found in both freshwater and marine environments globally.

Shorthorn Sculpin

Myoxocephalus scorpius

Authority: (Linnaeus, 1758)
Other Names: Also known as black sculpin, daddy sculpin, Greenland sculpin
Description: The dorsal surface ranges from greenish to reddish or brown, with various markings or bars. The ventral side is yellowish to white. Several large blotches are found on the undersides of males. Its body tapers markedly, which makes this species look "front heavy." The anal fin is comprised of thirteen to fourteen rays.
Size: Length to 36" (90 cm)
Habitat/Ecology: On rocky shores and in tidepools; low intertidal zone to water 360' (110 m) deep
Geographic Range: Labrador to New Jersey; Great Britain; Siberia; Greenland
Notes: The shorthorn sculpin adapts well to water turbulence and a wide range of salinities and temperatures. It is capable of living in many environments and will eat almost anything that is available.
Similar Species: Grubby (*Myoxocephalus aenaeus*) is similar in shape and coloration but is smaller—only reaching 6" (15 cm) in length. It can be identified by counting a total of ten or eleven anal fin rays.

Rock Gunnel

Pholis gunnellus

Authority: (Linnaeus, 1758)
Other Names: Also known as butterfish, gunnel, rock eel, tansy
Description: The color of the body ranges from reddish to yellowish or greenish. It is elongated, with small pectoral fins. Dark spots are present along the back and the dorsal fin. A dark bar frequently runs from behind the mouth through the eye, eventually reaching the dorsal fin.
Size: Length to 12" (30 cm)
Habitat/Ecology: On algae-covered rocks and in tidepools; to water 600' (182 m) deep
Geographic Range: Labrador to Delaware Bay
Notes: The rock gunnel is covered with a thick slime layer that is likely useful in escaping from predators but even more useful in keeping this species moist while out of water. In North America, this species leaves the intertidal areas around December 1 and do not return until it warms up in early March. This species is known to reach four years of age.

Sargassum Anglerfish

Histrio histrio

Authority: (Linnaeus, 1758)
Other Names: Also known as angler-fish, frog fish, sargassum fish, sargassumfish
Description: The color is quite variable, from pale cream to greenish and dark brown, closely resembling the gulf-weed algae this species lives in. Fleshy weed-like appendages are present, and the skin is smooth. The mouth is upturned with an illicum and esca (see below) over the eyes.
Size: Length to 7.8" (20 cm)
Habitat/Ecology: In pelagic gulfweed; to water 35' (11 m) deep
Geographic Range: Gulf of Maine to Uruguay; tropical and subtropical waters of the globe
Notes: The sargassum anglerfish is a member of the frogfishes (family Antennariidae). It bears an illicum and esca—a long narrow tentacle with a tip that holds a swelling. This adaptation is often referred to as a "fishing rod and lure" used to capture its prey. It has also been discovered that this species can actually leap out of the water onto the top of an algal mat where it can remain out of water for some time.

Reptiles
(Class Reptilia)

Most reptiles live on land. A few, however, live in the ocean, but since they must breath air to survive, they must reach the surface on a regular basis. Sea turtles live in the earth's oceans, but females come to land during brief periods of time to lay their eggs. These species are very vulnerable at this time of their lives.

SEA TURTLES
(Families Cheloniidae and Dermochelyidae)

Worldwide there are only seven species of sea turtles—of which all are members of two separate families (Cheloniidae and Dermochelyidae). All sea turtles live their entire adult lives in our oceans. The only time they venture onto land is when the females come to the beach to lay their eggs. Female sea turtles are known to return to the same beach that they hatched from.

Loggerhead Sea Turtle

Caretta caretta

Newly emerged young from nest

Authority: (Linnaeus, 1758)

Other Names: Also known as logger-head turtle; formerly classified as *Testudo caretta*

Description: The color of the adult's carapace, head, and upper side of the flippers is reddish brown. The plastron, neck, and lower side of the flippers are yellow. The head is larger than most sea turtles with a thicker horny beak.

Size: Length of adult to approximately 3' (1 m); weight 250 lbs. (113 kg)

Habitat/Ecology: On sand during egg laying—between the high tide line and the dune front; pelagic otherwise

Geographic Range: North Carolina to Brazil; tropical and subtropical waters of the globe

Notes: The loggerhead sea turtle is a rare species that makes its way onto

Adult female emerging from water to lay eggs

Adult female's tracks on beach

our coastline to nest. Females nest between April and September, laying about three to five nests per season. They are long-lived and reach sexual maturity at approximately thirty-five years old.

Loggerheads obtained their common name from their large heads, which hold powerful jaws that enable them to feed on hard-shelled prey, including whelks and conches. This species is truly a long-distance traveler—known to swim as far as 3000 miles (4,828 km) between nest site and feeding grounds.

Eggs in nest

Green Sea Turtle

Chelonia mydas

Authority: (Linnaeus, 1758)

Other Name: Also known as green turtle

Description: The carapace is pale to dark green, with yellow, brown, and green tones and radiating stripes. The underside is yellowish white. The head is small, blunt with a serrated jaw. The carapace does not have any ridges.

Size: Length of adult to approximately 3' (1 m); weight 350 lbs. (150 kg)

Habitat/Ecology: On sand during egg laying—between the high tide line and the dune front; pelagic otherwise

Geographic Range: Connecticut to the Gulf of Mexico; tropical and subtropical waters of the globe

Notes: The green sea turtle is an endangered species that reaches our Atlantic shores in Florida and occasionally farther north. Females lay their eggs every two to four years. They are long-lived and it is not known how old they are before they are sexually mature. They come to the beach between June and September to lay their eggs. The average nest contains 135 eggs that remain in the sand for about two months before hatching. It is estimated that along the southeast coast of Florida between 200–1100 females nest annually.

Seaweeds

The Atlantic, like the other oceans, contains a large number of organisms that use sunlight to sustain themselves. This group is collectively called algae. Within this group are minute algae which are referred to as microscopic algae. The species in this group are too small to be included in this account. Only the macroscopic algae or seaweeds are included here. There are three phyla of seaweeds that have no flowers, stems, or leaves. They do have a root-like holdfast that attaches the alga to a solid substrate but derives no nutrients from the substrate. The seaweeds include: green algae (Phylum Chlorophyta), brown algae (Phylum Ochrophyta), red algae (Phylum Rhodophyta).

GREEN ALGAE (Phylum Chlorophyta)

Like land plants, green algae contain chlorophylls a and b, the dominant pigments that provide these organisms with their characteristic color. These pigments capture sunlight and convert it to chemical energy used to fix carbon dioxide into sugars (during the process of photosynthesis).

Maiden Hair Sea Lettuce

Ulva intestinalis

Authority: Linnaeus, 1753

Other Names: Also known as green grass seaweed, hollow green weed, hollow green algae, link confetti, maiden hair; formerly classified as *Enteromorpha intestinalis*

Description: The bright green elongated tubes are smooth, unbranched, and grow in clusters.

Size: Height normally to 16" (40 cm); diameter to 0.5" (12 mm)

Habitat/Ecology: On rocks, sand, shells, wharves, and in tidepools; high intertidal zone to shallow subtidal depths

Geographic Range: Canadian Arctic to Florida; Aleutian Islands to Mexico; Russia to Portugal

Notes: This green alga is composed of a tube that is a single cell thick and often bleached white by the sun. It may require close inspection to reveal its hollow tube construction. This cosmopolitan species is often present where freshwater channels reach the ocean. Maiden hair sea lettuce is an edible species that is often added to stews.

Similar Species: Flat-tube Sea Lettuce (*Ulva linza*) (see p. 283)

Flat-tube Sea Lettuce

Ulva linza

Authority: Linnaeus, 1753
Other Names: Also known as water-gut, sea grass, maiden hair; formerly classified as *Enteromorpha linza*
Description: The bright green blades are ribbon-like, with wavy edges, and may be twisted spirally. This species is tubular, with a tapering stipe, and only the upper portion is flattened.
Size: Height to 16" (40 cm); width to 1" (2.5 cm)
Habitat/Ecology: On rocks, jetties, and seawalls; high intertidal zone
Geographic Range: Arctic to South Carolina; Russia to Portugal
Notes: This species is common in the spring. It has similarities to maiden hair sea lettuce (see p. 282) since they are both hollow. Flat-tube sea lettuce is only hollow at its base, however. If you carefully roll the base of the blade between your fingers, you can feel the hollow nature of its base—unlike common sea lettuce (see below) which has a flat base.
Similar Species: Common Sea Lettuce (*Ulva lactuca*) (see below)

Common Sea Lettuce

Ulva lactuca

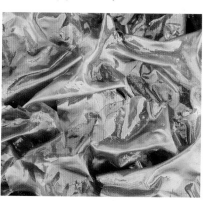

Authority: Linnaeus, 1753
Other Names: Also known as sea lettuce, green laver
Description: This bright green alga is sheet-like and often displays ruffled edges with a thallus that is two cells thick. Older specimens may be perforated.
Size: Height to 24" (60 cm); width to 6" (15 cm); normally much smaller
Habitat/Ecology: On rocks, shells, or in tidepools; an epiphyte (lives on other seaweed species); low intertidal zone
Geographic Range: Newfoundland to Florida
Notes: Common sea lettuce is an alga with the consistency of wax paper, permitting the beachcomber to view his or her fingerprints indistinctly through it (see the similar species section below). This seaweed is added to soups, salads, and many other dishes around the globe. It grows well in areas that are high in nitrogen, including many areas affected by pollution: sewer pipes, broken sewers, septic tank leakage, lawn fertilizers, and agricultural runoff. Always be cautious with any edible species when there's potential for contaminants to be absorbed by the species in question.

Similar Species: Green Laver (*Monostroma oxyspermum*) is thinner (only one cell thick) and often compared to the thickness of tissue paper. A beachcomber can clearly see his or her fingerprints through it. Green laver grows to reach 8" (20 cm) in length. You may also encounter other species of sea lettuce, but you'll need a microscope for their identification.

Green Beaded Filaments

Chaetomorpha melagonium

Authority: (F. Weber and Mohr) Kützing, 1845
Other Name: Also known as green cord seaweed
Description: This yellow-green species is filament-like, stiff, and unbranched; it looks like chain of narrow beads.
Size: Height to 12" (30 cm); width to 0.06" (1.6 mm)
Habitat/Ecology: On rocks in quiet waters, in moist areas and in tidepools; low intertidal zone to water 3' (1 m) deep or greater
Geographic Range: Arctic to New Jersey
Notes: This alga is a cold water species that often goes unnoticed due to the nature of its thin filaments. Its thallus consists of a single row of large cells easily viewed with the naked eye. Green beaded filaments are algae with immense cells that, because of their size, a wide variety of scientists use to investigate cells.
Similar Species: Green Tangled Filaments (*Chaetomorpha linum*) is another bead-shaped coarse alga that is unbranched. It resembles fishing line and grows to 4" (10 cm). The yellowish green cells can be viewed with a hand lens. It is commonly found in tangles. Other similar species may also be encountered. A microscope is required for correct identification.

Green Rope Seaweed

Acrosiphonia spp.

Authority: J. Agardh, 1846
Other Names: Formerly classified as *Codiolum* spp., *Spongomorpha* spp.
Description: The green filaments appear rope-like, and they have microscopic hooks on their branches that become twisted and tangled. This species has a disc-shaped holdfast to attach it to a substrate.
Size: Height to 6" (15 cm)
Habitat/Ecology: On rocky shores and in tidepools; low intertidal zone to subtidal depths

Geographic Range: Arctic to New Jersey

Notes: Green rope seaweed is often believed to be a sponge rather than an alga, and its former scientific name *Spongomorpha* means "sponge shape." The rope-like strands of this alga occur in only the gametophyte (sexual) stage of its life cycle. The sporophyte (asexual) stage looks very different, so much so that it was originally described as another species of algae, *Codiolum*, when first discovered. The gametophyte (sexual) stage is illustrated here. You may encounter several species of green rope seaweed, but you will need a microscope for their identification.

Tufted Sea Moss

Cladophora rupestris

Authority: (Linnaeus) Kützing, 1843

Other Name: Also known as mermaid's hair

Description: The dark green or bluish green filaments are long, soft, and profusely, irregularly branched. No hooklets are present, and this species appears moss-like. A close look reveals the filaments are smooth but not bead-like.

Size: Height to 24" (60 cm)

Habitat/Ecology: On rocks and on exposed coasts; mid intertidal zone to shallow subtidal depths

Geographic Range: Newfoundland to Massachusetts

Notes: This alga is found throughout the year. The fronds of tufted sea moss are easily separated since they lack microscopic hooks. A hand lens allows this characteristic to be viewed. The dense filamental nature of sea moss enables it to hold large volumes of water, preventing it from drying out when the tide recedes. This common species is one of several sea mosses found on the Atlantic Coast.

Similar Species: Green Rope Seaweed (*Acrosiphonia* spp.) (see p. 284)

Plumed Green Seaweed

Bryopsis plumosa

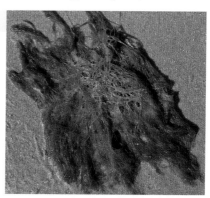

Authority: (Hudson) C. Agardh, 1823

Other Name: Also known as evenly branched mossy feather weed

Description: The color ranges from light to dark green. Branching filaments form an irregular radial pattern around the branches in erect clumps. This branching has been described as "feather-like."

Size: Height to 0.5" (12 cm) tall

Habitat/Ecology: On rocks, wood, jetties, and seawalls; low intertidal zone and lower

Geographic Range: Newfoundland to Mexico; Venezuela to Argentina; Alaska to Pacific Mexico; Asia, Australia, and New Zealand

Notes: The plumed green seaweed lives in protected sites. Its erect, bright green fronds are comprised of large, branching filaments.

Ⓘ Sea Staghorn

Codium fragile

Authority: (Suringar) Hariot, 1889

Other Names: Also known as dead man's fingers, felty fingers, green fleece, green sea velvet, sponge seaweed

Description: The fronds are bright green. Each branch is cylindrical and felt-like in texture. When picked up, it is always super-saturated with water.

Size: Height to 36" (91 cm); branch diameter to 0.75" (19 mm)

Habitat/Ecology: Attached to rocks, mid intertidal to upper subtidal zones; also often found in large tidepools

Geographic Range: Maine to North Carolina; Alaska to Mexico; Japan

Notes: Sea staghorn was accidentally introduced from Europe or the North Pacific in approximately 1957. In Japan this seaweed is considered a delicacy. "Miru," as it is called there, is prepared in a special way by first bleaching it in the sun, and then soaking it in a sugar solution before consuming it.

This species lives for several years, but it has been classified as a perennial, and biennial.

Microscopic fibers run lengthwise along the entire stipe of this alga, branching and re-branching to eventually turn outward and swell at the tips. Only the tips of the fibers display its green color, signifying that photosynthesis is taking place there. These fibers are dense, absorbing a high volume of water and becoming heavy as a result.

BROWN ALGAE
(Phylum Ochrophyta, Class Phaeophyceae)

Brown algae were formerly considered to be part of the phylum Phaeophyta, but due to recent DNA studies they are now placed in the Class Phaeophyceae within the Phylum Ochrophyta. Not all brown seaweeds are brown in color: in fact, they may be yellowish, blackish, or greenish as well. The golden-brown pigment fucoxanthin masks the green of chlorophyll. Consequently, brown algae range in color from yellow through golden brown to almost black.

Tufted Fringe

Elachista spp.

Authority: Duby, 1830
Other Names: Also known as little seaweed; formerly classified as *Elachistea*
spp.
Description: Brown filaments form
dense clumps from a central base.
Size: Height to 0.6" (16 mm) tall

Habitat/Ecology: On large seaweeds such as rockweed (see pp. 293–294) and
knotted wrack (see p. 295); mid to low intertidal zone
Geographic Range: Arctic to Virginia
Notes: This epiphytic alga is common and can be abundant at times. The tufted fringe
is sometimes compared to a man's beard made of clumps of dark brown whiskers.
The bases of this species actually penetrate into the tissue of the host alga, forming a
rather firm "button" that is easily felt when handled.

Sea Cauliflower

Leathesia marina

Authority: (Lyngbye) Decaisne, 1842
Other Names: Also known as sea
potato, cauliflower seaweed, brain seaweed, golden spongy cushion, rat's
brain; formerly classified as *Laethesia
difformis*
Description: The yellowish brown alga
is essentially spherical in shape as well
as convoluted, hollow, and spongy.
Size: Diameter to 5" (12 mm)
Habitat/Ecology: In rocky areas; also epiphytic (growing on other species of algae);
on exposed and protected sites; high to low intertidal zones
Geographic Range: Newfoundland to North Carolina; Bering Sea to Mexico;
Europe; Chile
Notes: The famous botanist and taxonomist Carolus Linnaeus first described this species, but he believed it to be a jelly fungus because of its unusual shape. It has also
been confused with an invertebrate egg sac. It certainly does not look like a "normal"
alga. This species is solid when it is young and small, but as it matures, it changes
dramatically, becoming hollow and convoluted.

Rough Tangle Seaweed

Stilophora tenella

Authority: (Esper) P. C. Silva, 1996
Other Names: Also known as rough tangle weed; formerly classified as *Stilophora rhizodes*
Description: The pale brown filaments are rough with a granular surface due to the presence of small clumps of hairs. The stiff branches are brittle. A disk-like holdfast is present for attachment to algae or other bases.
Size: Height to 12" (30 cm) tall
Habitat/Ecology: In protected waters; low intertidal zone to water approximately 15' (4.5 m) deep
Geographic Range: Prince Edward Island to North Carolina
Notes: Rough tangle seaweed is often found unattached and drifting. This is likely due to its habit of attaching itself loosely to the bases of other algae and common eelgrass (see p. 307).
Similar Species: Slippery Tangle Seaweed (*Sphaerotrichia divaricata*) is a slender bushy alga with fine branches and branchlets attached with wide-angles. It has a soft texture and is often slimy. The largest filaments are less than 0.06" (1.6 mm) thick and 20" (50 cm) tall.

Stringy Acid Weed

Desmarestia viridis

Authority: (O. F. Müller) J. V. Lamouroux, 1813
Other Names: Also known as mermaid's hair, sea sorrel, soft sour weed
Description: The color varies from light to dark brown when under water; olive to green when out of water. Numerous branches hold an opposite branching pattern, ultimately reaching the final filaments (a series of single cells).
Size: Height to 24" (60 cm), occasionally to 39" (100 cm)
Habitat/Ecology: On rocks, shells, or wood and in tidepools; low intertidal zone to water 40' (12 m) deep
Geographic Range: Arctic to New Jersey

Notes: The soft, bushy appearance of this alga does not reveal the harsh nature of its cellular make-up. Stringy acid weed produces sulfuric acid ions inside its cells, and as long as the plant is alive and healthy, it manages to keep the ions from combining with seawater to produce sulfuric acid, which would dissolve or digest its own cells. This species emits a distinctive odor that relates to cell's high acid content. The presence of sulfuric acid in this alga may simply be a method of deterring herbivorous snails and sea urchins from feeding on its tissues.

Similar Species: Wiry Acid Weed (*Desmarestia aculeata*) has a stiff appearance with a pinnate or alternate branching pattern from a central axis. Its range is similar to the stringy acid weed and it is found from the Arctic to Long Island Sound. Some of the common names for this species show a great deal of imagination: witch's hair, crisp color changer, and landlady's wig.

Sausage Seaweed

Scytosiphon spp.

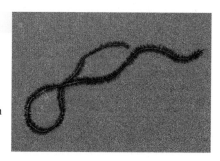

Authority: C. Agardh, 1820
Other Names: Also known as leather tube, sausage weed, soda straws, whip tube
Description: The color of the upright phase varies from golden brown to olive. The fronds are slender, hollow, and constricted at somewhat regular intervals. They normally form clumps from a central base.
Size: Height to 24" (60 cm)
Habitat/Ecology: On rocks and jetties at somewhat exposed sites; low intertidal zone to shallow subtidal waters
Geographic Range: Subarctic to Florida; Bermuda
Notes: This species has two stages in its life history: a crust stage and an upright stage. Sausage seaweed is well named, as the obvious stage resembles a miniature chain of sausages. The crust stage is not as obvious but only present in late summer. This is a common alga that produces an annual fruiting from winter to late spring, often lasting until early summer.

Rough Cord Weed

Halosiphon tomentosus

Authority: (Lyngbye) Jaasund, 1957
Other Names: Also known as cord weed, dead men's ropes, devil's shoe-lace, sea lace, mermaid's tresses, rough hollow weed; formerly classified as *Chorda tomentosa*

Description: The overall color is brown, and there is no branching on the slender whip-like filament. A dense covering of short, dark hairs, to 0.75" (19 mm) long, is present over the entire thallus.

Size: Height to 3.3' (1 m), occasionally to 26.4' (8 meters)

Habitat/Ecology: On rocks, docks, and pilings; low intertidal zone to shallow subtidal waters

Geographic Range: Arctic to Long Island

Notes: This northern annual is present primarily in the winter and spring. In the southern portion of its range, it normally disappears before the beginning of summer. The tiny fur-like hairs that cover its whip-like thallus give it a gritty appearance and are present throughout its lifespan. They sometimes seem to disappear when removed from water, but they have simply bent, lying flat next to the thallus.

Similar Species: Smooth Cordweed (*Chorda filum*) lacks a hair covering on the thallus.

Sugar Kelp

Saccharina latissima

Authority: Druehl and G. W. Saunders, 2006

Other Names: Also known as southern kelp, common southern kelp; formerly classified as *Laminaria saccharina*, *L. agardhii*

Description: The blade is a rich yellowish brown color and has a small, stem-like stalk (stipe). It has a somewhat wrinkled area in the midblade section. Its holdfast is root-like.

Size: Height to 11' (3.5 m); width to 10" (25.4 cm)

Habitat/Ecology: On rocks, pilings, and ledges; low intertidal zone to water 60' (18 m) deep

Geographic Range: Arctic to New Jersey; Alaska to California; Europe

Notes: Sugar kelp actively grows at an amazing rate. In cold northern waters, the entire blade will replace itself at least five times in one year. This common kelp gets its name from the presence of mannite, a sugar alcohol, which gives it a sweet taste. This alga is used as a stabilizing agent for some of our sweeter treats—candies, puddings, and ice creams. This large, impressive kelp is only found at the lowest of tides or washed ashore from subtidal depths. Recent DNA studies have determined that this species is not a member of the genus *Laminaria*, where it was once classified. As a result it is now included in the genus *Saccharina*, a classification that was used historically.

Finger Kelp

Laminaria digitata

Authority: (Hudson) J. V. Lamouroux, 1813

Other Names: Also known as horsetail kelp, fingered kelp, tangle

Description: The dark brown to olive brown thallus is blade-shaped and split into six to thirty finger-like sections. The stalk is very stiff and wood-like.

Size: Height to 6.5' (2 m); width to 4.7" (120 cm)

Habitat/Ecology: On rocks and in tidepools; low intertidal zone

Geographic Range: Arctic to Long Island; Russia; Europe

Notes: Finger kelp is an annual that prefers to live in areas with strong currents and cold water. The scientific name of finger kelp is easy to remember: *digitata* refers to the digits or fingers. Under the right conditions, this kelp will form large patches.

Winged Kelp

Alaria esculenta

Authority: (Linnaeus) Greville, 1830

Other Names: Also known as edible kelp, henware, dabblerlocks, winged kelp; formerly classified as *Laminaria esculenta*

Description: The yellowish brown blade is elongated, and a distinct midrib is found along its entire length. A group of reproductive bladelets, called sporophylls, are present on the lower portions of the stipe. A root-like holdfast anchors this alga to its substrate.

Size: Height to 10' (3 m); width to 6" (155 mm)

Habitat/Ecology: On rocks in areas of exposed surf; in tidepools; low intertidal zone to water 25' (7.5 m) deep

Geographic Range: Arctic to Long Island Sound

Notes: Winged kelp has a long history of being eaten, as it has been added to soups and is fabulous raw in salads (very similar to Japanese wakame). This species is also used as an additive in animal feed and as a fertilizer or soil conditioner.

This large seaweed, like several other algae, alternates phases in its life history, with a microscopic filament that attaches to rocks and similar substrates which in turn produces sperm cells and eggs. After fertilization these miniature kelp grow into the larger form that we recognize as winged kelp.

Sieve Kelp

Agarum clathratum

Authority: Dumortier, 1822

Other Names: Also known as devil's apron, sea colander, shotgun kelp; formerly classified as *Agarum cribrosum*

Description: The blade is dark brown to olive and heavily perforated. It is noticeably ruffled, somewhat leathery, and graced with a flattened midrib.

Size: Height normally to 1.5' (43 cm) occasionally to 12' (3.6 m); width to 12" (30 cm);

Habitat/Ecology: On rocks of protected shorelines and deep tidepools; low intertidal zone to water 30' (9 m) deep and lower

Geographic Range: Arctic to Cape Cod; Bering Sea to Washington (state)

Notes: Looking like an alga that has been riddled with holes by voracious herbivores, sieve kelp is easily identified. It often washes ashore after storms. This species is known to live to six years in Alaska.

Pecock's Tail Alga

Padina pavonica

Authority: (Linnaeus) Thivy, 1960

Other Names: Also known as trumpet petticoat alga; formerly classified as *Fucus pavonicus*

Description: The blades are yellowish brown, with whitish bands. They are fan-shaped, leafy, and low-growing, and they display concentric zonation in the banding.

Size: Diameter of each blade to 1" (25 mm)

Habitat/Ecology: On rocks, shells, roots of the red mangrove in tidal flats at sandy sites or in beds of seagrass; low intertidal zone to water 66' (20 m) deep

Geographic Range: North Carolina to Brazil; Africa; Europe; Australia

Notes: This low-lying alga is common in tropical areas and makes its way as far north as North Carolina. It is commonly found growing in clusters. This is one of several similar-looking species of algae; however, this is the only one to grow at intertidal levels.

Northern Rockweed

Fucus vesiculosus

Authority: Linnaeus, 1753
Other Names: Also known as bladder
focus, bladder wrack, bladderwrack,
dyers' focus, paddy tang, red fucus
rockweed, sea wrack, swine tang,
wrack

Description: The blades vary in color
from golden-yellow to dark green. A prominent midrib is present, and the blades
divide dichotomously (equally). Pairs of pea-shaped air bladders may be present
inside the blade. A disk-shaped holdfast is present to anchor the alga to a solid
substrate.

Size: Height to 3' (0.9 m)

Habitat/Ecology: On rocks, shells, pilings, wharves, and in estuaries; mid to low
intertidal zone

Geographic Range: Arctic to North Carolina

Notes: You can find several species of rockweed along the Atlantic shorelines. The
northern rockweed is the most common species of rockweed found along our Atlantic coastline. Its round, paired receptacles or swollen reproductive structures are
distinctive when present. When mature, most *Fucus* species contain receptacles with
mucilage inside during winter and spring. If a receptacle is opened, it is yellowish
orange in males and green in females. Each receptacle releases its gametes into the
water at high tide. Air bladders are also found in some species, and these help to
keep the blades afloat when submerged.

    Northern rockweed has been used to treat numerous ailments, including goiter; this
treatment has not been tested, however, and is not recommended.

Similar Species: **Spiral Rockweed** (*Fucus spiralis*) (see below) displays winged
receptacles.

    Flat Rockweed (*Fucus distichus*) (see p. 294) has long, flattened receptacles on its
blades.

Spiral Rockweed

Fucus spiralis

Authority: Linnaeus, 1753
Other Names: Also known as rockweed, spiraled wrack, spiral wrack;
formerly classified as *Fucus vesiculosus* var. *spiralis*

Description: The color of the thallus
varies from olive green to yellow
brown. The blades are flat, with a
prominent midrib, and contain receptacles that are normally swollen but not

paired. This species displays "winged receptacles" or receptacles with a distinct ridge that may be found on twisted branches.

Size: Height to 3' (0.9 m)

Habitat/Ecology: On rocks, often in relatively quiet water; high intertidal zone

Geographic Range: Arctic to North Carolina; Alaska to California; Europe; Africa

Notes: This is an easy species to misidentify if you are relying on the receptacles alone. Older specimens often lack the ridge of tissue found around the receptacles. Northern rockweed is also known to display the ridge around "new" receptacles. Use as many characteristics as possible for accurate identifications.

Spiral rockweed is normally present above northern rockweed (see p. 292) and knotted wrack (see p. 295) in the high intertidal zone.

Similar Species: Toothed Rockweed (*Fucus serratus*) is similar, except that its blades have a distinctive saw-toothed edge with no air-bladders. It can be found in the low intertidal zone from the Gaspé Peninsula, Quebec, to Bar Harbor, Maine. This species is thought to be introduced from Europe.

Flat Rockweed

Fucus distichus

Authority: Linnaeus, 1767

Other Names: Also known as seawrack; formerly classified as *Fucus distichus* ssp. *distichus*, *Fucus gardneri*

Description: The color varies from olive green to yellowish green. A midrib is present on the blade. The receptacles are long, flattened, and range in size from 2–4" (51–102 mm) long. Each receptacle displays a pointed tip.

Size: Height to 24" (60 cm)

Habitat/Ecology: On rocks; low intertidal zone to shallow subtidal depths

Geographic Range: Arctic to New York; Alaska to California; Europe, Asia

Notes: Recently, DNA studies have been conducted on several species of rockweeds on both the Atlantic and Pacific Coasts. These studies determined that a species found on the Pacific, *Fucus gardneri*, is actually the same species that is found on the Atlantic Coast, *Fucus distichus*. We also now know that flat rockweed (*Fucus distichus*) is found on many continents and oceans around the globe. In protected areas, this seaweed can live for five years.

Knotted Wrack

Ascophyllum nodosum

Authority: (Linnaeus) Le Jolis, 1863

Other Names: Also known as knot weed, rockweed, sea whistle, yellow tang

Description: The fronds are olive green, and in spring the receptacles are yellowish, stalked, and warty. The round fronds have no midrib. Conspicuous, swollen air bladders are present along the fronds at various intervals. Branching is irregular, and a disk-shaped holdfast is present.

Size: Height normally to 24" (60 cm), occasionally to 10' (3 m)

Habitat/Ecology: On rocks and mud shorelines; mid to low intertidal zone

Geographic Range: Arctic to New Jersey; Europe; Iceland

Notes: In northern areas of our coastline, knotted wrack is the dominant species of algae. This species only establishes itself where other algal species are present because it is the final stage of algal succession in the intertidal zone of the Atlantic Northeast. Knotted wrack is a long-lived species, normally to fifteen years, and it is believed that some holdfasts may be up to 400 years old! This is the equivalent of an old-growth forest at our seashore.

Knotted wrack is a perennial that is harvested in the Atlantic Northeast and in Norway, Ireland, and Iceland. Its uses include emulsifiers, thickening agents, animal fodder, and fertilizers. This species is often the host to a red alga called wrack fringe tubeweed (see p. 303). Knotted wrack is an abundant, slippery species that often completely covers the rocks that it grows on, making it a thick, treacherous carpet to walk over.

Shallow-water Gulfweed

Sargassum filipendula

Authority: C. Agardh 1824

Other Name: Also known as floating seaweed

Description: The overall color is golden brown to light brown. The main stipes are long, narrow, and generally smooth and divided along its length. Lance-shaped leaves that have saw-toothed edges, along with a distinct midrib, are also present. Small grape-like bladders may be found on slender, short, stalks. It also has a holdfast that is attached to a rock or shell.

Size: Length to 39" (100 cm) occasionally to 79" (200 cm)

Habitat/Ecology: On rocks or shells; from just below low tide to water 95' (28.5 m) deep

Geographic Range: Massachusetts to Florida; Gulf of Mexico; Caribbean; Brazil; West Africa

Notes: This species can be difficult to tell apart from two similar species that often have some of their characteristics lacking or not visible. As a result identifications are often not reliable, and all three species can be found as far north as Massachusetts.

This is a shallow-water species that is more likely to be found in the mid-Atlantic. The two similar species listed below are free-floating pelagic species originating from the Caribbean (specifically, the Sargasso Sea—an area of approximately two million square miles). These species often make their way to our shores with hitch-hikers, which include sargassum nudibranch (see p. 134), gulfweed crab (see p. 244), sargassum swimming crab (see p. 238), sargassum bryozoan (see p. 252), and others.

Similar Species: Broad-toothed Gulfweed (*Sargassum fluitans*) displays oval floats and smooth stalks that are often winged with a ridge of tissue. This species lacks a holdfast, as it is pelagic.

Common Gulfweed (*Sargassum natans*) displays floats with pointed tips or spines. This species lacks a holdfast, as it is pelagic.

RED ALGAE (Phylum Rhodophyta)

The majority of red algae are some shade of red; however, some species can exhibit a wide variety of colors, from yellow through blue to nearly black. This color variation results from the dominant accessory pigments phycoerythrin (red) and phycocyanin (blue), which actually mask the blue-green of chlorophyll a. Red algae absorb green, blue, and red portions of the light spectrum.

Twig Seaweed

Polyides rotundus

Authority: (Hudson) Gaillon, 1828

Other Names: Also known as discoid forked weed, goat tang

Description: The color of living specimens ranges from dark red to nearly black, and they change to black when they dry out. Several erect, stiff stalks originate from a single disk-like holdfast. Each stalk branches up to eight times dichotomously. The diameter of the round branches remains approximately the same along its entire length.

Size: Height to 12" (30 cm) tall

Habitat/Ecology: On rocks and in tidepools; low intertidal zone to subtidal depths of 66' (20 m)

Geographic Range: Arctic to Long Island; Europe; Russia

Notes: Twig seaweed can be found in low intertidal tidepools, but it is more common at subtidal levels. Some plants have barely noticeable swellings in the upper branches when they are at reproductive maturity. The species name *rotundus* refers to the round or spherical nature of its branches.

Red Crust Algae

Hildenbrandia spp.

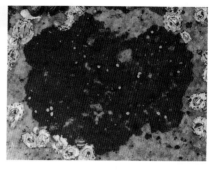

Authority: (Sommerfelt) Meneghini, 1841

Other Names: Also known as red crust, red rock crust, rusty rock

Description: The color varies from bright brownish red to orange or purple. Very thin, irregular patches form on rocks.

Size: Width to 3" (76 mm); several individuals may merge at subtidal sites

Habitat/Ecology: On rocks; low intertidal zone to subtidal water 70' (21 m) deep

Geographic Range: Arctic to Florida

Notes: This crust is closely attached to its substrate with an amazing tenacity. This species starts out with a bright coloration and becomes noticeably darker with age.

Coralline-crust Algae

Clathromorphum spp.

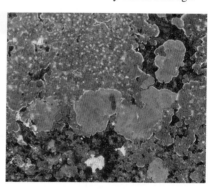

Authority: Foslie, 1898

Other Names: Also known as coralline alga; formerly classified as *Phymatolithon* spp.

Description: The color varies from yellowish pink to purplish pink. The crust-like, calcareous thallus varies from smooth to very irregular and imbricate.

Size: Width to 4" (10 cm)

Habitat/Ecology: On rocks; low intertidal zone to water 50' (15 m) deep

Geographic Range: Arctic to Gulf of Maine

Notes: Coralline-crust algae produces some truly beautiful patterns on the rocks to which the algae clings. A camera or paintbrush is ideal for recording this species' designs, as it cannot be removed from its substrate. This species also loses its fabulous color when removed from its habitat and left in the sun. The tortoiseshell limpet (see p. 55) is a specialized feeder, with iron-capped teeth, that eats this algae.

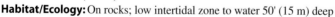

Knobby Coralline-crust Alga

Lithothamnion glaciale

Authority: Kjellman, 1883

Other Names: Also known as knobby red crust, stone shrub

Description: The color ranges from pink to purplish, but it often bleaches to white. This crustose alga forms a thick, calcareous crust covered with numerous rounded, rough, nipple-like protuberances on the surface.

Size: Height to 12" (30 cm); width to 0.75" (2 cm)

Habitat/Ecology: On rocks, shells, or free-living; low intertidal zone to subtidal depths of 180' (55 m)

Geographic Range: Arctic to New Jersey; Europe; Australia

Notes: The distinctive appearance of the knobby coralline-crust alga makes it one of the easiest alga to identify in the field. Its crust is formed from calcium and magnesium carbonate. Its conceptacles (sunken cavities where the reproductive structures are located) are produced from spring to early winter. Coralline algae in general are among some of the longest-lived algae known—some specimens as old as fifty have been recorded.

Branching Coralline Alga

Corallina officinalis

Authority: Linnaeus, 1758

Other Names: Also known as common coral weed, coral weed

Description: Overall color varies from whitish pink to lilac. The fronds are calcified, articulated, and repeatedly pinnate (irregularly), with a cylindrical axis that arises from a disc-like base.

Size: Height normally to 2.75" (70 mm), occasionally to 4.7" (120 mm)

Habitat/Ecology: On rocks, shells, or similar hard objects and in tidepools; low intertidal zone to subtidal depths of 50' (15 m)

Geographic Range: Arctic to Caribbean; Bermuda; Chile; Europe; China; Australia

Notes: This feather-like alga contains deposits of calcium and magnesium carbonate precipitated from the water. It is unknown why some red algae include calcium carbonate in their tissues. This calcareous layer may protect them against damage from various herbivorous animals, but this is only a theory. Branching coralline alga is often found growing in dense masses.

Purple Claw Seaweed

Cystoclonium purpureum

Authority: (Hudson) Batters, 1902

Other Names: Also known as bushy red seaweed, bushy red weed, purple claw weed

Description: The color of the fronds varies from purplish pink to deep purple or almost black. The fronds are soft and cylindrical, with many alternate branchlets that taper at both ends. Long, twisting tendrils may be present at the ends of some fronds. The fronds have a characteristically fleshy and firm texture.

Size: Height to 24" (60 cm) tall; diameter of each frond to 0.1" (3 mm)

Habitat/Ecology: On rocks, shells, and in tidepools; low intertidal zone to subtidal waters 45' (13.5 m) deep

Geographic Range: Newfoundland to New Jersey; Europe; Australia

Notes: The purple claw seaweed is a common red alga that prefers sheltered sites. Its genus *Cystoclonium* is translated "branches with bladders," which refers to the reproductive structures found on the branches of mature plants. This common summertime species often has an onion-like smell when freshly collected.

Variable Graceful Seaweed

Gracilaria tikvahiae

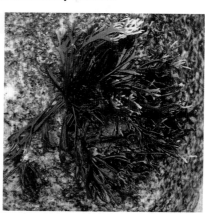

Authority: McLachlan, 1979

Other Name: Also known as graceful red weed

Description: The color varies widely from dark green to purplish red or brown. The numerous short, pointed branches grow in one plane, producing a relatively flat alga that is somewhat bushy. A small disc-like holdfast attaches to rocks or similar objects.

Size: Height to 14.4" (37 cm)

Habitat/Ecology: On rocks, shells, and jetties; also free-living; low intertidal zone to water 158' (48 m) deep

Geographic Range: The Maritime Provinces to Florida; Gulf of Mexico; Colombia

Notes: Much work has been done in the scientific world regarding seaweeds. *Gracilaria*, for instance, once contained at least a hundred species. Today, we now recognize only seven around the world. That figure will possibly change too as more information comes to light from the scientific community.

As its common name suggests, variable graceful seaweed is a highly variable species. It is also an opportunistic species that is common in areas where nutrient-loading leads to either seasonal or year-round eutrophication. This alga is also found year-round in protected bays, as well as in high-energy coastlines.

Irish Moss

Chondrus crispus

Authority: Stackhouse, 1797

Other Names: Also known as carragheen, carrageen, carrageen moss

Description: The color varies widely from purplish red to dark purple at shaded sites. At sites exposed to bright sunlight, the color ranges from yellow-ish green to yellow or white. Under-water, a bluish iridescence is often present. The flattened blades are carti-laginous and extend in tufts from a disk-like holdfast—each repeatedly dividing dichotomously.

Size: Height normally to 6" (155 mm), height in sheltered sites to 10" (250 mm); width to 4" (102 mm)

Habitat/Ecology: On rocks, shells, or wood and in tidepools; mid intertidal zone to water 230' (70 m) deep

Geographic Range: Arctic to New Jersey; Europe

Notes: Irish moss is a common perennial that requires three to five years to reach maturity. It is harvested commercially for its carrageenan—an important thickening agent for foods such as ice cream, syrups, puddings, and dairy products. You can also make a great pudding from Irish moss yourself. Avoid harvesting it from areas that have contaminants, such as near agricultural runoff or industrial sites. To make Irish moss pudding (a white dessert jelly), simply add ¼ cup of dried Irish moss to 1¼ pint of whole milk, and let sit for twenty minutes before placing in a double boiler to simmer for half an hour. Stir the mixture to ensure it does not stick to the bottom. Add three tablespoons of sugar and strain the mixture before letting it cool. It's great served with bits of chocolate or fresh fruit.

Similar Species: **False Irish Moss** (*Mastocarpus stellatus*) (see p. 301) is covered with papillae, or small bumps.

False Irish Moss

Mastocarpus stellatus

Authority: (Stackhouse) Guiry, 1984
Other Names: Blade Phase: carra-gheen, carrageen moss, tufted red weed; formerly classified as *Gigartina stellata* or *G. cornopifolia*; previously spelled *Mastocarpus stellata*
  Crust Phase: formerly classified as *Petrocelis cruenta*

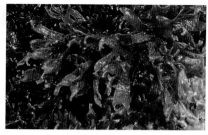
Blade phase

Description: During the blade phase, the purplish red to brown blades are firm, cartilaginous, flattened, and dichotomously branched one or more times. The surfaces of the blades are usually covered with numerous papil-lae, or small bumps, on female plants. Male plants lack papillae and are rare to find. Fronds form dense tufts, arising from a disk-like holdfast.

Tar or crust phase

During the crust phase, the purplish black crust is tar-like and glossy, with a smooth surface. Its shape is more or less random.

Size: Blade Phase: Height to 8" (20 cm)
  Crust Phase: Diameter to 4.75" (12 cm); thickness to 0.04" (1 mm)
Habitat/Ecology: On rocks; low intertidal zone to water 99' (30 m) deep
Geographic Range: Newfoundland to North Carolina; Europe; northern Russia
Notes: False Irish moss is often confused with Irish moss (see p. 300). They are often collected together when harvested for carrageenan. The life cycle of false Irish moss consists of two distinct stages or phases. These phases are easily distinguished, and originally, they were even considered to be separate species. We know now that the blade phase and crust phase are part of the life cycle of the same species, although they look totally unrelated. The blade phase is often found immediately above Irish moss in the low intertidal zone because it is more frost tolerant. The tar-like crust phase is often referred to as the Petrocelis-phase because it was formerly believed to be a separate species named *Petrocelis cruenta*.

Variable Tube Seaweed

Devaleraea ramentacea

Authority: (Linnaeus) Guiry, 1982
Other Names: Also known as sea bag; formerly classified as *Devaleraea ramentaceum*, *Halosaccion ramentaceum*

Description: The color varies from purple to reddish overall. The tubular fronds may be branched or unbranched. A small basal holdfast keeps the alga in place. The stipes are generally short, with bag-like ends.

Size: Length to 16" (40 cm)

Habitat/Ecology: On rocks and shells, and in tidepools; at or near the low intertidal zone

Geographic Range: Arctic to Massachusetts

Notes: This alga is a variable species that has a long history of scientific names—each of which was once believed to be a separate species. Today, we now realize just how variable this species can be.

Similar Species: Dumont's Tubular Weed (*Dumontia contorta*) is similar, with a yellowish to purple coloration. It may reach 19.5" (50 cm) in length, with irregular swellings on the fronds.

Agardh's Red Weed

Agardhiella subulata

Authority: (C. Agardh) Kraft and M. J. Wynne, 1979

Other Name: Formerly classified as *Agardhiella tenera*

Description: The color varies from greenish or brownish to rose-red, with a rather translucent look to it. The main axis is cylindrical and cartilaginous; it may be branched with few or many branches, which taper at both ends.

Size: Height to 18" (45 cm) tall

Habitat/Ecology: On shells, stones, or jetties; low intertidal zone to water 149' (45 m) deep

Geographic Range: Massachusetts to Brazil

Notes: This species was named after G. Agardh, a Swedish psychologist. The branches of this species are actually the germlings of the sexual stage of this species. This species is much more common intertidally than subtidally.

Purple Dulse

Palmaria palmata

Authority: (Linnaeus) Weber and Mohr, 1805

Other Names: Also known as dulse; formerly classified as *Rhodymenia palmata*

Description: The thallus is made up of several separate leaflets attached to its short stipe. Its blades are leather-like, wide, and divided into finger-like extensions.

Size: Height to 20" (50 cm) tall

Habitat/Ecology: On rocks, pebbles, and other seaweeds; low intertidal zone to water 10' (3 m) deep

Geographic Range: Arctic to New Jersey

Notes: Dulse is renowned for its uses as a food. It is used in soups, chowders, sandwiches, and salads, or added to pizza dough.

The life cycle of purple dulse is somewhat different than most other algae. Scientists have known about the asexual plants and the male gamete-producing stage for a long time, but the female gamete-producing stage was never found. Eventually female gamete-producing individuals were discovered to be much smaller than the large male gamete-producing stage, and the full life cycle was found to be unique to purple dulse and other members of the genus *Palmaria*. This species is a common intertidal seaweed in the northern part of its range.

Rosy Fan Alga

Rhodymenia pseudopalmata

Authority: (J. V. Lamouroux) P. C. Silva, 1952

Other Name: Formerly classified as *Rhodymenia pseudopalmata* var. *caroliniana*

Description: The fronds are light brownish red to rose-red in color, fanshaped, flattened, and rather stiff; they divide diochotomously several times. The stipe is short in intertidal specimens.

Size: Height to 7" (180 mm); width to 0.4" (10 mm)

Habitat/Ecology: On rocks and in tidepools; low intertidal zone to water 99' (30 m) deep

Geographic Range: North Carolina to Florida; Brazil; Europe; Mediterranean; Africa

Notes: This beautiful widespread species is more common intertidally in North Carolina. It actually grows both epilithic (grows on the surface of rock) and epiphytic (grows on another plant or alga).

Wrack Fringe Tubeweed

Vertebrata lanosa

Authority: (Linnaeus) T. A. Christensen, 1967

Other Name: Also known as tubed red weed, tubed weed; formerly classified as *Polysiphonia lanosa*; occasionally misspelled *P. lanora*

Description: The fronds are reddish brown to dark brown or black in color. They are cylindrical, cartilaginous, densely tufted, and repeatedly branched. The wrack fringe tubeweed attaches to its host by creeping rhizoids that penetrate into the host plant.

Size: Height to 3" (75 mm) tall
Habitat/Ecology: On knotted wrack (see p. 293) but never on rock; mid intertidal zone
Geographic Range: Arctic to New Jersey
Notes: Wrack fringe tubeweed is a tough, hemiparasite (an organism that is partially parasitic but largely independent and photosynthetic) of knotted wrack (see p. 295) and occasionally northern rockweed (see p. 293). It is normally very abundant when present.

    This epiphyte obtains amino acids, phosphates, and other minerals from its host. In addition, there is also a mutual exchange of fixed carbon compounds through photosynthesis. Wrack fringe tubeweed wounds its host's tissues and may actually stunt its growth.

Grinnell's Pink Leaf

Grinnellia americana

Authority: (C. Agardh) Harvey 1853
Other Name: Formerly classified as *Delesseria americana*
Description: The striking color of this species ranges from delicate rose to pink. The blades are lanceolate to ovate in shape and composed of a thin, translucent membrane that can be found in three forms. A prominent midrib is present on the blade in all forms. Male plants are small and not noticeably marked. Female plants display small round patches of color, with numerous tiny pin-holes over the entire blade. Spore-bearing plants are dotted throughout with numerous small, irregular, elongate patches of stronger color.
Size: Length to 2' (60 cm); width to 4" (10 cm)
Habitat/Ecology: On shells, rocks, or wharves; in quiet waters; low intertidal zone to water 40' (12 m) deep
Geographic Range: Massachusetts to southern Florida and Caribbean
Notes: Grinnell's pink leaf is a seasonal seaweed that can be totally absent on one day and flourishing a few days later. Its population will often explode in August, and it may last for as long as six weeks. The reason for this sudden appearance is unknown, just as with several other species of seaweeds.

    The thallus of this beautiful seaweed is often used to produce art cards and similar artworks.
Similar Species: Laver (*Porphyra* spp.) is darker, thicker, and lacks a midrib.

Elegant Chenille

Dasya baillouviana

Authority: (Gmelin) Montagne 1841

Other Name: Also known as chenille weed

Description: Color ranges from vivid rose to wine or deep purple, and may bleach with age. The branches are elongated and bushy, with fine fur-like branched filaments of equal length that extend in all directions creating a cylindrical, chenille-like appearance. These filaments collapse when brought out of the water. Some plants bear small, dark, berry-like attachments among the filaments which are the reproductive structures. This species arises from small, flat, and round holdfasts.

Size: Length to 36" (90 cm)

Habitat/Ecology: In protected areas with good tidal flow; subtidal depths of 59–132' (18–40 m) deep

Geographic Range: Prince Edward Island to Florida and Gulf of Mexico; Caribbean; Brazil; widespread in warm temperate to tropical seas

Notes: Although this species is a subtidal alga, it often washes up on the beach. It is truly a delicate and beautiful species, especially when viewed underwater. The elegant chenille is often used as the main subject for artwork as wall pieces.

Flowering Plants
(Phylum Anthophyta)

Flowering plants are also found at the seashore; however, only a few species are able to live there. These are members of the same phylum that we are all familiar with around us. They typically have flowers, roots, and leaves. These plants use chlorophyll to capture sunlight and convert it to chemical energy used to fix carbon dioxide into sugars during the process of photosynthesis.

Smooth Cordgrass

Spartina alterniflora

Authority: Loisel, 1807

Other Names: Also known as erect cordgrass, cordgrass, marsh grass, salt-marsh cordgrass, salt marsh grass, saltwater cordgrass, tall cordgrass

Description: Fresh leaves are dark green, long, tapering, and flat, with maroon-colored sheaths at their bases. The flower clusters reach up to 12" (30 cm) long.

Size: Height often to 14" (35 cm) tall, occasionally to 9.9' (3 m) tall; width of leaves 0.2" (0.5 cm) or wider

Habitat/Ecology: In mudflats next to an estuary or tidal creek; mid intertidal zone

Geographic Range: Newfoundland to Florida

Notes: Smooth cordgrass has the greatest salt tolerance among grasses. This species is a tall, smooth grass that grows to a height of 6 inches or 7 feet, depending upon its location at the seashore. Near the water, it grows the tallest, and as it grows in the high intertidal zone, its height is the shortest. Smooth cordgrass blooms late in the summer and has inconspicuous, terminal green flowers. It reproduces by extending its rhizomes, or horizontal stems, beneath the marsh mud. This species stabilizes mudflats and aerates the heavy soils.

Similar Species: **Salt Meadow Cordgrass** (*S. patens*) grows above smooth cordgrass in the high intertidal zone. This shorter species reaches a height of 24" (60 cm) with narrower leaves, less than 0.2" (0.5 cm) wide, that are rolled. This species, also called salt meadow hay, is less salt tolerant than smooth cordgrass.

Common Eelgrass

Zostera marina

Authority: Linnaeus, 1753
Other Names: Also known as barnacle grass, eel-grass, eel grass, eelgrass, grass wrack
Description: The green leaves are elongated and characteristically flat, growing from a rhizome in sand or mud.
Size: Height to 8' (2.5m); width to 0.5" (1.2 cm)
Habitat/Ecology: In quiet bays with sand or mud bottoms; low intertidal zone to water 100' (30 m) deep
Geographic Range: Arctic to South Carolina; Alaska to Mexico

Notes: Common eelgrass often grows in large beds, which are a critical habitat for a wide range of marine species, including invertebrates and fishes. The roots stabilize the substrate, ensuring that the area is protected from erosion. In the early 1930s, common eelgrass experienced widespread, catastrophic losses due to a blight. The Atlantic eelgrass limpet (*Lottia alveus*) once made this plant its host from Labrador to New York. Today, the Atlantic eelgrass limpet is extinct, likely due to the drastic reduction of its host species, common eelgrass. The brant (*Branta bernicla*) was also negatively impacted by the loss of much of its food from this blight; however, it has recovered, as has common eelgrass.

Pickleweed

Salicornia spp.

Authority: (Linnaeus, 1753)
Other Names: Also known as glasswort, saltwort, samphire, sea asparagus
Description: A green, fleshy succulent that changes its colors in late summer to a mix of green and red. Its narrow stems are jointed, and the leaves are reduced to minute scales. The green flowers are tiny and inconspicuous, and they begin to bloom in August.
Size: Height to 20" (50 cm); stems may trail to 39" (1 m)
Habitat/Ecology: On sheltered shores at and above the high tide mark; especially common in saltwater marshes and tidal flats
Geographic Range: New Brunswick to Florida; Gulf of Mexico

Notes: Pickleweeds have been used traditionally as food and as an external medicinal plant for a variety of ailments. As food, they are served as a fresh (and very salty) veggie, and they are preserved as pickles. Several species are found along the Atlantic Coast. Woody pickleweed (*Salicornia pacifica*) is a woody perennial that is also found along the Pacific coast. Additional species are also present. Much confusion surrounds the identification of *Salicornia* that may be encountered in North America.

Seaside Plantain

Plantago maritima

Authority: (Linnaeus, 1753)
Other Names: Also known as goose-tongue seashore plantain, sea plantain
Description: The leaves are light green to brown, the stem is reddish brown, and the flowers are greenish, changing to golden brown. The leaves are long, narrow, and tapered to a point at the tips, and they grow from a taproot. One or more flowering stems are present, each producing numerous, tiny flowers in crowded spikes.
Size: Height to 10" (25 cm)
Habitat/Ecology: On moist beaches, in crevices of large boulders, sandy or gravel beaches, and salt marshes
Geographic Range: Arctic to Virginia; Alaska to California; Eurasia; Patagonia; the Galapagos Islands
Notes: This species produces its tiny flowers from June to October. Various native peoples of North America ate the young, salty leaves of the seaside plantain.

Sea Purslane

Sesuvium portulacastrum

Authority: (Linnaeus, 1759)
Other Names: Also known as perennial sea-purslane, shoreline seapurslane
Description: The green or red leaves are positioned opposite each other on a stem. This sprawling, fleshy perennial has inflated leaves, and its star-like, purplish pink flowers have five sepals and no petals.
Size: Height to 24" (61 cm)
Habitat/Ecology: The face of dunes to the upper beach
Geographic Range: Florida to the Gulf of Mexico; Hawaii
Notes: Sea purslane is an edible species with stems and leaves that taste something like a salty green bean. In Asia this plant

is sold in vegetable markets and considered a source of vitamin C. Some believe sea purslane helps with kidney troubles and scurvy. Propagation is simple—push a cut stem into moist soil, and it will produce new roots. This species blooms all year round.

Red Mangrove

Rhizophora mangle

Authority: Linnaeus, 1753

Other Names: Also known as American mangrove, mangle rojo, mangrove

Description: Their leaves are dark green, to 6" (15 cm) long, and generally larger and shinier than other mangroves. The flowers are white to cream, and the fruit is a dark brown oval berry. Prominent prop roots extend into the water from higher up on the trunk of the plant than other mangroves. Their seeds, or propagules, are long and pencil-shaped.

Size: Height to 115' (35 m)

Habitat/Ecology: In sand or mud; brackish or saline coastal shorelines that are protected from large waves; at the water's edge

Geographic Range: North Carolina to Brazil; Guatemala to Panama; Colombia; Ecuador

Notes: The red mangrove is the most common mangrove found in the Atlantic tropical and subtropical region. This species flowers all year long. It reproduces by propagules, floating seeds which are actually embryonic roots. When they are released from the tree, they have grown up to 10" (25 cm) long and have already germinated.

Similar Species: Black Mangrove (*Avicennia germinans*) lives higher on the shoreline and has long underground cable roots, which produce numerous thin, upright pneumatophores on the ground beside the tree. Its propagules are bean-like and flattened in shape.

Spire

Whorl

Axial rib

Aperture

Body whorl

Outer lip

Inner lip

Canal

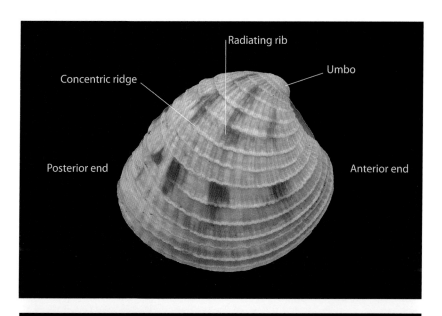

Radiating rib

Umbo

Concentric ridge

Posterior end

Anterior end

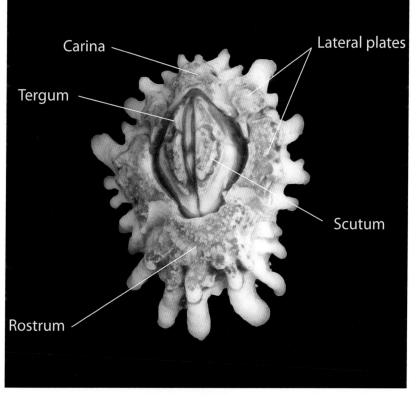

Carina

Lateral plates

Tergum

Scutum

Rostrum

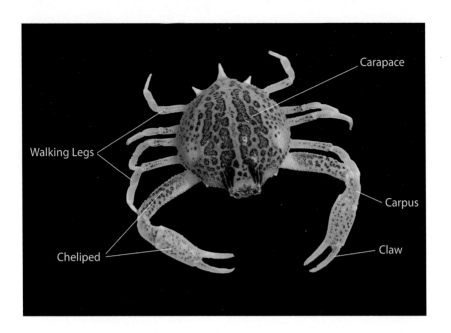

Carapace

Walking Legs

Carpus

Cheliped

Claw

GLOSSARY

Acontia: Thin threads that contain nematocysts for use defensively by many anemones.

Alga (plural algae): Plants that live in an aquatic environment and lack a root system.

Antenna (plural antennae): A slender, sensory appendage that projects from the cephalic (head) area.

Aperture: The opening into which the entire body of a snail can withdraw.

Apex: The top of a shell in a snail, limpet, or other gastropod.

Atrium: A chamber of the heart.

Beak: The projecting part of the hinge in bivalves.

Byssal threads: See **Byssus**.

Byssus: Tough silk-like threads secreted by a gland in the foot of some bivalves to anchor their valves to a solid substrate.

Callus: A tongue-like covering of the umbilicus.

Carapace: The hard covering or exoskeleton that protects the upper portion of a shrimp or crab.

Carpus: The wrist-like joint of crustaceans, such as shrimp; the third from last segment of a leg.

Ceras (plural cerrata): One of the elongated projections found on the back of aeolid nudibranchs used in gas exchange as well as extensions of the digestive gland.

Cheliped (plural chelipeds): The leg of an arthropod, such as crabs, that bears large pincers.

Cilia: Minute hair-like structures used for locomotion, food gathering, and other functions.

Ctenes: The comblike tufts of comb jellies.

Columella: The central axis of true snails.

Commensal: The relationship between two different organisms in which one benefits and the other is not affected.

Conceptacles: Sunken cavities where the reproductive structures are located in red algae.

Chondrophore: A spoon-shaped projection found near the hinge on one of the shells of a bivalve.

Dactylus (plural dactyli): The segment of the crab's leg that is farthest from the body; claw(s).

Detritus: Debris that contains organic particles.

Dextral: A right-handed spiral or clockwise coil.

Epiphyte: A plant that lives on another plant but not as a parasite.

Exoskeleton: An external skeleton, such as the shell of a crab.

Filter feeder: An organism that strains particles of food from the water.

Flagellum (plural flagella): One of the whip-like extensions found on some cells, used for motility and feeding.

Gametophyte: The sexual (gamete-forming) stage of algae.

Girdle: The muscular tissue that surrounds the eight valves of a chiton.

Gonads: Reproductive organs.

Gnathopod: A leg-like appendage of a crustacean.

Gorgonin: A tough, fibrous, flexible protein present in soft corals.

Holdfast: The root-like part of algae.

Ligament: The tough, elastic part of the hinge that joins the two valves of a bivalve.

Madreporite: The sieve plate or a porous plate that allows water to pass both in and out.

Mantle: A fold in the body wall that lines the shell of a mollusk. Also, the sac-like hood that is present behind the eyes of an octopus.

Midden: A pile of refuse.

Nematocyst: A cell that releases a stinging or entangling thread for the protection of jellies, sea anemones, and related organisms (Phylum Cnidaria).

Ocelli: Eyespots on ribbon worms.

Operculum: The calcareous or horn-like door that covers a snail for protection when it has retreated inside its shell.

Oral disk: A disk with a central mouth for feeding, as found in sea anemones.

Osculum (plural oscula): The large pore through which water exits from a sponge.

Ostium (plural ostia): A minute incurrent pore through which water enters a sponge.

Pallial sinus: The indentation at the hind end of the pallial line on the inner surface of the valves of bivalves.

Papillae: The finger-like projections used in respiration on the dorsal side of nudibranchs.

Parapodia: The lateral extensions on the side of each segment of segmented worms.

Pedal laceration: A form of asexual reproduction in sea anemones that consists of the pedal disc broadening, then moving away and leaving small particles of itself behind, which become new individuals.

Pedicellariae: Pincer-like appendages found on sea stars and sea urchins.

Pelagic: Free-swimming in the ocean.

Periostracum: The thin skin-like coat of organic material secreted by various mollusks on the outside of their shells.

Pheromone: A chemical secreted by an animal that influences the behavior or physiology of others of the same species, often by attracting members of the opposite sex.

Physa: A swollen, bulb-like burrowing structure at the base of the column of an anemone.

Planula: Free-swimming larvae of many cnidarians.

Polychaete: Segmented worms that have paddle-like appendages, well-developed sense organs, and many setae.

Polygynous: A male having more than one female mate.

Polyp: An elongated individual organism (in the Phylum Cnidaria) with a mouth surrounded by tentacles at one end and attached to a substrate at the other end.

Proboscis: The organ found at the "snout" of ribbon worms that can be extended. The anterior end of the digestive tract that can be found in some annelids; this organ can be everted. Also, a muscular tube found at the anterior end of the digestive tract in some snails used for feeding.

Radula: A toothed, tongue-like ribbon in the mouth of mollusks used to rasp food from a hard surface.

Rhinophore: One of a large pair of antennae-like sensory organs found on the head of nudibranchs.

Roe: The eggs or ovaries of an invertebrate. Also, the eggs of fish.

Rostrum: An elongated, usually pointed structure found at the front of the carapace in various crustaceans.

Sessile: Lacking a stalk.

Setae: Short bristles found on annilid worms.

Sinistral: A left-handed spiral or counter-clockwise coil.

Spicule: A lime or glass rod that provides support for sponges.

Sporophyte: The asexual or vegetative stage of algae.

Stipe: The stalk of an alga.

Telson: The last abdominal segment in crustaceans.

Test: The round internal skeleton of the sea urchin or sand dollar.

Thallus (plural thalli): The main body of algae, lichens, and other organisms that lack roots. The holdfast or its equivalent is not included.

Tubercle: A nodule or small protuberance on the surface of a plant or animal.

Tubiferous: Containing hollow chambers.

Umbilicus: The navel-like opening in the center of the columella at the base of true snails.

Umbo (or umbone): The "beak" or prominent portion of the hinge on a bivalve.

Uropod: The last pair of appendages in crustaceans.

Valve: One of two calcareous coverings found on a bivalve; one of the eight shells covering the dorsal portion of a chiton.

Velum: A veil-like ring that hangs on the underside of a jelly.

Vesicles: Bladder in seaweeds; a membranous pouch in a plant or animal.

Viviparous: Producing living young.

Zooecium (plural zooecia): Living chamber(s) constructed by a colony of zooids.

Zooid: An individual bryozoan or moss animal within a colony.

SELECTED REFERENCES

Abbott, R. T. 1974. *American Seashells: The Marine Molluska of the Atlantic and Pacific Coasts of North America*. Van Nostrand Reinhold Co., New York, New York.

Bertness, M. D. 1999. *The Ecology of Atlantic Shorelines*. Sinauer Associates, Inc., Sunderland, Massachusetts.

Bigelow, H. B. and W. C. Schroeder. 1953. *Fishes of the Gulf of Maine*. United States Department of the Interior, Fishery Bulletin of the Fish and Wildlife Service 53, Washington, D.C.

Bird, C. J., and J. L. McLachlan. 1992. *Seaweed Flora of the Maritimes: 1. Rhodophyta— The Red Algae*. National Research Council of Canada, Halifax, Nova Scotia.

Bleakney, J. S. 1996. *Sea Slugs of Atlantic Canada and the Gulf of Maine*. Nimbus Publishing and the Nova Scotia Museum, Halifax, Nova Scotia.

Bousfield, E. L. 1960. *Canadian Atlantic Sea Shells*. National Museum of Canada, Ottawa, Ontario.

Clark, A. M., and M. E. Downey. 1992. *Starfishes of the Atlantic*. Chapman and Hall, New York, New York.

Corke, J. 2012. *Identification Guide to Sharks, Skates, Rays and Chimaeras of Atlantic Canada*. WWF Canada, Toronto, Ontario.

DeVictor, S. T., D. M. Knott, and S. E. Crowe. 2010. *South Carolina Beachcomber's Guide: A Guide to the Common Invertebrates, Plants and Natural Artifacts of the South Carolina Seashore*. Southeastern Regional Taxonomic Center, South Carolina Department of Natural Resources, Columbia, South Carolina.

Gibson, M. 2003. *Seashores of the Maritimes*. Nimbus Publishing Limited, Halifax, Nova Scotia.

Gosner, K. L. 1978. *Atlantic Seashore: A Field Guide to Sponges, Jellyfish, Sea Urchins, and More*. Houghton Mifflin Company, New York, New York.

Hartmann, Trish. 2006. *Bivalve Seashells of Florida: An Identification Guide to the Common Species of Florida and the Southeast*. Anadara Press, Tampa, Florida.

Hendler, Gordon, John E. Miller, David L. Pawson & Porter M. Kier. 1995. *Sea Stars, Sea Urchins, and Allies: Echinoderms of Florida and the Caribbean*. Smithsonian Institution Press, Washington, D.C.

Kaplan, Eugene H. 1988. *A Field Guide to Southeastern and Caribbean Seashores: Cape Hatteras to the Gulf Coast, Florida, and the Caribbean*. Roger Tory Peterson Institute. Houghton Mifflin Company, Boston and New York.

Keates, H. 1995. *Beachcomber's Guide from Cape Cod to Cape Hatteras: Marine Life of Massachusetts, Rhode Island, Connecticut, New York, New Jersey, Delaware, Maryland, Virginia, and North Carolina*. Gulf Publishing Company, Houston, Texas.

Kingsbury, J. M., and P. Sze. 1997. *Seaweeds of Cape Cod and the Islands*. Bullbrier Press, Jersey Shore, Pennsylvania.

Lee, T. F. 1986. *The Seaweed Handbook: An Illustrated Guide to Seaweeds from North Carolina to the Arctic*. Dover Publications, New York, New York.

Martinez, A. J. 2003. *Marine Life of the North Atlantic: Canada to New England*. Aqua Quest Publications Inc., New York, New York.

Meinkoth, N. A. 1981. *The Audubon Society Field Guide to North American Seashore Creatures*. Knopf, New York, New York.

Pollock, L. W. 1998. *A Practical Guide to the Marine Animals of Northeastern North America*. Rutgers University Press, New Brunswick.

Potter, H. J. and L. Houser. 2000. *Seashells of North Carolina*. North Carolina Sea Grant College Program, North Carolina State University, Raleigh, North Carolina.

Rehder, H. 1981. *The Audubon Society Field Guide to North American Seashells*. Knopf, New York, New York.

Ruppert, E. E. and R. Fox. 1988. *Seashore Animals of the Southeast: A Guide to Common Shallow-water Invertebrates of the Southeastern Atlantic Coast*. University of South Carolina Press, Columbia, South Carolina.

Scott, W. B., and M. G. Scott. 1988. *Atlantic Fishes of Canada*. University of Toronto Press, Toronto, Ontario.

Sears, J. R. 2002. *NEAS Keys to Benthic Marine Algae*. Northeast Algal Society. Express Printing, Fall River, Massachusetts.

Smith, R. I. 1964. *Keys to Marine Invertebrates of the Woods Hole Region*. Contribution No. 11, Marine Biological Laboratory, Woods Hole, Massachusetts.

South, G. R. 1975. *Common Seaweeds of Newfoundland*. Oxen Pond Botanic Park, Marine Sciences Research Laboratory, Memorial University, St. John's, Newfoundland.

Taylor, W. R. 1957. *Marine Algae of the Northeastern Coast of North America*. University of Michigan Press, Ann Arbor, Michigan.

Watling, L., J. Fegley, and J. Moring. 2003. *Life Between the Tides: Marine Plants and Animals of the Northeast*. Tilbury House Publishers, Gardiner, Maine.

Voss, Gilbert L. 1976. *Seashore Life of Florida and the Caribbean: A Guide to the Common Marine Invertebrates of the Atlantic from Bermuda to the West Indies and of the Gulf of Mexico*. E. A. Seemann Publishing, Inc., Miami, Florida.

Williams, A. B. 1984, *Shrimps, Lobsters, and Crabs of the Atlantic Coast of the Eastern United States, Maine to Florida*. Smithsonian Institution Press, Washington.

Witherington, B. and D. Witherington. 2006. *Florida's Living Beaches: A Guide for the Curious Beachcomber*. Pineapple Press, Inc., Sarasota, Florida.

———. 2011. *Living Beaches of Georgia and the Carolinas: A Beachcomber's Guide*. Pineapple Press, Inc. Sarasota, Florida.

ACKNOWLEDGMENTS

I would like to thank several people who assisted with this project in so many ways. Without their help, this project would not have been possible.

First and foremost, I would like to thank Stackpole Books for accepting this project. I would also like to thank Tim Gahr for his careful and insightful editing.

A number of individuals were kind enough to give freely of their time and expertise to identify specimens or photographs, confirm identifications, review text, update current scientific names, or otherwise assist with this project in additional ways. These include: Dennis M. Allen (University of South Carolina), Diana Marcela Bolanos (University of Cartagena, Cartagena, Bolívar, Colombia), Terri Bremer (Cape Cod Museum of Natural History), Ana I. Dittel (University of Delaware), Stephen Fegley (University of North Carolina), Evan Gwilliam (Cape Cod National Seashore), Andrew Hebda (Nova Scotia Museum of Natural History), Gretchen Lambert (California State University, Fullerton), Charlene Mayes (University of New Brunswick), Jon Norenburg (National Museum of Natural History, Washington, D.C.), Leslie Pezzack (Nova Scotia Museum of Natural History), Gerhard Pohle (Huntsman Marine Science Centre, St. Andrews, NB), Gary W. Saunders (University of New Brunswick), Jim Simon (Fisheries & Oceans Canada).

Site suggestions and other helpful on-site assistance were freely given by many individuals within various organizations. These include: Randy Newman (Fort Macon State Park, NC), the naturalists at the Nova Scotia Museum of Natural History (Halifax, NS), the park staff at Reid State Park (ME), the visitor center staff and volunteers at Cape Cod National Seashore (Wellfleet, MA), and Joel Wooster (S. Daytona, FL).

PHOTOGRAPHIC CREDITS

All photographs by J. Duane Sept except the following:

Caroline Longtin: p. 294

North Carolina Parks
S. Bland: p. 11t, p. 43b, p. 130b , p. 193t, p. 196b, p. 256t
John Fullwood: p. 27
Anna Kellner: p. 29b, p. 77b, p. 79t, p. 147t, p. 183t, p. 195b
S. McElhone: p. 278m
Randy Newman: p. 13m, p. 17b, p. 30, p. 42t, p. 42m, p. 47, p. 59b, p. 134b,
p. 192t, p. 204m, p. 204b, p. 206t, p. 213t, p. 214b, p. 215b, p. 216t, p. 217t,
p. 218b, p. 224t, p. 226b, p. 231t, p. 233t, p. 236b, p. 239t, p. 244b, p. 246t,
p. 255b, p. 263t, p. 277b, p. 278b, p. 279t, p. 279b, p. 280t, p. 280m,
p. 285b, p. 288t, p. 295b, p. 299b, p. 302m, p. 303m, p. 304, p. 305
Randy Newman and Garrett Newman: p. 216b, p. 242t
P. Pearson: p. 212t

The Southeastern Regional Taxonomic Center (SERTC), South Carolina, Department of Natural Resources: p. 19t, p. 24t, p. 34t, p. 44t , p. 44m, p. 46m, p. 68t,
p. 136t, p. 208b, p. 217b, p. 218m, p. 221t, p. 228t, p. 229t, p. 230t, p. 237t,
p. 237b, p. 238t, p. 238b, p. 243b, p. 247t

Joel Wooster: p. 31b, p. 58t, p. 64b, p. 138t, p. 149b, p. 152, p. 180t, p. 198, p. 204t,
p. 243t, p. 256b, p. 273b

INDEX

barnacle-eating dorid (*Onchidoris bilamellata*), 131–32

barnacles (*Cirripedia*), 200–206

barndoor skate (*Raja laevis*), 275

bay barnacle (*Amphibalanus improvisus*), 202

beaded periwinkle (*Cenchritis muricatus*), 70

beaded sundial (*Heliacus bisulcatus*), 72

beautiful topsnail (*Calliostoma pulchrum*), 58

Beroe's common comb jelly (*Beroe cucumis*), 29

bigclaw skeleton shrimp (*Caprella equilibra*), 208

bigclaw snapping shrimp (*Alpheus heterochaelis*), 217–18

bivalves (*Bivalvia*), 137–96

black mangrove (*Avicennia germinans*), 309

blood ark (*Lunarca ovalis*), 142

blotched swimming crab (*Achelous spinimanus*), 238

blue button (*Porpita porpita*), 22

blue crab (*Callinectes sapidus*), 236

blue land crab (*Cardisoma guanhumi*), 247

blue mussel (*Mytilus edulis*), 145

blue mussel pea crab (*Tumidotheres maculatus*), 243

bocourt swimming crab (*Callinectes bocourti*), 237

bony fishes (*Osteichthyes*), 276–77

boreal awningclam (*Solemya borealis*), 139

Bowerbank's halichondria (*Halichondria bowerbanki*), 4

branching coralline alga (*Corallina officinalis*), 298

bread crumb sponge (*Halichondria panicea*), 3

brilliant sea fingers (*Titanideum frauenfeldii*), 10

brittle stars (*Ophiuroidea*), 258–59

broad-ribbed cardita (*Cardites floridanus*), 165

broad-toothed gulfweed (*Sargassum fluitans*), 296

broadback mud crab (*Eurytium limosum*), 240–41

brown algae (*Phaeophyceae*), 286–96

brown baby ear (*Sinum maculatum*), 96–97

brown-band wentletrap (*Epitonium rupicola*), 78

brown finger sponge (*Axinella pomponiae*), 7

brown rock shrimp (*Sicyonia brevirostris*), 214

brown ruffle-edged flatworm (*Phrikoceros mopsus*), 31

brown shrimp (*Farfantepenaeus aztecus*), 213

bruised nassa (*Nassarius vibex*), 115–16

bushy-backed nudibranch (*Dendronotus frondosus*), 134–35

buttercup lucine (*Anodontia alba*), 162

by-the-wind sailor (*Velella velella*), 22

C

Cabrit's murex (*Vokesimurex cabritii*), 101

calico box crab (*Hepatus epheliticus*), 229

calico clam (*Callista maculata*), 188–89

campeche angelwing (*Pholas campechiensis*), 193

cannonball jelly (*Stomolophus meleagris*), 26

Caribbean land hermit crab (*Coenobita clypeatus*), 224–25

Caribbean vase snail (*Vasum muricatum*), 123

carnation worm (*Hydroides dianthus*), 42

Carolinian ghost shrimp (*Callichirus major*), 220

carpet tunicates (*Didemnum spp.*), 271

caterpillar fireworm (*Amphinome rostrata*), 43

Catherine's mole crab (*Albunea catherinae*), 229

cayenne keyhole limpet (*Diodora cayenensis*), 51–52

channeled duckclam (*Raeta plicatella*), 174

channeled whelk (*Busycotypus canaliculatus*), 114

charrua mussel (*Mytella charruana*), 149

checkered nerite (*Nerita tessellata*), 63

cherry-striped porcelain crab (*Petrolisthes galathinus*), 227

chestnut latirus (*Leucozonia nassa*), 118

chestnut turban (*Turbo castanea*), 60

Chinese mitten crab (*Eriocheir sinensis*), 241

chitons (*Polyplacophora*), 48–50

chocolate tunicate (*Didemnum psammatodes*), 271

clams (*Bivalvia*), 137–96

clearnose skate (*egg case*) (*Raja eglanteria*), 275–76

club-finger sponge (*Desmapsamma anchorata*), 6

cnidarians (*Cnidaria*), 9–27

coffee bean trivia (*Niveria pediculus*), 88

coffee melampus (*Melampus coffea*), 129–30

collared bamboo-worm (*Clymenella torquata*), 38

colorful moonsnail (*Naticarius canrena*), 95

comb jellies (*Ctenophora*), 28–29

common Atlantic bubble snail (*Bulla striata*), 128

common Atlantic marginella (*Prunum apicinum*), 124–25

common Atlantic octopus (*Octopus vulgaris*), 196–97

common Atlantic slippersnail (*Crepidula fornicata*), 81

common broom worm (*Pherusa affinis*), 40–41

common bugula (*Bugula neritina*), 253

common dovesnail (*Columbella mercatoria*), 105–6

northern rock barnacle (*Semibalanus balanoides*), 201

northern rockweed (*Fucus vesiculosus*), 293

northern rosy margarite (*Margarites costalis*), 58

northern sea pork (*Aplidium constellatum*), 273

northern sea roach (*Ligia oceanica*), 211

northern sea star (*Asterias rubens*), 255

northern spotted moonsnail (*Euspira triseriata*), 94

northern star coral (*Astrangia poculata*), 12

northern sun star (*Solaster endeca*), 258

northern white crust (*Didemnum candidum*), 271

nudibranchs (*Opisthobranchia*), 130–37

O

octopods (*Cephalopoda*), 196–97

olive nerite (*Neritina reclivata*), 64

olive-pit porcelain crab (*Euceramus praelongus*), 228

onion anemone (*Paranthus rapiformis*), 17–18

orange-footed sea cucumber (*Cucumaria frondosa*), 265

orange sea grape tunicate (*Molgula citrina*), 267–68

orange-striped anemone (*Diadumena lineata*), 15–16

ornate spaghetti-worm (*Amphitrite ornate*), 40

ovate comb jelly (*Beroe ovata*), 29

oyster pea crab (*Zaops ostreum*), 242

P

painted anemone (*Urticina felina*), 14

painted fifteen-paired scaleworm (*Harmothoe imbricata*), 34–35

paintsplash tunicate (*Didemnum duplicatum*), 271

pale anemone (*Aiptasia pallida*), 18

pale sea cucumber (*Pentamera pulcherrima*), 265

pallid janthina (*Janthina pallida*), 76

paralytic shellfish poisoning (*PSP*), vi

parchment tubeworm (*Chaetopterus variopedatus*), 42–43

parchment-worm crab (*Pinnixa chaetopterana*), 244

peanut worms (*Sipuncula*), 45

pear whelk (*Busycotypus spiratus*), 115

pecock's tail alga (*Padina pavonica*), 292

pentogonal porcelain crab (*Megalobrachium soriatum*), 226

peppermint shrimp (*Lysmata wurdemanni*), 213

pickleweed (*Salicornia spp.*), 307–8

pink beach hopper (*Maera danae*), 207–8

pink conch (*Lobatus gigas*), 86

pink shrimp (*Penaeus duorarum*), 213

pitted murex (*Favartia cellulosa*), 104

pleated sea squirt (*Styela plicata*), 269–70

plumed green seaweed (*Bryopsis plumosa*), 285–86

plumed worm (*Diopatra cuprea*), 37

pointed venus (*Anomalocardia cuneimeris*), 186–87

polychete worms (*Polychaeta*), 33–44

ponderous ark (*Eontia ponderosa*), 143–44

Portuguese man-of-war (*Physalia physalis*), 21

Potter spaghetti-worm (*Amphitrite figulus*), 40

prickly jingle (*Heteranomia squamula*), 154

purple claw seaweed (*Cystoclonium purpureum*), 299

purple dulse (*Palmaria palmata*), 302–3

purple encrusting sponge (*Haliclona cinerea*), 3

purple march crab (*Sesarma reticulatum*), 245

purple-spined sea urchin (*Arbacia punctulata*), 261

purplish tagelus (*Tagelus divisus*), 183

Q

queen quahog (*Arctica islandica*), 183

R

rainbow tellin (*Tellina iris*), 179

ram's horn squid (*Spirula spirula*), 197

red algae (*Rhodophyta*), 296–305

red boring sponge (*Cliona celata*), 8

red-brown ark (*Barbatia cancellaria*), 140

red colonial tunicate (*Symplegma rubra*), 270

red crust algae (*Hildenbrandia spp.*), 297

red-finger aeolis (*Flabellina verrucosa*), 135

red lineus (*Lineus ruber*), 32

red mangrove (*Rhizophora mangle*), 309

red-ridged clinging crab (*Mithraculus forceps*), 233

red-spotted anemone (*Aiptasiogeton eruptaurantia*), 18

red tide, vi

red velvet mite (*Neomolgus littoralis*), 199

redbeard sponge (*Clathria prolifera*), 6

redjointed fiddler (*Uca minax*), 248–49

regal sea fan (*Leptogorgia hebes*), 11

Rehder's baby-bubble (*Acteon candens*), 128

reptiles (*Reptilia*), 278–80

reticulated cowrie-helmet (*Cypraecassis testiculus*), 98

ribbed barnacle (*Tetraclita stalactifera*), 204

ribbed mussel (*Geukensia demissa*), 148

ribbon worms (*Nemertea*), 32–33

rice olive (*Olivella cf. prefloralia*), 122

rock boring peanut worm (*Themiste alutacea*), 45

rock-boring urchin (*Echinometra lucunter*), 263

rock gunnel (*Phollis gunnellus*), 277

solitary bubble snail (*Haminoea solitaria*), 129
sooty sea hare (*Aplysia fasciata*), 130–31
south Atlantic lugworm (*Arenicola cristata*), 38
south Atlantic moon jelly (*Aurelia marginalis*), 26
southern gribble (*Limnoria tripunctata*), 209
southern horsemussel (*Modiolus squamosus*), 146
southern quahog (*Mercenaria campechiensis*), 184–85
southern surfclam (*Spisula raveneli*), 171–72
speckled crab (*Arenaeus cribrarius*), 235
speckled flatworm (*Pleioplana atomata*), 31
speckled snapping shrimp (*Synalpheus fritzmuelleri*), 219
speckled tellin (*Tellina listeri*), 176
spiny papercockle (*Papyridea soleniformis*), 168
spiny pelagic goose barnacle (*Lepas pectinata*), 206
spiny-skinned animals (*Echinodermata*), 254–66
spiny slippersnail (*Bostrycapulus aculeatus*), 82–83
spiral margarite (*Margarites helicinus*), 57
spiral rockweed (*Fucus spiralis*), 293–94
sponges (*Porifera*), 2–8
spoonworms (*Thalassema spp.*), 45–46
spotted bumblebee shrimp (*Gnathophyllum modestum*), 217
spotted limpet (*Eoacmaea pustulata*), 55
spotted oyster flatworm (*Stylochus oculiferus*), 30
spotted porcelain crab (*Porcellana sayana*), 226
spotted slippersnail (*Crepidula maculosa*), 82
squids (*Cephalopoda*), 196–97
starred barnacle (*Chthamalus stellatus*), 201
stiff penshell (*Atrina rigida*), 150
Stimpson whelk (*Colus stimpsoni*), 108
stocky cerith (*Cerithium litteratum*), 75
stone crab (*Menippe mercenaria*), 239–40
stout tagelus (*Tagelus plebeius*), 182
straight sea whip (*Leptogorgia setacea*), 11
striate cup-and-saucer (*Crucibulum striatum*), 80
striate piddock (*Martesia striata*), 194
stringy acid weed (*Desmarestia viridis*), 288–89
striped acorn barnacle (*Amphibalanus amphitrite*), 203
striped falselimpet (*Siphonaria pectinata*), 56–57
striped hermit crab (*Clibanarius vittatus*), 223–24
striped snapping shrimp (*Alpheus formosus*), 218

sugar kelp (*Saccharina latissima*), 290
sulfur sponge (*Aplysilla longispina*), 5
sun sponge (*Hymeniacidon heliophila*), 4–6
sunray venus (*Macrocallista nimbosa*), 188
synaptas (*Leptosynapta spp.*), 265

T

Tampa tellin (*Tellina tampaensis*), 179
ten-ridged whelk (*Neptunea decemcostata*), 109
thick-lip drill (*Eupleura caudata*), 104–5
thick lucina (*Phacoides pectinata*), 162
three-lined basketsnail (*Ilyanassa trivittata*), 117
tidal spray crab (*Plagusia depressa*), 242
tide-pool scud (*Gammarus oceanicus*), 207
tides, description of, v
tiger lucina (*Codakia orbicularis*), 163
tinted cantharus (*Gemophos tinctus*), 103, 110
titan acorn barnacle (*Megabalanus coccopoma*), 203
toothed rockweed (*Fucus serratus*), 294
tortoiseshell limpet (*Testudinalia testudinalis*), 55
translucent sea squirt (*Ascidia interrupta*), 268–69
transverse ark (*Andara transversa*), 141
true jellies (*Scyphozoa*), 23–27
true tulip (*Fasciolaria tulipa*), 119
truncated softshell-clam (*Mya truncata*), 191
tufted fringe (*Elachista spp.*), 287
tufted sea moss (*Cladophora rupestris*), 285
tufted twelve-paired scaleworm (*Lepidonotus squamatus*), 33
tunicates (*Urocordata*), 267–73
turkey wing (*Arca zebra*), 139
turtle barnacle (*Chelonibia testudinaria*), 204–5
tusk shells (*Scaphopoda*), 137
twig seaweed (*Polyides rotundus*), 296–97
two-gilled bloodworm (*Glycera dibranchiata*), 35
two-toned tree-oyster (*Isognomon bicolor*), 153

V

variable coquina (*Donax variabilis*), 181
variable dwarf olive (*Olivella mutica*), 122
variable graceful seaweed (*Gracilaria tikvahiae*), 299–300
variable tube seaweed (*Devaleraea ramentacea*), 301–2
violet chain ascidian (*Botrylloides violaeus*), 272–73
virgin nerite (*Neritina virginea*), 64

W

warty sea anemone (*Bunodosoma cavernatum*), 13–14
waved whelk (*Buccinum undatum*), 107–8
wavy astarte (*Astarte undata*), 166
well-ribbed dovesnail (*Cotonopsis lafresnayi*), 106–7
West Indian fighting conch (*Strombus pugilis*), 85
western Atlantic wentletrap (*Epitonium occidentale*), 77
wharf crab (*Armases cinereum*), 245
white Atlantic cadlina (*Cadlina laevis*), 131
white baby ear (*Sinum persectivum*), 96
white crested telllin (*Tellidora cristata*), 180
white-fingered mud crab (*Rhithropanopeus harrisii*), 241
white globe trivia (*Niveria nix*), 89
white hoofsnail (*Hipponix antiquatus*), 79
white lace bryozoan (*Membranipora membranacea*), 251
white nassa (*Nassarius albus*), 116–17
white northern chiton (*Stenosemus albus*), 48
white skate (*egg case*) (*Leucoraja ocellata*), 275
whitecross hydromedusa (*Staurostoma mertensii*), 23
wine-glass hydroid (*Campanularia spp.*), 20
winged kelp (*Alaria esculenta*), 291
wiry acid weed (*Desmarestia aculeata*), 289
worms, marine, 30–47
wrack fringe tubeweed (*Vertebrata lanosa*), 303–4

Y

yellow boring sponge (*Cliona celata*), 8
yellow false doris (*Adalaria proxima*), 133
yellow pricklycockle (*Dallocardia muricata*), 167–68

Z

zebra periwinkle (*Echinolittorina ziczac*), 68
zig-zag wine-glass hydroid (*Obelia geniculata*), 19–20
zigzag scallop (*Euvola ziczac*), 156–57